Airport Marketing Strategies

Airport Marketing Strategies: Aviation and Tourism Perspectives

BY

Dr. Lázaro Florido-Benítez
University of Málaga, Spain

United Kingdom – North America – Japan – India – Malaysia – China

Emerald Publishing Limited
Emerald Publishing, Floor 5, Northspring, 21-23 Wellington Street, Leeds LS1 4DL

First edition 2024

Copyright © 2024 Lázaro Florido-Benítez.
Published under exclusive licence by Emerald Publishing Limited.

Reprints and permissions service
Contact: www.copyright.com

British Library Cataloguing in Publication Data
A catalogue record for this book is available from the British Library

ISBN: 978-1-83608-083-1 (Print)
ISBN: 978-1-83608-082-4 (Online)
ISBN: 978-1-83608-084-8 (Epub)

INVESTOR IN PEOPLE

I dedicate this book to my mother Manuela, my two daughters Alba and Nerea and my wife Dolores for their continuous support. Finally, I would like to make a special dedication to my dog named Maddie; she is my faithful travel companion. For over 7 years, she has been accompanying me while I worked in my research projects and this special book. My wife and two daughters are happily aware of that.

Dr Lázaro Florido-Benítez
Lecturer of Tourism, Air transport, Economics and Business Administration
University of Málaga, Spain
Málaga 29013
The better I get to know men, the more I find myself loving dogs (Charles De Gaulle).

Contents

List of Figures and Tables

Figures

Tables

List of Abbreviations

3R	Restart, Rebuild and Redesign
4Cs	Customer, Cost, Communication, Convenience
4Ps	Product, Price, Promotion, Place
7Ps	Product, Price, Promotion, Place, Physical Evidence, Processes, People
ACI	Airports Council International
ACRP	Airport Cooperative Research Programme
AENA	Spanish Airport and Air Navigation
AI	Artificial Intelligence
AIF	Airport Improvement Fee
AMA	American Marketing Association
APP	Application
AR	Augmented Reality
ARFF	Aircraft Rescue and Firefighting
ASQ	Airports Service Quality
ATAG	Air Transport Action Group
B2B	Business-to-Business
B2C	Business-to-Consumer
BTME	Business Traveller Middle East Awards
CAA	Civil Aeronautics Administration
CAA	Civil Aviation Authority
CAG	Changi Airport Group
CAPEX	Capital Expenditures
CCCI	Creative Connections & Commons Inc.
CEO	Chief Executive Officer
COO	Chief Operating Officer
CTK	Global Cargo Ton-Kilometre
CWA	Clean Water Act
DDoS	Distributed Denial-of-Service

DEA	Data Envelopment Analysis
DMO	Destination Marketing Organization
DMUs	Denominated Decision-Making Units
DoS	Denial-of-Service Attacks
EASA	European Union Aviation Safety Agency
EC	European Commission
ENISA	European Union Agency for Network and Information Security
ESG	Environment Social and Governance
EU	European Union
EWOM	Electronic Word of Mouth
FAA	Federal Aviation Administration
FBI	Federal Bureau of Investigation
GDP	Gross Domestic Product
IATA	International Air Transport Association
ICAO	International Civil Aviation Organization
ICT	Information and Communication Technology
ID	Identification Document
IMF	International Monetary Fund
INE	National Statistical Institute
IoT	Internet of Things
ITA	International Trade Administration
KPI	Key Performance Indicator
LCC	Low-Cost Carrier
NAVAID	Navigation Aid
OAG	Official Airline Guide
OECD	Organization for Economic Co-operation and Development
OPEX	Operating Expenses
OTA	Online Travel Agency
PFC	Passenger Facility Charge
PKF	Passenger Kilometres Performed
PMR	Passenger with Reduced Mobility
PPE	Personal Protective Equipment
QR	Quick Response

ROI	Return on Investment
ROIC	Return On Invested Capital
RT PCR	Reverse Transcription Polymerase Chain Reaction
SAFs	Sustainable Aviation Fuels
SITA	Société Internationale de Télécommunications Aéronautiques
SuM4All	Sustainable Mobility for All
SWOT	Strengths, Weaknesses, Opportunities and Threats
UK	United Kingdom
UNTWO	United Nations World Tourism Organization
US	United States of America
VIP	Very Important Person
VR	Virtual Reality
WHO	World Health Organization
WTO	World Trade Organization
WTTC	World Travel & Tourism Council
YoY	Year-over-Year

About the Author

Lázaro Florido-Benítez holds a PhD in Tourism and Marketing from the University of Malaga, Spain, and a Master's in Management of Airports–Aeronautics from the European Business School. He is a Lecturer and a Researcher in the Economics and Business Administration Department. His main research interests include tourism, digital marketing, airport marketing and air transport connectivity. In the area of tourism, he has investigated the promotion of tourist destinations, how airports and destinations promote marketing strategies through digital marketing, mobile marketing, the impact of mobile marketing at airports and the impact of airports and airlines on the tourist destination, among many others. He has published in many peer-reviewed journals on topics such as tourism, airports, marketing and cybersecurity.

Preface

This book provides an updated global vision of airport marketing strategies in the context of the aviation and tourism sectors. There are many books and articles on marketing and airport marketing, but there is not one yet that speaks directly to airport marketing strategies. This book will substantiate the academic literature regarding the role of airports and their marketing strategies in the aviation and tourism industries. One of the purposes of this book is to understand and document the nature of the airport's management and business through marketing strategies, the distinct challenges that airport and airline operators and Destination Marketing Organizations (DMOs) currently face during these difficult times of economic, social and pandemic periods and how airport operators should try to cope with a global crisis through in coherent, well-planned, coordinated and comprehensive manner. Alone or together? Can airport and airline operators work and address this pronounced fall in passenger and freight volumes for 5 or 6 years more? What are the marketing strategies used in aviation and tourism activities? These are some of the questions we can ask ourselves, and there are probably many more that we could think of in this book.

Many studies have been conducted to examine the direct effects of marketing on tourism, international markets and human behaviour areas. However, in spite of the growing interest on airports and marketing relationships by researchers, academics and practitioners alike, there is no specific literature on airport marketing strategies, where researchers and airport operators can obtain relevant information in which to project their investigations and joint marketing strategies with other partners. To fill this gap, the purpose of this groundbreaking book is to introduce students, researchers and practitioners to the new methods of airport marketing strategies in the digital innovation era, strategies that enhance commercial revenues, promotion campaigns, the effectiveness of marketing actions and the airport's brand image. Further, this book is intended to provide some awareness and understanding of the various interactions and interdependencies between airports, DMOs, airlines, marketing tools and stakeholders.

Indeed, this book shows real examples of airport marketing strategies around the world to help airport and airline operators, marketers and DMOs improve their marketing strategies in a competitive and environmentally sustainable market, as is the case with aviation and tourism activities. Opportunities to develop mutually beneficial relationships in cities between DMOs and airports are plentiful but often largely untapped by both parties due to miscommunication and the common interests of business operators. Strategy is the art of asking, 'Why?'

Establish and conduct a good strategy by the airport operator or company, which provides a road map for managers and indicates what must be done to survive, be profitable and grow as an organisation in an industry as competitive as the aviation sector. A good strategy must be based on clearly identified and framed challenges by airport operators. Strategy is science because it requires analytical skills, the ability to organise and analyse information and the ability to make well-informed decisions.

The marketing strategy of diversification is critical to reviving in times of economic downturn. Indeed, during the pandemic crisis, the use of digital channels to promote products and services is experimenting with an unprecedented boom in promotion and communication marketing campaigns. Airports such as Los Angeles (IATA code: LAX) in the United States, Orlando International (IATA: MCO) in the United States, Schiphol Amsterdam (IATA: AMS) in the Netherlands or Changi airport (IATA: SIN) in Singapore are pioneers and recognised experts in marketing communication and technical aspects of promotion campaigns.

The aviation industry has been a very restricted and rather endogamic sector for aeronautical engineers, operators and governments; they monopolised the aeronautical and safety activities from 1970 to 2000, and for them, the non-aeronautical and marketing operations were only residual income for airports. Fortunately, this trend is slowly changing thanks to tourism and marketing experts, who have provided a joint vision and a clearer picture of the interrelationship between the aviation and tourism industries to increase commercial revenue and passenger arrivals at airports worldwide. The management of marketing campaigns through digital channels by airport operators, marketing departments, airlines and DMOs has to be targeted with a clear, relevant and attractive message of products and services offered to users/passengers/tourists, to reach a high conversion rate and return on investment of marketing campaigns. This is one of the reasons why airport operators and the rest of their partners are turning to a range of evaluation measures for aviation and tourism promotion campaigns.

The concluding Chapter 9 tackles cybersecurity as a sociotechnical phenomenon in airport marketing activities. The cybersecurity issues at organisations marketing campaigns (e.g. phishing attacks, URL poisoning, man-in-the-middle, distributed denial of service or drone denial attacks) through digital channels are increasingly frequent and dangerous to companies and customers because of the digitisation of business (websites and apps) that has become in companies' main showcase. The European Aviation Safety Agency (EASA) estimated a monthly average of 1,000 airport cyberattacks in 2020. For instance, the Airbus Group is hit by up to 12 cyberattacks per year, mostly in the form of ransomware and hostile actions carried out by state-sponsored attackers.

Digital development, new technologies, cybersecurity and information technologies are speeding up the transformation of airports into new business models, where they must stratify their portfolio of businesses with the aim of providing diversified and replacement revenue streams and enabling them to increase non-aeronautical revenues. These great changes at airports have created a world full of opportunities between the aviation and marketing industries, where passengers and companies operating in and around the airport will be the main beneficiaries.

The book maintains a thoroughly strategic perspective in the context and terms of marketing. Importantly, the author offers innovative perspectives on which airport marketing strategies and resulting examples and ideas might evolve in everyday practice at airports and airlines all around the world, as well as in academic research. As such, this book should be a must-read for everyone in the aviation and tourism industries.

Dr Lázaro Florido-Benítez

Acknowledgements

I would like to thank Emerald's editors and reviewers for giving me this opportunity to edit this refereed book as part of the Emerald Editorial. I also thank in particular Sheena Reghunath and Thomas Felix Creighton for their helpful and constructive comments in the editorial process.

Dr Lázaro Florido-Benítez
Lecturer of Tourism, Air transport, Economics and Business Administration
University of Málaga, Spain
Málaga 29013

Chapter 1

Introduction

Abstract

This chapter introduces the evolution of airports from the Airlines Deregulation Act of 1978 in the United States to the present day. Starting with a description of airports and their surroundings, the tourists' perceptions concerning airports, and how airports and airlines have become the cornerstones of the tourism and aviation industries, especially in the period of pandemic for later retrieval. During the 1980s and 1990s, airport operators worked under an established monopoly, and they did not consider marketing strategies to increase and maximise business revenue. Since then, airport operators have been constantly looking for new business models to increase aeronautical and commercial revenues. This chapter ends with a description of how digitalisation represents not only a world full of opportunities in the airport and marketing relationship but also a great challenge to operators and marketers in terms investment and innovation.

1.1 When Airport Operators Were Reluctant to Implement Marketing Tools

The perception of airports by tourists and companies has improved over the last 25 years, thanks to marketing strategies and promotion campaigns developed by airport operators with the aim of establishing their real place inside and outside of the transportation, tourism and logistics sectors. But not always has the airport been considered the cornerstone for transporting passengers and goods; in 1995, most tourists and companies kept seeing airports as a simple transport infrastructure where they got on a plane to take a vacation, do business or go home. As stated by Gretzel et al. (2008), the emergence of travel as a significant economic activity began after World War II, as travel became widely accessible to the general population.

Airport operators soon understood that passengers and airlines were not just their primary source of income or aeronautical revenue; they too could get more income from non-aeronautical activities like retail services, shopping, personalised

Airport Marketing Strategies, 1–10
Copyright © 2024 Lázaro Florido-Benítez
Published under exclusive licence by Emerald Publishing Limited
doi:10.1108/978-1-83608-082-420241001

products and services, sales databases to attract new customers or customer segmentation, very important person (VIP) services, duty-free shops, quality of services as an added value, sporting, leisure and gastronomy activities, collaboration with partners to increase the number of customers and revenue, logistics and business platforms for e-commerce companies (i.e. Amazon, Zara, eBay, or Nike), among many others.

Before the introduction of the Airlines Deregulation Act of 1978 in the Unites States, most airport operators were focused on aeronautical revenue from air carriers through aircraft landing fees, handling charges and passenger service charges (Doganis, 2019; Graham, 2013). Airport operators worked under a monopoly established based on the legal regulations of governments, and they were not interested in commercial revenues and much less in marketing strategies. The traditional belief was that airport operators could not influence passenger demand and air traffic. A study carried out by the International Air Transport Association (IATA) and Deloitte (2017) revealed that from the 1980s and 1990s, governments' central responsibility was to ensure the best interests of passengers, cargo customers and the continued development of the regional economy. After 1990, everything changed substantially in cost, revenue and benefit terms for airports and airlines, and since then, Choo (2014) indicates that the aviation industry has become very competitive, and air fares have come down considerably, leading to lower profit margins. Operators have increasingly concentrated on revenue from passengers rather than airlines (Puls & Lentz, 2018).

Indeed, due to the high competitiveness in the air transport sector and the continuous economic crisis, airline companies have experienced extreme difficulties continuing operate, particularly low-cost carriers (LCCs) due to the low-cost model, and many of them have declared bankruptcy or ceasing operations, especially in the period of the COVID-19 pandemic (see Fig. 1). In May 2022, South African Mango airlines, a state-owned carrier, was rescued by the government with 225 million rands (~ $14 million) to continue operating in this

Fig. 1.   Airlines Ceased Operations and Airlines That Continue to Operate Under File for Administration/Declared Bankruptcy to Avoid Going Bankrupt From 2015 to 2022. *Source:* Compiled by the author. *Note:* Black box shows airlines were operating under declared bankruptcy (Use Chapter 11 bankruptcy) or filed for administration to avoid going bankrupt between 2021 and 2022. The rest of the airlines have ceased operations due to liquidation, insolvency or bankruptcy. *Source:* Own elaboration.

region (Mahlaka, 2022). The Spanish government approved a €200 million ($214 million) rescue loan to the privately owned Spanish airline Volotea to help it recover from the pandemic crisis (Reuters, 2022). As stated by Florido-Benítez (2021a), from 2015 to 2021, more than 40 airlines worldwide ceased operations for bankruptcy or insolvency, such as Monarch Airlines, Air Berlin, Thomas Cook and Cobalt Air, among many others, governments, airports, and airline operators need to rebuild the number of connections to pre-pandemic levels. The International Air Transport Association (IATA) (2021) and the World Bank (2022) reported that 1.8 billion passengers flew in 2020, a decrease of 60.2% compared to the 4.5 billion who flew in 2019; thus, this is the worst year on record in airline industry statistics (see Fig. 2).

After that, the World Health Organization (WHO) declared the coronavirus a global pandemic on 11 March 2020. From January 2022 on, many airlines reduced operating costs to obtain liquidity, according to the legally established criteria by governments. In addition, most low-cost and legacy carriers launched promotion campaigns for cheap flights to increase passenger demand throughout the year 2022. The big questions that now divide researchers and governments are the length of time of this pandemic, the airlines' survival, the high uncertainty in the tourism and aviation sectors and the pessimistic prospects in developed countries. The great challenge of the aviation industry, which had virtually closed over the last 2 years, is highlighted by there were 16% fewer seats in their pre-pandemic and an increase of 31% over 2021. For instance, the scale of recovery for some airlines like Ryanair or EasyJet has been truly amazing in 2022; both airlines have close passenger numbers and flight data to the year 2019, according to the Official Airline Guide (OAG, 2022), although in 2023, both airlines have recovered their traffic to pre-pandemic levels.

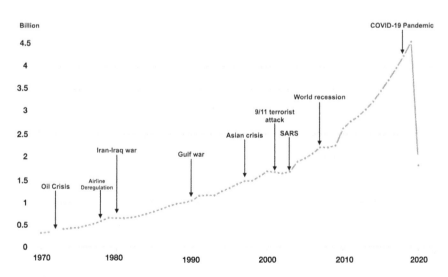

Fig. 2.   Passengers Carried by Airlines From 1970 to 2020. *Source:* Adapted from The World Bank (2022).

Nevertheless, the Airlines Deregulation Act of 1978 allowed free entry into airports and routes for airlines, and it also encouraged millions of passengers to enjoy air travel around the world. Deregulation spurred the creation of dozens of new airlines and prompted many smaller airlines to expand, in fact, in this new commercial environment was born hub and spoke airports, and known LCCs, which established the concept of point-to-point services. For all these reasons and for some others that are examined in the next chapters, commercial or non-aeronautical revenues and marketing strategies are needed to ensure the profitability of airport operators. Previous studies claim that it is not easy to date the beginning of the implementation of marketing activities at airports because airport marketing budgets and activities are linked to other costs, sales or even costs of administration (see Halpern & Graham, 2022; Thelle et al., 2012). The tourism development within a destination and airport provides a context where goals and economic interests overlap among Destination Marketing Organizations (DMOs), airports, airlines and stakeholders, and sometimes, it is very hard to advance a common set of interests (Florido-Benítez, 2022a).

The generation of revenue is a crucial output for airports and airlines, but in the case of airports, the airport's output value is related to the generation of aeronautical and non-aeronautical revenues. Airport revenues are those incomes generated from air traffic operations, aeronautical revenue and other passenger-dependent activities like retail concessions, retail businesses, catering, parking, advertising and rental cars; all of them are considered non-aeronautical revenue (Doganis, 2019; Senguttuvan, 2007). Digital development, new technologies, cybersecurity and information technologies are speeding up the transformation of airports into new business models, where they must stratify their portfolio of businesses with the aim of providing diversified and replacement revenue streams and enabling them to increase non-aeronautical revenues. These great changes at airports have created a world full of opportunities between the aviation and marketing industries, where passengers and companies that are operating in and around the airport will be the main beneficiaries.

1.2 There Is a World Full of Opportunities Between the Aviation and Marketing Sectors

The evolution of airports and their business models has developed favourably from an economic and technological point of view. Airport operators are constantly looking for new business models to increase aeronautical and commercial revenues. In spite of that, the airport as an infrastructure for transport and an intermodal transport node does not make any sense nowadays. As stated by Battal and Bakir (2017), airports have undergone a structural transformation with liberalisation, commercialisation and globalisation; in fact, both the revenue sources and revenue types of the airports have increased in the last 20 years, especially in non-aeronautical revenues. This type of income is where marketing activities are more functional and productive in return on investment (ROI) terms than aeronautical revenues because airport marketing strategies are not limited by stringent and complex environmental, health and safety standards that restrict passengers' access to airports.

Airports have a greater extent of operability in marketing activities, and they can lay out joint marketing strategies with other partners such as DMOs, airlines, tourist destinations, amusement and theme parks, museums, large online companies, logistics companies or even big international events like the Olympics, World Expo and the FIFA World Cup. Airport operators should also 'think big' to bring about positive changes and beneficial results. At the end, airport operators must implement marketing strategies if they want to increase their enplanements and bring on additional carriers. We all must understand the importance of airports and airlines for cities and their tourist attractions (e.g. Disney and Universal theme parks, the British Museum, the Metropolitan Museum or the National Museum of China) in terms of accessibility, connectivity and flight frequencies because these tourist attractions receive millions of visitors annually from around the world. In 2020, North American, Chinese, Japanese and Brazilian visitors made up three quarters of the total visits to the Louvre Museum, and probably most of them arrived in Paris by aeroplane (Florido-Benítez, 2023). For example, in May 2021, operators of Brussels airport invested in marketing campaigns through digital media to encourage consumers to book their travel in the summer after the Belgium government lifted the travel ban abroad. This marketing strategy focused basically on direct business-to-consumer (B2C) communication and diversification of marketing promotion campaigns between business-to-business (B2B) like own website promotions, advertising campaigns of new routes in radio, digital channels, TV, online travel agencies (OTAs) and influencers (Routes, 2021).

Airport marketing strategies have evolved and gained importance in the aviation and tourism industries in the last years, thanks to new technologies, the growth and democratisation of air travel among citizens, the accessibility and connectivity provided by LCCs and legacy carriers and the notable evolution of airports in large cities worldwide. Fig. 3 displays the evolution of airports from

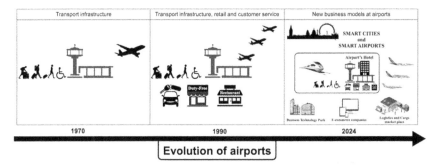

Fig. 3.   Evolution of Airports in the Last 50 Years. *Source:* Own elaboration.

1970 to 2024. As we can see, in 1970, airports were seen as a simple transport infrastructure to support airlines. After the Airlines Deregulation Act of 1978, many airports began to implement a growth strategy in commercial revenues, which would include a wide range of activities like restaurants, rent cars, retail outlets and duty-free shops. Today's airports are authentic shopping malls, and they have diversified and oriented their business model on those commercial activities associated with sustainable and lasting development in the long term. Airports have segmented much more volume and variability in their product and service lines, with the aim of adapting themselves to different customers and partners. Most airports have redesigned their terminals to minimise the transfer time of passengers, and they have more time to purchase and consume products and services within the airport's terminal. Nowadays, many airports are becoming smart airports inside smart cities to provide more personalised service through robots or the Internet of Things (IoT).

For instance, the airport of Málaga Costa del Sol (IATA code is AGP) in Spain was a tourist airport focused principally on luxury and mass tourism, but since Technology Park of Andalusia, Amazon, DHL, Vodafone, Google, Oracle, Virus Total, Aertec Solutions, Fujitsu, Caterpillar, San Miguel, Mayoral, high-speed train, museums, logistics companies, agri-food businesses, e-commerce and technology companies were introduced in Málaga city. Today, this airport has been set up as a multifunctional and attractive infrastructure for big companies worldwide (see Fig. 4), and Málaga's airport is one of the most important airports in Europe in accessibility and connectivity terms (Florido-Benítez, 2021b). All airports have a common denominator; they must improve their performance and competitiveness against their main competitors. Nowadays, airports are more proactive and innovative in their marketing strategies, and they have become more sophisticated in their segmentation of the market. Following the Federal Aviation Administration (FAA), Morrison and Maxim (2021) suggest

Málaga multifunctional airport

TERRITORY	OPERABILITY	PRESENT CARGO MARKET	ADDED VALUE

• Accesibility rate-time
• Location
• Local supply and customized
• Origin-destination demand
• Airport capacity
• Andalusia Techo-Park
• Intermodal airport
• Good weather, beach ,
  gastronomy
	• 24/7 all year
	• International connectivity
	• Physical and digital accesibility
	• International Business Network
	• 2 runways
	• Low costs
	• Multifunctional logistics
	• Digital transformation
	• Security Operations Centre
	  (SOC)
		• Forwarders and Integrators
		• Wide body capacity
		• Consolidation
		• Multimodal transport means
		• Regulated agent
		• Full freighter capacity
		• Frequency comercial-
		  cargo airlines
		• Less than 20 minutes
		  warehouses from airport
			• Opportunities for
			  Import/Export
			• Cooperation Airport-DMO-
			  Logistic
			• Reputation
			• Cybersecurity measures
			• Marketing & Business
			  development
			• Specialized supra-structure
			• Improved air cargo
			  connectivity-distribution

Fig. 4.   Factors That Have Transformed Málaga Airport in Multifunctional. *Source:* Adapted from Florido-Benítez (2021b).

that the effects of the pandemic on the tourism and aviation sectors require new challenges and future opportunities. Indeed, airports and commercial airlines are an essential part of smart tourist destinations (STDs), particularly if a tourist destination wants to be certified as an STD, and these want to provide excellent air accessibility and connectivity to residents and tourists (Florido-Benítez, 2024).

1.3 Airports in the Digital Innovation Era

The aviation and tourism industries are very sensitive to social, economic, market uncertainty, national security and economic crisis effects, which impact the nature of airports' operability and passengers' behaviour. These two industries mostly provide products and services related to the leisure and entertainment sectors, and they are not goods considered necessities by citizens. The COVID-19 pandemic is a living example of how airports, airlines and hotels have been affected by the effects of the pandemic, and many large operators worldwide have declared bankruptcy or been financially supported by governments. In 2021, global passenger traffic fell by 58.4% compared to the year 2019, although these data show an improvement compared to 2020 versus 2019, which fell by 65.8% (IATA, 2022). This is one of the major reasons why airports and airlines are going through a period of unprecedented change in economic, technological, innovation and marketing activities, and it is a dominant theme running through this book.

The 21st century is becoming known as the Digital Innovation Era, and all organisations want to be well positioned in digital media to get the consumer's attention, and they will provide their products and services. Airports are obviously not exempt of this disruptive digitalisation. On the contrary, according to a report by Airports Council International (ACI) in 2017, it claims that airport operators are constantly launching new digital initiatives, especially in safety and security, and marketing activities to make airport business and operations more efficient, safer and productive (see FAA, 2022; Florido-Benítez, 2021c; Halpern et al., 2021; Remencová & Sedláčková, 2021; Zaharia & Pietreanu, 2018). Digitalisation not only represents a world full of opportunities in the airport and marketing relationship but also a great challenge to operators and marketers in terms of investment and innovation.

Airports and airlines are highly dependent on the tourism industry. The growing demand for tourists' flow requires support in marketing actions through digital media and social-network marketing. As stated by Florido-Benítez (2022b), users who are familiar with digital media and their own smartphones move more efficiently and comfortably during the pandemic. Florido-Benítez (2022b) calls these users Human-Mobile-App (HuMobAp) humans move-mobile phone according to their needs and incentives that apps provide to them, such as flight apps (Delta Air Lines), travel apps or online travel agencies (Booking.com), review information apps (Tripadvisor), hotel reservation apps (Hilton Hotels), supermarket apps (Tesco) or even to track all departing and arriving flights and receive updates about gate changes, delays and airport updates through the airport's apps (Schiphol Amsterdam Airport).

Many studies have been conducted to examine the direct effects of marketing on tourism, international markets and human behaviour. However, in spite of the growing interest in airports and marketing relationships by researchers, academics and practitioners alike, there is no specific literature on airport marketing strategies, where researchers and airport operators can obtain relevant information that projects their investigations and joint marketing strategies with other partners. To fill this gap, the purpose of this groundbreaking book is to introduce students, researchers and practitioners to the new methods of airport marketing strategies in the digital innovation era, strategies that enhance commercial revenues, promotion campaigns, the effectiveness of marketing actions and the airport's brand image. Further, this book is intended to provide some awareness and understanding of the various interactions and interdependencies between airports, DMOs, airlines, marketing tools and stakeholders.

Airport marketing strategies are shown in a business, marketing and technological context, with the aim of highlighting the importance of this tool in the internationalisation of airports. To increase airports' sales and online presence through digital channels is a priority for airport operators, not a choice to boost their benefits and remain competitive after the pandemic crisis. Moreover, this book provides updated information, is accessible and is an in-depth textbook that introduces readers to the principles and practice of marketing, marketing tools, airport marketing strategies, different marketing techniques as well as the major changes and future marketing challenges facing airports in the coming years. That is why we must start out defining marketing within an airport industry context in Chapter 2.

References

ACI. (2017). *News and events from the voice of the world's airports.* https://issuu.com/aciworld/docs/aci_world_report_july_2017. Accessed on January 17, 2024.

Battal, U., & Bakir, M. (2017). The current situation and change in airport revenues: Research on the Europe's five busiest airports. *International Journal of Academic Research in Business and Social Sciences, 7*(7), 287–303.

Choo, Y. Y. (2014). Factors affecting aeronautical charges at major US airports. *Transportation Research Part A: Policy and Practice, 67,* 54–62.

Doganis, R. (2019). *Flying off course. Airline economics and marketing.* Routledge.

FAA. (2022). Smart cockpit technology. https://www.faa.gov/newsroom/safety-briefing/smart-cockpit-technology. Accessed on February 5, 2024.

Florido-Benítez, L. (2021a). The effects of COVID-19 on Andalusian tourism and aviation sector. *Tourism Review, 76*(4), 829–857.

Florido-Benítez, L. (2021b). How Málaga's airport contributes to promotes the establishment of companies in its hinterland and improves the local economy. *International Journal of Tourism Cities, 8*(2), 393–411.

Florido-Benítez, L. (2021c). New marketing strategy: Mobile applications as a marketing tool in airports. In *Chapter of book: Handbook of research on applied AI for international business and marketing applications* (pp. 14–29). IGI GLOBAL Publisher of Timely Knowledge.

Florido-Benítez, L. (2022a). The pre/on/post of low-cost carriers in Spanish tourist destinations. *Revista de Turismo Estudos & Prácticas, 11*(1), 1–26.

Florido-Benítez, L. (2022b). International mobile marketing: A satisfactory concept for companies and users in times of pandemic. *Benchmarking: An International Journal, 29*(6), 1826–1856.

Florido-Benítez, L. (2023). Air connectivity and proximity airports as an added value for museums. *Museum World, 11*, 136154.

Florido-Benítez, L. (2024). Constructing Spanish smart destinations: A new guide for the tourism industry. *International Journal of Tourism Cities, 10*(1), 261–279. https://doi.org/10.1108/IJTC-09-2023-0193

Graham, A. (2013). Understanding the low-cost carrier and airport relationship: A critical analysis of the salient issues. *Tourism Management, 36*, 66–76.

Gretzel, U., Wang, Y., & Fesenmaier, D. (2008). Travel and tourism. In H. Bidgoli (Ed.), *The handbook of computer networks. Distributed networks, network planning, control, management, and new trends and applications* (Vol. 3, pp. 943–961). Wiley.

Halpern, N., Budd, T., Suau-Sanchez, P., Bråthen, S., & Mwesiumo, D. (2021). Conceptualizing airport digital maturity and dimensions of technological and organizational transformation. *Journal of Airport Management, 5*(2), 182–203.

Halpern, N., & Graham, A. (2022). *Airport marketing* (2nd ed.). Routledge.

IATA. (2021). Airline industry statistics confirm 2020 was worst year on record. https://www.iata.org/en/pressroom/pr/2021-08-03-01/. Accessed on February 2, 2024.

IATA. (2022). Passenger demand recovery continued in 2021 but Omicron having impact. https://www.iata.org/en/pressroom/2022-releases/2022-01-25-02/. Accessed on February 1, 2024.

IATA and Deloitte. (2017). Airport ownership and regulation. https://www.iata.org/contentassets/4eae6e82b7b948b58370eb6413bd8d88/airport-ownership-regulation-booklet.pdf. Accessed on January 1, 2024.

Mahlaka, R. (2022). Mango collapse averted (for now) as government throws airline a financial lifeline. https://www.dailymaverick.co.za/article/2022-06-07-mango-collapse-averted-for-now-as-government-throws-airline-a-financial-lifeline/. Accessed on June 13, 2023.

Morrison, M. A., & Maxim, C. (2021). *World tourism cities. A systematic approach to urban tourism*. Routledge.

OAG. (2022). More restriction-free travel destinations join the path to recovery. https://www.oag.com/blog/restriction-free-destinations-join-path-recovery?hsLang=en-gb. Accessed on May 31, 2023.

Puls, R., & Lentz, C. (2018). Retail concessions at European airports: Commercial strategies to improve non-aeronautical revenue from leisure travelers. *Journal of Air Transport Management, 71*, 243–249.

Remencová, T., & Sedláčková, N. (2021). Modernization of digital technologies at regional airports and its potential impact on the cost reduction. *Transportation Research Procedia, 55*, 18–25.

Reuters. (2022). Spanish government bails out airline Volotea with 200-million-euro loan. https://www.reuters.com/article/spain-airlines-volotea-idINKBN2NP0GF. Accessed on June 8, 2023.

Routes. (2021). Brussels airport to invest in crucial marketing efforts to stimulate summer bookings. https://www.routesonline.com/news/29/breaking-news/295771/

brussels-airport-to-invest-in-crucial-marketing-efforts-to-stimulate-summer-bookings/. Accessed on January 11, 2023.

Senguttuvan, P. S. (2007). *Principles of airport economics*. Excel Books.

The World Bank. (2022). *Air transport, passenger carried.* https://data.worldbank.org/indicator/IS.AIR.PSGR?end=2020&start=1970&view=chart. Accessed on January 6, 2023.

Thelle, M. H., Pedersen, T. T., & Harhoff, F. (2012). *Airport competition in Europe*. Copenhagen Economics.

Zaharia, S. E., & Pietreanu, C. V. (2018). Challenges in airport digital transformation. *Transportation Research Procedia, 35,* 90–99.

Chapter 2

Marketing Activity and Its Relationship With Airports

Abstract

This chapter describes the importance of marketing activities at airports. The link between marketing and airports has been reinforced by new technologies and digital marketing tools. This technological combination has had a high penetration in the user's smartphones and airport activities, particularly in non-aeronautical revenue. Moreover, this chapter introduces a new conceptualisation of airport marketing, a definition more updated and aligned with airports' business needs in the time of a pandemic crisis. The rest of the chapter shows the mobile marketing tool and its interaction with passengers, as well as how this helps airport operators design new products and services, and increase commercial revenue through digital channels.

2.1 Marketing Approaches and Alternatives

The term marketing connotes to marketers, researchers and company operators a function that belongs to commercial enterprises. Marketing is seen as the task of finding and stimulating buyers for the firm's output. It involves product development, pricing, distribution and communication of goods in the more progressive firms, as well as continuous attention to the changing needs of customers and the development of new products, with product modifications and services to meet these needs (Kotler & Levy, 1969). In 2004, the American Marketing Association (AMA) defined the concept of marketing as an organisational function and a set of processes for creating, communicating and delivering value to customers, and for managing customer relationships in ways that benefit the organisation and its stakeholders (Keefe, 2004). However, the AMA (2017) redefined the concept of marketing as the activity, set of institutions and processes for creating, communicating, delivering and exchanging offerings that have value for customers, partners and society at large.

Airport Marketing Strategies, 11–35
doi:10.1108/978-1-83608-082-420241002

An updated version by Iacobucci (2021) defines marketing as an exchange between a firm and its customer; thus, an exchange relationship. In this context of exchange, airports seek to generate aeronautical and non-aeronautical revenue and provide high-value products and services to customers and organisations inside and outside of airports, like airlines, cargo carriers, online and logistics companies, Destination Marketing Organisations (DMOs) and business and technology parks, among many others. But we would go even further in the definition of the marketing term. Carvalho and Costa (2011) place higher emphasis on the organisational level, like new customised services, new customer relationship support and service delivery, with new technological opportunities through e-marketing. According to Labanauskaitė et al. (2020) e-marketing is defined as an integrated process, which a company sends a marketing message to a target segment by using internet and digital marketing tools such as sales promotion, advertising, viral messages, social media, blogs and mobile communications, among others, with the aim of reaching the target user and encouraging the use of offers. These types of marketing tools are examined in more detail in 5, 6 and 7 chapters.

Nevertheless, from a marketing research point of view, AMA (2017) considers that marketing research is the function that links the consumer, customer and public to the marketer through information. This information is used to identify and define marketing opportunities and problems; generate, refine and evaluate marketing actions; monitor marketing performance; and improve understanding of marketing as a process. Marketing research specifies the information required to address these issues, designs the method for collecting information, manages and implements the data collection process, analyzes the results and communicates the findings and their implications. Understanding the operation of airport marketing tools can represent a useful starting point for managing airport marketing strategies within the airport's terminal, airlines, logistics and cargo carriers and e-commerce firms. These marketing tools will help to design policy interventions and joint marketing strategies by airport operators, DMOs (understood local and national authorities) and stakeholders.

The theme of this book is that in dealing with airport marketing strategies, we must review again the main concepts of marketing with the aim of projecting the airport and marketing relationship and its present and future alternative scenarios. Besides, airports are an integral part of cities' marketing strategies as they support and lead the tourism development of tourist destinations, where they operate both physically and digitally. Hence, airports and commercial airlines are related to the situational analysis factors, objectives and strategies of cities (Baker & Cameron, 2008). For this reason, airport operators and their marketing teams must be constantly iterating new business models and joint marketing strategies to improve passengers' experiences at airports, redefine marketing decisions, minimise possible risks and maximise profit in Return on Investment (ROI) terms.

2.2 Airports Are an Integral Part of the Success of Destination Marketing

Due to the growing demand for air transport worldwide at tourist destinations, airports have become a privileged infrastructure in cities. The IATA (2022) points out that air transport is key to global economic development; this provides direct connections between cities, enabling the flow of goods, people, capital, technology, ideas and falling air transport costs. In the last few years, cities and countries have negotiated with airlines, airports and other tourist destinations around the world about opening new commercial air routes to attract market niches, new partners and potential investors through effective marketing strategies. Depending on the goals and market niches, airport operators may lay out joint marketing strategies with DMOs or airlines, their final objective is to attract passengers at airports and airlines and tourists in cities. But airport operators also have their own goals, interests and strategies to improve operability, income and their international brand image.

In 2020, for instance, the National Tourism Board of Spain, known as Turespaña, launched a new marketing campaign entitled 'Spain is part of You' (see Fig. 5), supported by the Spanish airport network, known more commonly as AENA (2021), a public operator attached to the Ministry for Public Works of Spain. This promotional campaign was designed to reinforce the positioning of Spain as the main holiday destination for the main outbound markets like the United Kingdom, France, Germany, Italy, Belgium, Sweden, the Netherlands, Hungary and Poland. The main goal of this campaign is to respond to the exceptional situation caused by the pandemic, in which Spanish airports provide confidence (see Fig. 6), security and hygiene to tourists, so they can plan their

Fig. 5.   Promotional Campaigns by Turespaña. *Source:* Courtesy of Spain.info official website.

Airports in Spain

Here at AENA we want you to come to our airports with complete confidence.

Fig. 6.   Campaign's Informational of Hygiene-Health Control Measures by AENA. *Source:* Courtesy of AENA.

holidays in all Spanish cities. In this promotional strategy, Spanish airports offer tourists the opportunity to fly to all the locations in Spain in 1 hour by plane (Turespaña, 2021).

The success of airports is reliant on the competitiveness of the destination in which they are located, and vice versa. There are a lot of opportunities to develop beneficial joint marketing strategies between airports, airlines, DMOs and stakeholders, but often they do not use these properly (Florido-Benítez, 2020). An understanding of this commercial interrelation enables stakeholders to take advantage of opportunities in promotion, distribution and new product development, thereby enhancing their own success as well as contributing to the effectiveness of their DMOs, because the main function of DMOs is to increase tourist visitation at tourist destinations (Pike, 2008). The role of DMO is to commercialise a tourism destination or city. Destination marketing and management is a complex issue that requires a comprehensive, holistic and systematic approach to understand it (Wang & Pizam, 2011). It is therefore important to consider the conceptualisation of destination marketing in this book, as an airport cannot be understood and addressed itself like an interdependent body without the trading environment that surrounds and the city where the airport is operating around the clock.

According to the United Nations World Tourism Organisation (UNTWO), destination marketing covers all the activities and processes to bring buyers and sellers together; focuses on responding to consumer demands and competitive positioning; is a continuous coordinated set of activities associated with efficient distribution of products to high potential markets; and involves making decisions about the product, branding, price, market segmentation, promotion, and distribution (UNWTO, 2004). In addition, incorporating the views of tourists brings a more comprehensive and nuanced approach to managing destinations and provides a means of assessing current practices and strategies (Pearce & Schänzel, 2013). A study carried out by Chang and Chiang (2022) demonstrated that the virtual reality (VR) tool improves tourists' experiences at destinations, and this is an effective tool for tourism destination marketing in promotion campaigns, brand image and sustainable marketing strategies. In the same vein, Balasubramanian and Rasoolimanesh (2022) suggest that the creation of augmented reality (AR) and VR products for tourism destinations will create new markets for the industry to survive this pandemic crisis. These marketing tools must be supervised by DMOs; Florido-Benítez (2024a) notes that DMOs need to serve as stewards for their destinations, including greater awareness of problems that emerge from the design and implementation of technologies, greater accountability and greater care exercised in decision-making (Florido-Benítez, 2024b).

2.3 Airport Marketing Conceptualisation

After the Airlines Deregulation Act of 1978 in the United States, and the progressive privatisation of airports around the world changed completely the operability of airports, especially in the US' airports. In the 1980s and 1990s of the 20th century, airport operators understood that in a complex and competitive environment like the aviation industry, it was very difficult to maximise profits with aeronautical revenue at the end of the year, and this was insufficient to cover airport costs. Operators were forced to adapt to the new market circumstances and opportunities, and they meanwhile introduced marketing activities for non-aeronautical services to augment revenue.

Marketing did not play a significant role in the management of airports until the 1980s. Deregulation of the airlines and other sectors of the air transport industry, however, motivated airports to begin competing for airline routing. Marketing was first introduced at airports that sought to either enlarge or protect their airline customer base. As air travelers became more sophisticated and demanding, airports came to believe that they could influence airline routing decisions through a pull strategy of directing marketing efforts to end users, offering enhanced services, or making the promise of exceptional levels of customer satisfaction (Fodness & Murray, 2007).

At this point, Freathy (2004) revealed that new commercial services and equipment were added to the airport's aeronautical functions, expressing the new airport vision as a platform for doing business. From a strategic and marketing perspective, airports have become key providers of vacation and business services to customers and companies, particularly perishable services that cannot be stored for later sale or use. That is one of the reasons why marketing strategies through promotion campaigns can influence customers' needs and decisions about 'customised or massive services' and respond to changes in supply and demand.

Today, most airports' planning and operation envisions the development of additional commercial activities through marketing activities that optimise infrastructure and bring revenue to the airport operators (Brilha & Nobre, 2019; Florido-Benítez, 2016a, 2016b). Halpern and Graham (2022) focus on airport marketing in three elements: internal (operator), micro (suppliers, customers and stakeholders) and macro (political-legal, economic and technological) environments, which play a key role in influencing the airport's marketing strategy and planning decisions by operators. According to the Airport Cooperative Research Program (ACRP), airport marketing is defined as an ongoing process of attracting users and tenants, developing services, managing community relations and positioning the airport worldwide against the competition (ACRP, 2009). Halpern and Niskala (2008) suggest that airport marketing uses several marketing techniques to exploit market trends and attract leisure carriers and target markets.

There is much scientific literature on marketing activity and its conceptualisation, but few that speak directly to airport marketing and its definition. For this reason, this book adds a new definition of airport marketing and defines it as a marketing multipurpose tool to design a wide range of strategies through marketing tools like traditional marketing, mobile and digital marketing, apps, promotion and customised messages, among many others, with the aim of attracting users and companies inside and around airports, which enables airport operators to increase aeronautical and non-aeronautical revenue, enhance customers' experiences and empower the airport's brand image globally. Fig. 7 shows a new global vision of airport marketing in the digital innovation era. Airport marketing is more interoperable and creative with users, partners, airlines and companies. The pandemic crisis has changed positively how organisations and people communicate, creating digital, inclusive and ubiquitous communication

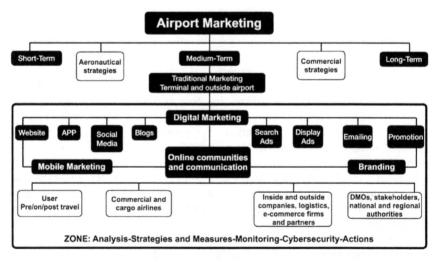

Fig. 7.   Airport Marketing Concept. *Source:* Own elaboration.

between them, which offers many more alternatives and opportunities for users and companies to choose from. Airports of the future will be smart, but also open safe spaces (understood as a cybersecurity term) to promote the innovation and technological development of firms at the service of people.

While marketing is now as fundamental to the success of the airport sector as any other business, airport marketing is also considered increasingly important due to the impact it can have on the economic and social development of the surrounding area. This is particularly the case when tourism or cargo traffic is being considered. For this reason, airport marketing undertaken by publicly owned airports may often have wider objectives than just enhancing the success of the airport operator. Due to these wider implications, collaboration with other interested stakeholders, such as tourism and regional development agencies is more commonplace within airport marketing than in many other industries (Graham, 2008). As a public infrastructure, one of the airport operator's main responsibilities is to generate economic benefits through commercial activities.

Airports operate in a highly competitive environment and are increasingly generating revenue through ancillary services (IATA, 2020). For instance, the International Civil Aviation Organization (ICAO) claims that airport operators must identify and reach their target audience through diverse marketing channels, while forging forward-looking relationships with potential business partners to make better decisions and put them into practice (ICAO, 2019). Marketing techniques like digital mobile marketing help to maximise profit within airports' hinterland by attracting retailers and service providers, as well as improving customers' experiences at airports.

2.4 Mobile Marketing as a Tool to Increase Passengers' Satisfaction and Experience Levels

The proliferation of mobile devices like smartphones and tablets has opened new opportunities for airports and companies operating within the airport's terminal and around the airport. Airports have implemented mobile marketing tools to improve passengers' satisfaction and experience within their facilities. Today, no one doubts that the internet is an important medium, and smartphones are with people all the time and have become an essential, personal and intimate tool for all users. This marketing channel promotes a product or service in a world in which people dedicate ever more time to the use of the mobile internet to organise their daily lives, from making reservations at restaurants to doctor appointments. It is not an exaggeration to say that buying and selling habits are rapidly transforming due to the powerful association between mobile devices and marketing (Florido-Benítez & del Alcázar, 2015).

Major airports are switching to a business model, following commercial management guidelines, and focusing on developing more creative environments in tune with the new technologies. Thus, airports are leaving behind the rigid image of the aerodrome as a mere intermodal node. The application of a business approach to airports implies an improvement in their financing capabilities. As stated by the

Société Internationale de Télécommunications Aéronautiques (SITA) improving passengers' experiences is the primary reason why airports and airlines invest in technology. In 2018, airports and airlines spent a record 50 billion euros on improving the passenger experience, and it is paying off, especially during the COVID-19 pandemic (SITA, 2019). Several researchers agreed that mobile marketing has the ability to reach their target market even faster than traditional advertising (Florido-Benítez, 2021; Hopkings & Turner, 2013; Tong et al., 2020). For this reason, the airport's apps are a key element in airport marketing, and because they have become important in the airport's portfolio, they cannot be considered a mere communication tool.

The app is a software programme designed for mobile devices, and this is seen as a tool in mobile marketing. The intention is to obtain great media coverage and promote a relevant interactive process using advertisements, offers, discounts, prizes, etc., thanks to the user's experience with the mobile device. Apps are being transformed into sales channels, where distribution is the key to entering the channel and enabling the sale of products and services (Florido-Benítez, 2016c). Florido-Benítez (2021) suggests that universalising the firm's brand app, with the aim of increasing the number of users in direct contact and promoting the products and services internationally in a more immediate and close way. In addition, the airport's app is used to collect users' data with their consent (i.e. personal data, surveys, location, personal tastes and preferences, among others). User interaction with the app is monitored by the airport's marketing department to analyse passengers' behaviour and lay out mobile marketing strategies to increase commercial revenue and be more effective in shopping. Leeflang et al. (2015) revealed that the massive growth in customer data has also lowered the costs of some traditional data sources while facilitating new data sources. For example, online survey tools make it extremely easy for firms to survey their own customers.

Airports such as Schiphol in Amsterdam saw the mobile marketing tool as a great opportunity not only to increase the overall satisfaction of passengers, but also to enhance the airport's brand image across the globe. The creation of the Schiphol Amsterdam airport mobile application (app) improved in all areas the experience of passengers at the airport, and this provides floor managers and the rest of the staff insight into your daily to-do list and other tools you need to help you do your job. Fig. 8 displays the two modalities of apps, Schiphol app to passengers and Schiphol Today app for the airport's staff. In 2013, Schiphol airport won the award for best airport in Europe and third in the world, and the Schiphol airport app played an important role in these two awards (World Airport Awards, 2013). It is important to highlight that the important thing about an application is not that it can geolocate you, instead, the essence of an application at the airport lies in personalising the passenger's experience and being able to offer them micro-segmented products (Florido-Benítez, 2021; Florido-Benítez & del Alcázar, 2014).

Although it may seem like the idea of mobile marketing was introduced a long time ago, this is a misconception. Its performance as a new marketing activity has been ongoing for less than a decade since it is a recent marketing modality. Furthermore, it is immersed in a field of new technologies that is subject to

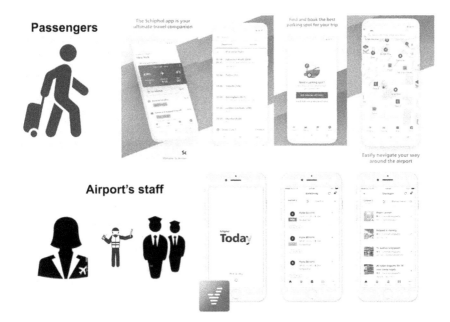

Fig. 8.   Airport's App as a Tool of Mobile Marketing and
Productivity. *Source:* Own elaboration.

continuous change (Florido-Benítez, 2014, 2021; Florido-Benítez et al., 2015). Mobile marketing has led to it being defined in different ways and with various interpretations. The literature review has shown a recent interest in the analysis of this tool since some researchers and associations like Mobile Marketing Association (MMA) differ in defining the idea; although authors like Okazaki (2012), Rodríguez-Carmona (2012) and Ström et al. (2014) claim that mobile marketing is a tool by which organisations can develop their designs, advertising, improve the experience of retailers' brands, reinforcing or adding valuable benefits, and it may create lasting competitive advantages.

The COVID-19 pandemic has changed travel patterns worldwide; consumers react more favourably to safety as compared to emotional advertising appeals (Garaus & Hudáková, 2022). Marketing strategies like app notifications help to continue using mobile payment apps during the pandemic crisis. Their compatibility with COVID-19 conditions, which require social distancing, usefulness and ease of use, work more effectively than the traditional payment methods (Rafdinal & Senalasari, 2021). The rapid growth in the use of smartphones and their respective apps has created new ways for the tourism and aviation industries to connect with their visitors while travelling. Understanding the opportunities currently provided by apps is also critical from a marketing perspective (Kennedy-Eden & Gretzel, 2012).

Nonetheless, authors and organisations such as MMA (2009), Tong et al. (2020) and Shankar and Balasubramanian (2009) define mobile marketing as a multidirectional channel of communication between companies advertising deals and customers using a mobile medium, device or technology. However, Müller et al. (2018) view this marketing modality as a sales channel through which customers are offered products and services. Mobile marketing represents all marketing activities like promotion, product design, service design, distribution and payment services, among many others (Fritz et al., 2017; Varadarajan, 2010). Diversified booking channels, including instant messaging tools, mobile phone clients, the official website of tourist attractions and telephone booking, among others, can provide tourists with a good travel experience and humanised service (Zhao et al., 2022). For example, loyal visitors to the destination and the knowledge of the tourist about the city are factors that have an impact on a longer length of stay at tourist destinations. These two indicators provide an integral perspective on tourism that includes territorial planning and management by operators (Gemar et al., 2022). Marketing problems are typically dynamic, involving multiple decision variables, and their outcomes are uncertain. A study carried out by Florido-Benítez (2016c) revealed that mobile marketing is a great communication and sale tool that is used in interactive wireless media, with the aim of promoting and selling personalised products and services, offering information and assistance to users and employees and universalising the brand image worldwide through mobile devices. In the digital innovation era, airport operators must manage their information and marketing strategies, so passengers have all the information necessary on their smartphones.

2.5 Social Media Is a Tool to Share Airports' Content and Passengers' Experiences

Social media has become an integral part of our lives, revolutionising the way we communicate, interact and consume information. The aviation industry, which plays a significant role in connecting people and bridging distances, has also recognised the immense potential of social media marketing. Social media platforms provide an opportunity for airport and airline operators to strengthen passenger relationships and foster loyalty. Airport and airline operators can engage with passengers on a personal level, responding to their queries, addressing concerns and providing timely assistance. By actively participating in conversations and demonstrating a genuine interest in customer needs, airports and airlines can build long-term relationships and turn customers into brand advocates (Medium, 2023).

For instance, community managers of airports and airlines can ask passengers to share their experiences and photographs on Facebook, Instagram, X or Tick Tock platforms to enhance airports and airlines' brand image visibility and their products and services. This marketing strategy can capture the attention of potential travellers and obtain immediate feedback on passengers' experiences and perceptions at airports and airlines. A study carried out by Sigurdsson et al. (2020) found that more than 70% of all Icelandair Facebook posts included a picture or video and that posts with pictures attracted the most engagement in terms of likes and comments, whereas posts with videos generated the most shares regarding consumer engagement with the airline brand. Passengers can post any complaints, compliments and suggestions about an airline on social media at any time by using their mobile devices. Social media can be used as an indicator of a company and its partners' reputation and service quality (Tian et al., 2020). For example, an airport operator is involved in a large, extended business network. An airport operator's success largely depends on the quality of the support provided by its suppliers, such as airline fuel and lubricant providers, catering service providers, aircraft storage and maintenance providers, among many others.

Instagram, TikTok and Facebook platforms are used by the younger generation, and this is known by commercial airlines. Therefore, airlines such as Emirates, Iberia, Qatar, Air Asia and Ryanair have completely focused on social media as another digital communication channel to promote their products and services. More than 40% of young people turn to social media for restaurant recommendations, socialising tips, entertainment ideas and even travel inspiration (Perez, 2023). Social media plays a crucial role in online marketing, as it helps customers to make better informed purchases, builds brand awareness, increases product acceptance and lowers the risks involved in consumption (Arica et al., 2022). As per a study by IAB on social networks in Spain, 62% of users are influenced by the opinions of third-party users on social media when making purchasing decisions (IAB, 2023). An active social media presence provides added value for users who trust brands with an engaging and dynamic social media account. Hence, incorporating social media networks into airport and airline marketing strategies is crucial to boost search engine positioning and build trust and credibility with the target audience. Madrigal (2017) notes that American Airlines receives more than 4,500 mentions per hour 70–80% of them on Twitter.

Panel A of Fig. 9 illustrates how 75% of low-cost carriers (LCCs) (Ryanair, Wizz Air, Vueling, Air Asia, Iberia Express and Spirit airlines) and 67% of legacy airlines (Emirates, Iberia, Delta, United Airlines, Saudia Arabia and Turkish airlines) have a presence on Facebook, Instagram, YouTube and TikTok, with only a small number not utilising TikTok (Smartvel, 2023). These findings suggest that airlines are recognising the importance of social media platforms in their marketing strategies, regardless of their category.

Nonetheless, Panel B of Fig. 9 shows how legacy airlines tend to showcase more corporate content, while LCCs opt for more controversial, humourous and trendy content. These differences are due to factors such as their target audience, brand image and reputation. For instance, airlines such as Ryanair, Wizz Air, Vueling, EasyJet, Iberia Express, Iberia and Turkish airlines are focused on destination contents because most of them operate in the main European tourist destinations, and these airlines and some destinations promote joint tourism campaigns on social media. On the contrary, legacy carriers prefer to promote the quality of their services and their brand image on social media as a key differentiating element. The airline industry is a part of the service division that plays an important role in tourist destinations, and commercial airlines provide their

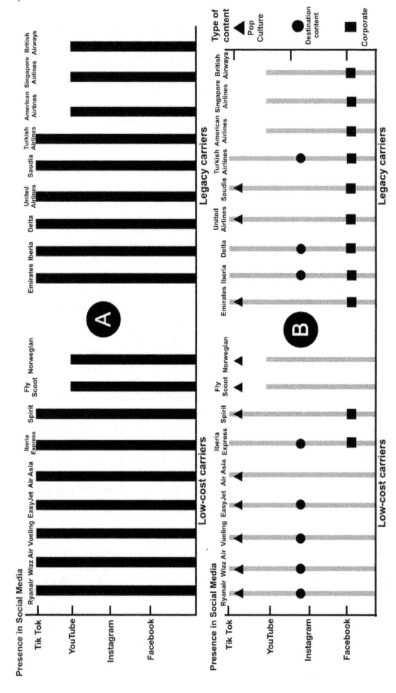

Fig. 9. The Presence of Airlines in TikTok, YouTube, Instagram and Facebook Platforms (Panel A), and Type of Content (Panel B). *Source:* Adapted from Smartvel (2023).

services through their website, app and social media platforms. Airport operators need new ways to create competitive advantages through social media for airlines to attract more passengers at airports' terminals (Seo et al., 2020).

2.6 Customer Loyalty Programmes Are Added Value for Airports and Airlines

Loyalty programs are structured marketing efforts that encourage consumers to return to companies where they frequently make purchases. Yi and Jeon (2003) define a loyalty programme as a marketing programme that is designed to build customer loyalty by providing incentives to profitable customers. Therefore, the role of a loyalty programme is to offer customers additional value, which can span beyond the actual value being exchanged (Kwiatek et al., 2020). Ninety percent of US consumers actively participate in some type of loyalty programme (Berman, 2006), and it involves the issuance of specially coded credit cards. Card usage can confer benefits, including immediate price discounts, members-only deals, free gifts at some threshold level of spending, redeemable points and/or eligibility for sweepstakes and contests (Kim et al., 2013).

Loyalty programs are a massive source of revenue for airlines, allowing them to act as de facto financial service companies by partnering up with credit cards and awarding points. The biggest loyalty programme in the United States and the world is managed by Delta airlines, with over 120 million members. This marketing programme called 'SkyMiles' increased by 8.5 million customers in 2022 (Pande, 2023). Not very far behind is United Airlines' MileagePlus program. The United company has over 110 million members across the globe. Coming in third place is Advantage. This loyalty program is managed by American Airlines, and it boasts over 100 million members, drawing strongly as the biggest carrier in the United States by flights, fleet size and destinations. While the airline has fewer international destinations than its two closest rivals, its domestic presence is massive and only growing. Crossing the Atlantic, Miles & More is the largest airline loyalty program in Europe. This loyalty program benefits by bringing together members from Lufthansa, LOT Polish, SWISS, Austrian, Brussels Airlines, Eurowings and even more carriers under one umbrella, totalling 36.6 million members (Pande, 2023). The ability to save up miles for flights is the first reason many customers enrol in airlines' loyalty programs. Eighty percent of all miles are redeemed for flights, and the rest are redeemed for hotel stays, car rentals and consumer products (McKinsey & Company, 2023).

Hotels and airlines are not the only travel-related organisations with appealing loyalty programs, airports have them, too. An airport reward programme can deliver some great benefits and encourage travellers to fly more from their favourite airports. Airports are competing for your business just like airlines, especially as passengers may be willing to drive longer distances to reach an airport with lower fares (Qubein, 2023). For instance, the airport of Heathrow (London) has its own loyalty programme called 'Heathrow Rewards'. The airport's loyalty programme offers discounts or vouchers at firms of retail brands, restaurants, bars and hotels, plus parking at Heathrow and Heathrow Express transportation. When the user registers her/his credit card during enrolment in the Heathrow Rewards, she/he'll collect 10 points for every $14 (£10) spent. She/he can also use her/his points towards your miles programme, including Miles & More by Lufthansa, British Airways Avios and Emirates Skywards, for example 250 Heathrow Rewards points equal 250 miles (Heathrow, 2024). These loyalty programmes are also used as a marketing tool by the Charles de Gaulle airport in Paris, the airport of Frankfurt in Germany, the airport of Schiphol in the Netherlands, the airport of Auckland in New Zealand, the airport of Changi in Singapore and most US airports. As an example of this marketing strategy, Copenhagen's airport has its CPH Advantage loyalty programme, which gives users free Wi-Fi (a $7 saving), parking discounts, lounge discounts, shopping discounts and free gifts. The membership is tiered, however, so you can work your way up to better and better perks the more you visit and spend.

We must be aware that airports are also designed as shopping malls by airport operators to increase non-aeronautical revenues through VIP services, restaurants, hotels, parking, duty-free stores, gyms, clothes and jewellery shops, among many others. Passengers spend quite a bit of time at the airport's terminals while they wait for their flight; in fact, they like to visit all establishments inside the terminal. On the other hand, people that visit the airport for different purposes, such as the families of passengers, local residents, spotters or even workers, must be considered by airport operators as another market niche for increasing commercial sales. Airports' loyalty programs enable passengers and/or visitors to accumulate reward points by shopping, dining or paying for other commercial activities at airports. For example, Changi airport has over 400 retail and service stores and 140 food and beverage outlets. The Changi airport's loyalty programme, called Changi Rewards, offers discounts or vouchers on most of these establishments to provide personalised products and services to passengers, as well as increase commercial revenues. Wu and Tsui (2020) revealed that the attractive benefits of Changi Rewards had a positive influence on arousing customers' intention to engage with the programme, as well as making them spend more time inside the terminals of airports and their establishments.

Moreover, airport and airline operators should implement customised loyalty programs to meet the needs of their most loyal customers. It would be a big mistake to consider a passenger that flies 20 times a year more than a tourist that flies once a year for holidays. Passengers want to participate in reward programs to obtain economic benefits (discounts), emotional benefits (sense of belonging), prestige or recognition and/or access to an exclusive treatment or service. Thus, loyalty programs must be considered an added value of the organisation, where customers feel rewarded for loyalty and commitment to the airport or airline selected. Creating a successful passenger loyalty programme in an airport requires a strategic and holistic approach that addresses passengers' needs and creates value for both passengers and airports.

Sometimes, airports' communication and reward strategies can be difficult to design and implement and may not always match passengers' needs and wants. Most loyalty programs are based on volume (e.g. your 10th flight is free).

Although it would be interesting for airport and airline operators to conduct online surveys to better understand the needs and profiles of passengers, this relevant information can help airport and airline operators design personalised loyalty programs to cover passengers' needs and preferences. To attract and retain loyal customers, airports need to offer unique and valuable benefits that differentiate them from their competitors. For example, airports can provide exclusive access to lounges, fast-track security, priority boarding, free parking, discounts on shopping and dining or personalised services through airports' loyalty programs. However, these benefits also require significant investments and resources. One of the main objectives of airport and airline loyalty programs is to enhance passenger relationships by offering high value to profitable market segments (Zakir-Hossain et al., 2017).

2.7 Airport Operators Need to Adapt Their Marketing Strategies to Changing Customer Needs

With the evolving landscape of business and technology, airports must adapt to innovative marketing strategies and changing customers' needs. It is no longer enough to rely solely on traditional marketing. Today, airports need to adopt marketing strategies that consider digital platforms and customer-centric approaches. Digital channels such as the metaverse, social media, TV or even artificial intelligence (AI) not only bring opportunities for growth and expansion but also challenges that require out-of-the-box solutions. Strategies alliances among airports, airlines, DMOs, tourist attractions and hotels are now widespread to meet the needs of all types of visitors throughout their holidays (Florido-Benítez, 2023a, 2023b). Notwithstanding, airports own interests sometimes are not aligned with airlines and DMOs' interests and marketing strategies because they all compete for the same customers and their spending capacity. For instance, airports' marketing strategies based on discounts and vouchers to increase sales of firms inside the airport's terminal can reduce the consumption of beverages and meals by passengers in-flight.

Therefore, it is necessary to clearly define airports' own interests and their marketing strategies, so as not to conflict with the economic interests of airlines and other airport partners. Fig. 10 shows how airports, airlines, cities, DMOs, tourist attractions, hotels and other companies have their own economic interests and marketing strategies, but all of them also develop joint marketing strategies to attract visitors and investments to the city. This is like playing a game of chess, but with different strategies to increase the benefits.

Strategic marketing alliances between airport operators, airlines and DMOs make more attractive in terms of tourism and foreign investment. Lufthansa, Munich airport and the DMO's Munich cooperate jointly improve the tourism industry and the city's air connectivity, as well as satisfy the new demands of passengers and airlines simultaneously (Albers et al., 2005).

Sometimes, airport and DMO economic interests are completely opposite to residents' needs and interests. For example, to attract millions of visitors annually

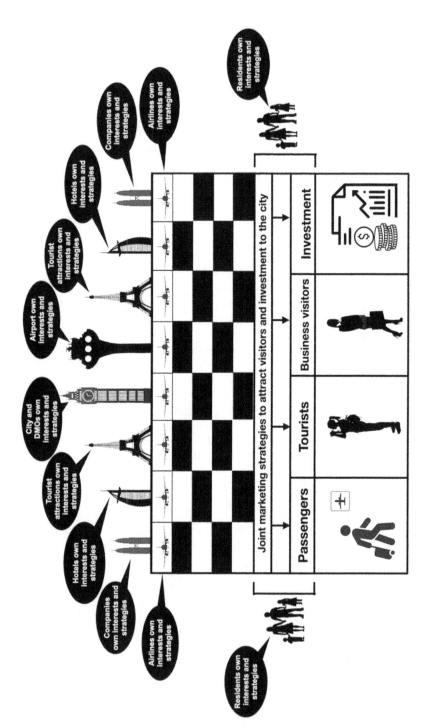

Fig. 10.   Individual and Joint Marketing Strategies by Organisations to Attract Visitors and Investment to the City. *Source:* Own elaboration.

through commercial airlines to European cities such as Barcelona, Venice, Amsterdam, Berlin, Copenhagen, Lisbon, Málaga, Palma de Mallorca, Paris, London or Munich is negatively affecting residents due to overtourism, gentrification, touristification of living space, inappropriate behaviour of tourists or tourists' acts of vandalism factors (Koens et al., 2018). People take shorter holidays but travel more often, while LCCs and sharing economy platforms allow people to reach different destinations, especially cities, at affordable prices (Żemła & Szromek, 2021). When airport operators design marketing strategies focused on customers' needs, they also must be aware of where they are operating and residents' preferences.

Airport and airline operators are increasing their sales, visibility and services thanks to e-commerce platforms and the internet. Consumer marketing strategy in e-commerce uses websites and app sites to create brand awareness and influence consumer behaviours and buying decisions (Florido-Benítez, 2016a).

Online businesses facilitate a consumer marketing strategy that is interaction and information-based to enhance users' efficiency, experiences and satisfaction (Rosário & Raimundo, 2021). For instance, airlines' websites consist of design features that ensure responsiveness, clarity, consistency and concision to enhance interactivity and engagement with their consumers. We live in an age where most customers have a smartphone in their pockets, and they are always connected.

In 2006, international passengers spent 75% of their time landside and 25% airside (Graham, 2009); thus, this information suggests that airport operators should improve the dwell time of passengers and offer customised products and services to boost non-aeronautical revenue.

Hence, the interaction between companies and users must be immediate, durable and fully satisfactory for both users and companies. When the passenger does arrive at the airport, an SMS notification could be triggered with the link to the airline or airport's app for instructions on where to go, how to use new self-check-in systems, notifications on gate numbers and a map of the airport. Furthermore, airport operators should implement a virtual assistant to improve and simplify the compensation process for delayed or cancelled flights. Passengers could use this virtual assistant or chatbot to submit all necessary information, such as flight numbers and airport car parking tickets that can be analysed in real-time, with basic checks being applied to the claim. Ethiopian airlines provide a chatbot called 'Lucy', accessible on Telegram and Messenger platforms. Passengers can book flights, make payments for services, complete check-ins and add other flight-related amenities online. At the end, each airport and airline should have at least one focal point for communication and information to meet passengers' needs and claims.

2.8 Regional Airports Need to Increase Revenue Through Corporate Aviation

Executive or corporate aviation is carried out by companies and aircraft dedicated to the efficient, comfortable and safe transport of people in small groups between any origin and destination. NetJets, Flexjet, Wheels Up, Vista Global and FlyExclusive serve as the five largest US private jet operators (Gollan, 2022), and these five private companies have helped to increase airports' revenues, such as Hartsfield-Jackson Atlanta, Dallas-Fort Worth, Denver, Chicago's O'Hare, Los Angeles and Orlando airports. Private aviation is considered an essential operational tool for business flyers. Global executive aviation moves more than $25 billion a year, and selling such aircraft also continues to grow, with China, North America and the Persian Gulf being the most commercial markets. These data also include the charter or aerotaxi sector, which, far from being a great luxury, also represents a necessary service for airport operators (EAS Barcelona, 2019).

During the pandemic, private aviation increased CO2 emissions by over 23% (Sobieralski & Mumbower, 2022). We are aware that ethical and environmental perspectives are not correct in terms of reducing substantially CO2 emissions and decarbonisation in the private aviation industry, but we expect that the use of alternative fuels will soon improve citizens' perceptions of the image of the public and private aviation industries. Private air companies encourage the local and regional economies at cities, as well as attract a tourism of quality and business, which improves the sustainability of regional airports. The private aviation sector represents a small part of the global air transportation market, reaching US$24billion in 2020 (Fortune Business Insights, 2013). The availability of flights in the departure and/or arrival destinations represents, for business flyers, one of the main reasons for flying on a private jet. Some cities are not directly connected by commercial flights to the needed destination, or the delays and inefficiencies of commercial aviation can represent another obstacle to satisfying the needs of customers with high purchasing power and business flyers (Klaus & Tarquini-Poli, 2022).

Private aviation is associated with luxury travel for ultra-high-net-worth individuals who place a high value on the time savings of flying private (Veloutsou et al., 2022). For this reason, airport operators can provide customised services to this type of client and business flyers to increase the airport's aeronautical and commercial revenue. Airports such as Paris Le Bourget, London Luton, Vienna-Schwechat, Rome Ciampino or Milan Linate airport offer exclusive access and customised services to private flights (e.g. VIP experiences, fixed base operators, personalised catering, among others). In the case of the Haneda airport in Tokyo, Japan, it has the highest landing fee for a private aircraft in the world. A private jet has to pay $6,850 just to land your aircraft in this airport (Travair, 2023).

Although, the private jet will never have priority over a commercial aircraft, particularly in hub-and-spoke airports like Dallas-Fort Worth International, it will cost an additional $500 or so for each private flight, whereas a regional airport like Dallas Love Field often carries lower costs (Paramount Business Jets, 2023). Private aviation companies prefer to use regional airports due to their low costs and they are often located closer to their destination. It is cheaper to use a regional airport, where landing fees cost around 90% less than commercial ones. That's why almost all private jets are stationed at regional airports (Paramount Business Jets, 2023).

Indeed, most private jet companies operate in regional airports because their customers want to fly from a specific airport to reach their destination. For these private firms, time savings are crucial in determining whether to fly private, leading many to avoid larger airports due to longer wait times during taxi, take-off and landing. In regional airports, wait times are often short or non-existent on account of the limited number of flights originating and arriving there. Regional airports are reconfiguring their operations to be more attractive for the private and commercial aviation sectors. Meanwhile, regional airport operators can introduce a service differentiation perspective, such as luxury services for corporate executives, celebrity artists, movie stars and football teams, among many others, who often travel in private jets. Choi (2021) notes that regional airport operators need a better understanding of their customers and flight characteristics to offer quality service and redefine their marketing strategies.

Obviously, executive aviation is a very lucrative sector for those regional airports that want to increase their operational incomes. In addition, providing this type of service and facility by regional airport operators to private aviation might be a distinct competitive advantage and added value over other airports. One of the main challenges for regional airports after COVID-19 is to restore air connectivity and economic and financial sustainability to generate benefits and liquidity. Most European regional airports did not receive economic financing during the pandemic, and they have great economic, liquidity and financial problems (Kazda et al., 2017).

From a financial point of view, liquidity is important to airports for two reasons. Firstly, while airlines collect airport charges from passengers at the time of booking, these are not paid to airports until after passengers have undertaken their flight. Secondly, airports have high capital expenditure requirements and associated capital costs given the nature of the infrastructure that they maintain (ACI, 2021). Regional airports need to design incentives to encourage productive efficiency and improve their business portfolios to increase revenue and reduce costs (Alber et al., 2013). Garcia (2024) notes that US airport operators are focusing on four key areas to improve revenue after the pandemic crisis: attracting new airlines and private aviation companies, enhancing the passenger experience, boosting passenger spending at the terminal and upgrading technology to manage operations. Also, it should be noted that regional airports should prioritise their efforts to attract private jet companies to minimise their high dependency on commercial airlines in the low season.

References

ACI. (2021). *Turnaround time: Airport financial recovery and restart following COVID-19.* https://www.aci-europe.org/downloads/resources/Turnaround%20Time_ACI%20EUROPE%20whitepaper%20on%20financial%20recovery%20from%20Covid-19.pdf. Accessed on December 1, 2023.

ACRP. (2009). *ACRP report 28. Marketing guidebook for small airports.* https://onlinepubs.trb.org/onlinepubs/acrp/acrp_rpt_028.pdf. Accessed on December 1, 2021.

AENA. (2021). Coronavirus: Everything you need to know at your airport. https:// www.aena.es/en/informationcovid19coronavirusairportsandflights.html. Accessed on December 27, 2021.

Alber, N., Ülkü, T., & Yazhemsky, E. (2013). Small regional airport sustainability: Lesson from benchmarking. *Journal of Air Transport Management, 33*, 22–31.

Albers, S., Koch, B., & Ruff, C. (2005). Strategic alliances between airlines and airports—Theoretical assessment and practical evidence. *Journal of Air Transport Management, 11*(2), 49–58.

AMA. (2017). Definition of marketing. https://www.ama.org/the-definition-of-marketing-what-is-marketing/. Accessed on February 3, 2022.

Arica, R., Cobanoglu, C., Cakir, O., Corbaci, A., Hsu, M.-J., & Della Corte, V. (2022). Travel experience sharing on social media: Effects of the importance attached to content sharing and what factors inhibit and facilitate it. *International Journal of Contemporary Hospitality Management, 34*(4), 1566–1586.

Baker, M. J., & Cameron, E. (2008). Critical success factors in destination marketing. *Tourism and Hospitality Research, 8*(2), 79–97.

Balasubramanian, K., & Rasoolimanesh, S. M. (2022). The progress of ICT applications in destination marketing in emerging economies. In I. Mensah, K. Balasubramanian, M. R. Jamaluddin, G. Alcoriza, V. Gaffar, & S. M. Rasoolimanesh (Eds.), *Marketing tourist destinations in emerging economies. Palgrave studies of marketing in emerging economies*. Palgrave Macmillan.

Berman, B. (2006). Developing an effective customer loyalty program. *California Management Review, 49*(1), 123–148.

Brilha, N. M., & Nobre, H. (2019). Airports as platforms: Towards a new business model. *International Journal of Business Performance Management, 20*(4), 297–312.

Carvalho, L., & Costa, T. (2011). Tourism innovation – A literature review complemented by case study research. *Tourism & Management Studies, 1*, 23–33.

Chang, H. H., & Chiang, C. C. (2022). Is virtual reality technology an effective tool for tourism destination marketing? A flow perspective. *Journal of Hospitality and Tourism Technology, 13*(3), 427–440.

Choi, J. H. (2021). Changes in airport operating procedures and implications for airport strategies post-COVID-19. *Journal of Air Transport Management, 94*, 102065.

EAS Barcelona. (2019). Corporate aviation, a sector in full development in Europe. https://easbcn.com/en/corporate-aviation-a-sector-in-full-development-in-europe/. Accessed on February 5, 2022.

Florido-Benítez, L. (2014). Managing relationship between business and tourists through mobile applications as a marketing tool tourist destinations. *TURyDES, 7*(17), 1–17.

Florido-Benítez, L. (2016a). Airport mobile marketing as a channel to promote cross-selling. *Journal of Airline and Airport Management, 6*(2), 133–151.

Florido-Benítez, L. (2016b). The impact of mobile marketing in airports. *Journal of Airline and Airport Management, 6*(1), 1–18.

Florido-Benítez, L. (2016c). *The implementation of mobile marketing as a multidisciplinary tool in the tourism and airport sector*. Editorial Académica Española.

Florido-Benítez, L. (2020). Seville airport: A success of good relationship management and interoperability in the improvement of air connectivity. *Revista de Turismo Estudos e Prácticas, 5*(2), 1–30.

Florido-Benítez, L. (2021). New marketing strategy: Mobile applications as a marketing tool in airports. In *Chapter of book: Handbook of research on applied AI for international business and marketing applications* (pp. 14–29). IGI GLOBAL Publisher of Timely Knowledge.

Florido-Benítez, L. (2023a). The location of airport an added value to improve the number of visitors at US museums. *Case of Studies on Transport Policy, 11*, 100961.

Florido-Benítez, L. (2023b). Air connectivity and proximity airports as an added value for museums. *Museum World, 11*, 136154.

Florido-Benítez, L. (2024a). Metaverse cannot be an extra marketing immersive tool to increase sales in tourism cities. *International Journal of Tourism Cities*. (in press). https://doi.org/10.1108/IJTC-01-2024-0001

Florido-Benítez, L. (2024b). Constructing Spanish smart destinations: A new guide for the tourism industry. *International Journal of Tourism Cities, 10*(1), 261–279. https://doi.org/10.1108/IJTC-09-2023-0193

Florido-Benítez, L., & del Alcázar, B. (2014). Analysis of mobile marketing in airports. In 7th World Conference for Graduate Research in Tourism, Hospitality and Leisure, Istanbul, Turkey (pp. 409–414).

Florido-Benítez, L., & del Alcázar, B. (2015). The effects of apps as a marketing tool in airport infrastructure and airlines. *International Journal of Leisure and Tourism Marketing, 4*(3/4), 222–240.

Florido-Benítez, L., del Alcázar, B., & González, E. (2015). The benefit of managing the relationship between companies and tourists through mobile applications as a marketing tool and a differentiating element of tourist destinations. *ARA-Journal of Tourism Research, 5*(2), 57–69.

Fodness, D., & Murray, B. (2007). Passengers' expectations of airport service quality. *Journal of Services Marketing, 21*(7), 492–506.

Fortune Business Insights. (2013). *Business jet market size*. www.fortunebusinessinsights.com/industry-reports/business-jet-market-101585. Accessed on February 7, 2022.

Freathy, P. (2004). The commercialization of European airports: Successful strategies in a decade of turbulence? *Journal of Air Transport Management, 10*(3), 191–197.

Fritz, W., Sohn, S., & Seegebarth, B. (2017). Broadening the perspective on mobile marketing: An introduction. *Psychology and Marketing, 34*(2), 113–118.

Garaus, M., & Hudáková, M. (2022). The impact of the COVID-19 pandemic on tourists' air travel intentions: The role of perceived health risk and trust in the airline. *Journal of Air Transportation, 103*, 102249.

Garcia, M. (2024). US airports struggle to raise revenue even as passenger numbers rise. https://www.forbes.com/sites/marisagarcia/2024/01/17/us-airports-struggle-to-raise-revenue-even-as-passenger-numbers-rise/. Accessed on February 22, 2024.

Gemar, G., Sánchez-Teba, E. V., & Soler, I. S. (2022). Factors determining cultural city tourists' length of stay. *Cities, 130*, 103938.

Gollan, D. (2022). 2021's 30 biggest charter/fractional private jet companies ranked (full year). https://privatejetcardcomparisons.com/2022/03/02/2021s-30-biggest-charter-fractional-private-jet-companies-ranked-full-year/. Accessed on February 6, 2024.

Graham, A. (2008). *Managing airports: An international perspective* (3rd ed.). Butterworth-Heinemann.

Graham, A. (2009). How important are commercial revenues to today's airports? *Journal of Air Transport Management, 15*, 106–111.

Halpern, N., & Graham, A. (2022). *Airport marketing* (2nd ed.). Routlegde.

Halpern, N., & Niskala, J. (2008). Airport marketing and tourism in remote destinations: Exploiting the potential in Europe's Northern Periphery. In A. Graham, A. Papatheodorou, & P. Forsyth (Eds.), *Aviation and tourism: Implications for leisure travel* (pp. 193–207). Ashgate.

Heathrow. (2024). Collect points when you spend. Enjoy the benefits of Heathrow rewards. https://www.heathrow.com/heathrow-rewards. Accessed on February 4, 2024.

Hopkings, J., & Turner, J. (2013). *Mobile marketing. Go mobile: Location-based marketing, apps, mobile optimized ad campaigns, 2D codes and other mobile strategies to grow your business.* Wiley.

IAB. (2023). IAB Spain's social media research 2023. https://iabeurope.eu/knowledge_hub/iab-spains-social-media-research-2023/. Accessed on November 6, 2023.

ICAO. (2019). *Aviation benefits reports.* https://www.icao.int/sustainability/Documents/AVIATION-BENEFITS-2019-web.pdf. Accessed on May 30, 2024.

Iacobucci, D. (2021). *Marketing management* (6th ed.). Cengage Learning.

IATA. (2020). Airport marketing & corporate communications strategies. https://iata.org.xy2401.com/training/courses/Pages/airport-marketing-tapg24.aspx.html. Accessed on October 6, 2023.

IATA. (2022). *Global outlook for air transport. Time of turbulence.* https://www.iata.org/en/iata-repository/publications/economic-reports/airline-industry-economic-performance—june-2022—report/. Accessed on May 6, 2023.

Kazda, A., Hromádka, M., & Mrekaj, B. (2017). Small regional airports operation: Unnecessary burdens or key to regional development. *Transportation Research Procedia*, *28*, 59–68.

Keefe, L. (2004). *What is the meaning of 'marketing'?* (pp. 17–18). American Marketing Association.

Kennedy-Eden, H., & Gretzel, U. (2012). A taxonomy of mobile applications in tourism. *E-review of Tourism Research*, *10*(2), 47–50.

Kim, H. Y., Lee, J. Y., Choi, D., Wu, J., & Johnson, K. K. (2013). Perceived benefits of retail loyalty programs: Their effects on program loyalty and customer loyalty. *Journal of Relationship Marketing*, *12*(2), 95–113.

Klaus, P., & Tarquini-Poli, A. (2022). Come fly with me: Exploring the private aviation customer experience (PAX). *European Journal of Marketing*, *56*(4), 1126–1152.

Koens, K., Postma, A., & Papp, B. (2018). Is overtourism overused? Understanding the impact of tourism in a city context. *Sustainability*, *10*, 4384.

Kotler, P., & Levy, S. J. (1969). Broadening the concept of marketing. *Journal of Marketing*, *33*(1), 10–15.

Kwiatek, P., Morgan, Z., & Thanasi-Boçe, M. (2020). The role of relationship quality and loyalty programs in building customer loyalty. *Journal of Business & Industrial Marketing*, *35*(11), 1645–1657.

Labanauskaitė, D., Fiore, M., & Stašys, R. (2020). Use of E-marketing tools as communication management in the tourism industry. *Tourism Management Perspectives*, *34*, 100652.

Leeflang, P. S. H., Wieringa, J. E., Bijmolt, T. H. A., & Pauwels, K. H. (2015). *Modeling markets: Analyzing marketing phenomena and improving marketing decision making.* Springer.

Madrigal, A. C. (2017). The people who read your airline tweets. https://www.theatlantic.com/technology/archive/2017/12/on-the-other-side-of-your-airline-travel-tweets/548693/. Accessed on January 1, 2024.

McKinsey & Company. (2023). *How to improve airline customer loyalty programs.* https://www.mckinsey.com/industries/travel-logistics-and-infrastructure/our-insights/travel-invented-loyalty-as-we-know-it-now-its-time-for-reinvention. Accessed on January 28, 2023.

Medium. (2023). The impact of social media marketing on the aviation industry. https://medium.com/a2digital/the-impact-of-social-media-marketing-on-the-aviation-industry-a650bf7e28dd#:~:text=Connecting%20with%20Customers%20in%20Real, and%20other%20relevant%20information%20promptly. Accessed on January 12, 2024.

MMA. (2009). MMA updates definition of mobile marketing. https://www.mmaglobal.com/news/mma-updates-definition-mobile-marketing. Accessed on January 17, 2024.

Müller, J. M., Pommeranz, B., Weisser, J., & Voight, K.-I. (2018). Digital, social media, and mobile marketing in industrial buying: Still in need of customer segmentation? Empirical evidence from Poland and Germany. *Industrial Marketing Management, 73*, 70–83.

Okazaki, S. (2012). *Fundamentals of mobile marketing.* Peter Lang International Academic Publishers.

Pande, P. (2023). Tope 5: The world's biggest airline loyalty programs by membership. https://simpleflying.com/top-5-the-worlds-biggest-airline-loyalty-programs-by-membership/#delta-skymiles-120-million. Accessed on January 26, 2024.

Paramount Business Jets. (2023). Will my private jet charter use the same airport as a commercial airline? https://www.paramountbusinessjets.com/faq/private-jet-commercial-use-same-airport. Accessed on January 31, 2024.

Pearce, D., & Schänzel, H. A. (2013). Destination management: The tourists' perspective. *Journal of Destination Marketing & Management, 2*(3), 137–145.

Perez, G. (2023). Airline trends: Leveraging social networks for business. https://www.smartvel.com/resources/blog/airline-trends-leveraging-social-networks-for-business. Accessed on January 29, 2024.

Pike, S. (2008). *Destination marketing: An integrated marketing communication approach.* Elsevier Butterworth-Heinemann.

Qubein, R. (2023). Airports have rewards programs, too. https://www.nerdwallet.com/article/travel/airports-have-rewards-programs-too. Accessed on January 27, 2024.

Rafdinal, W., & Senalasari, W. (2021). Predicting the adoption of mobile payment applications during the COVID-19 pandemic. *International Journal of Bank Marketing, 39*(6), 984–1002.

Rodríguez-Carmona, L. M. (2012). Valuing mobile marketing. Vivat academia. *Revista de Comunicacion, 117E*, 51–62.

Rosário, A., & Raimundo, R. (2021). Consumer marketing strategy and E-commerce in the last decade: A literature review. *Journal of Theoretical and Applied Electronic Commerce Research, 16*(7), 3003–3024.

Seo, E. J., Park, J.-W., & Choi, Y. J. (2020). The effect of social media usage characteristics on e-WOM, trust, and brand equity: Focusing on users of airline social media. *Sustainability, 12*, 1691.

Shankar, V., & Balasubramanian, S. (2009). Mobile marketing: A synthesis and prognosis. *Journal of Interactive Marketing, 23*(2), 118–129.

Sigurdsson, V., Larsen, N. M., Sigfusdottir, A. D., Fagerstrøm, A., Alemu, M. H., Folwarczny, M., & Foxall, G. (2020). The relationship between the firm's social media strategy and the consumers' engagement behavior in aviation. *Managerial and Decision Economics, 41*(2), 234–249.

SITA. (2019). Airlines and airports spend a record $50 billion on improving the passenger experience, and it is paying off. https://www.sita.aero/pressroom/news-releases/airlines-and-airports-spend-record-$50-billion-on-improving-the-passenger-experience-and-it-is-paying-off/. Accessed on January 10, 2024.

Smartvel. (2023). Airline trends: Leveraging social networks for business. https://www.smartvel.com/resources/blog/airline-trends-leveraging-social-networks-for-business. Accessed on January 31, 2024.

Sobieralski, J., & Mumbower, S. (2022). Jet-setting during COVID-19: Environmental implications of the pandemic induced private aviation boom. *Transportation Research Interdisciplinary Perspectives, 13*, 100575.

Ström, R., Vendel, M., & Bredican, J. (2014). Mobile marketing: A literature review on its value for consumers and retailers. *Journal of Retailing and Consumer Services, 21*(6), 1001–1012.

Tian, X., He, W., Tang, C., Li, L., Xu, H., & Selover, D. (2020). A new approach of social media analytics to predict service quality: Evidence from the airline industry. *Journal of Enterprise Information Management, 33*(1), 51–70.

Tong, S., Luo, X., & Xu, B. (2020). Personalized mobile marketing strategies. *Journal of the Academy of Marketing Science, 48*, 64–78.

Travair. (2023). Top 10 private airports for use with your private jet. https://www.travair.com.au/blog/top-10-private-airports. Accessed on February 6, 2024.

Turespaña. (2021). You deserve Spain, the new campaign from Turespaña to attract international tourists. https://www.lamoncloa.gob.es/lang/en/gobierno/news/Paginas/2021/20210512deserve-spain.aspx. Accessed on February 6, 2024.

UNWTO. (2004). *Survey of destination management organisations.* United Nations World Tourism Organisation.

Varadarajan, R. (2010). Strategic marketing and marketing strategy: Domain, definition, fundamental issues, and foundational premises. *Journal of the Academy of Marketing Science, 38*(2), 119–140.

Veloutsou, C., Christodoulides, G., & Guzmán, F. (2022). Charting research on international luxury marketing: Where are we now and where should we go next? *International Marketing Review, 39*(2), 371–394.

Wang, Y., & Pizam, A. (2011). *Destination marketing and management: Theories and applications.* CABI.

World Airport Awards. (2013). World's best airport. https://www.worldairportawards.com/the-worlds-top-100-airports-2013/. Accessed on February 9, 2024.

Wu, H., & Tsui, K. W. T. (2020). Does a reward program affect customers' behavioural intention of visiting the airport? A case study of Singapore Changi Airport. *Journal of Air Transport Management, 82*, 101742.

Yi, Y., & Jeon, H. (2003). Effects of loyalty programs on value perception, program loyalty, and brand loyalty. *Journal of the Academy of Marketing Science, 31*(3), 229–240.

Zakir-Hossain, M., Kibria, H., & Farhana, S. (2017). Do customer loyalty programs really work in airlines business?—A study on air Berlin. *Journal of Service Science and Management, 10*, 360–375.

Żemła, M., & Szromek, A. R. (2021). Influence of the residents' perception of over-tourism on the selection of innovative anti-overtourism solutions. *Journal of Open Innovation: Technology, Market, and Complexity, 7*(3), 202.

Zhao, Y., Wang, H., Guo, Z., Huang, M., Pan, Y., & Guo, Y. (2022). Online reservation intention of tourist attractions in the COVID-19 context: An extended technology acceptance model. *Sustainability, 14*(16), 10395.

Chapter 3

Airport Costs and Revenues to Consider by Airport Operators

Abstract

The airport operators' management is a complex process, especially in terms of airport cost and revenue factors, because it requires a basic understanding of economics, marketing, logistics, the current legal framework of the airport according to national and international bodies and the evaluation of the airport's operational processes and infrastructure every day. In addition, this chapter presents how these factors affect airport pricing, which has increased significantly after the COVID-19 pandemic in response to new measures of security and hygiene, higher fuel prices and the introduction of new government measures to combat the spread of the COVID-19 virus in countries, airports and airlines. To sum up, this section is intended to provide readers with an overview of the management of airport costs and revenue distribution by operators and alert them to key issues and their effects on airport economics, strategies marketing and long-term survivability.

3.1 The Main Cost Structure at Airports

In relation to airport business portfolios and marketing strategy management by operators, it is important to consider the cost structure of airports to return on invested capital (ROIC) in these infrastructures. Obviously, the cost and capital invested depend on the size of the airport (large, medium and small), category (tourist, national, regional, cargo and logistics) and location (urban, islands, capital, near the coastline). The capital employed at airports is considerably high because of the cost of land and construction of infrastructure, airport maintenance, personnel costs, safety-security and hygiene costs and retail marketing, among many others. For instance, a 30% ROIC tells us that for every dollar we were to invest in a business project, it would generate 30 cents in income.

Airport Marketing Strategies, 37–54

Copyright © 2024 Lázaro Florido-Benítez

Published under exclusive licence by Emerald Publishing Limited

doi:10.1108/978-1-83608-082-420241003

Airports are complex infrastructures in which many inputs and output processes are linked to the main potential costs of the structure and operation of
airports. Moreover, scholars and airport operators use the Data Envelopment
Analysis (DEA) model to assess the performance of homogeneous units that are
denominated decision-making units (DMUs), with the aim of measuring airport
efficiency and identifying causes of inefficiencies related to DMUs. Tavassoli et al.
(2021) and Storto (2018) suggest that the DEA model must include the financial
and operational activities of the airport to have an accurate efficiency measure-
ment and the effective understanding of the determinants of scarce performance.
Wittmer et al. (2011) claim that the airport's cost and revenue depend on the
interdependency between the airport and its catchment area, including its
geographical location and proximity to the city center and tourism and logistics
activities. Airports are facilities requiring public investment, and they are
frequently part of a national airport system designed and financed to produce
maximum benefit from public funding (Ashford et al., 2013).

A comprehensive data coverage from a sample of over 800 commercial airports worldwide by ACI (2014) shows that operating expenses represent 62% of
total airport costs and capital costs by 38% in 2013. These are the two main costs
at airports (see Fig. 11). Capital costs or capital expenditures (CAPEX) are those
capital investments that are necessary over time so that the airport can generate
substantial proceeds. It involves investment in a fixed asset or improving an
existing asset like infrastructure, equipment, patents, property or land, among
many others. In Fig. 11, we can see that the main three capital costs are:
depreciation and amortisation with 60%, followed by interest expenses with 36%
and other capital costs with 4%. These three indicators play a very important role
in the overall accounting of airports' costs. ACI (2021) reported that the global
airport sector will need approximately $2.4 trillion in capital investments to
address the long-term trend in passenger demand by 2040.

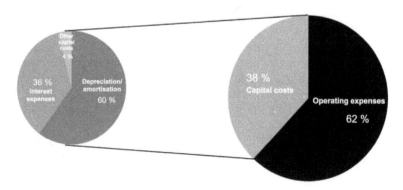

Fig. 11.   Capital Costs and Its Costs' Distribution and Operating
Expenses. The Two Main Airport Costs in 2013. *Source:* Adapted from ACI
(2014).

We do not forget that airport operators need to invest a huge amount of capital to provide basic services such as the movement of aircraft, passengers and cargo activities with the aim of facilitating the future growth in passenger, company and airline demand at airports. Although airports are not always responsible for the services and prices provided by airport operators, in-route charges, government taxes, new safety-hygiene costs and rules, ground handling services or new cybersecurity initiatives can be levied for flying to and from an airport. For instance, in 2014, Singapore Changi Airport Group invested $80 million to trim costs for airlines and boost passenger traffic to reduce reliance on foreign labour and raise productivity (Reuters, 2014). Sometimes airports do not have a great facility to move their assets, and they need to respond to changes taking place in their wider business environment by altering their prices (Halpern & Graham, 2022). Airports and airlines not only bring passengers, but these infrastructures are also drivers of productive synergies. Destinations must see airports as a market where you can exchange, send and receive products and services that you produce. Let us take as examples the three main cargo airports in the world: Hong Kong, Memphis and Shanghai airports (Florido-Benítez, 2020, 2023).

Operating expenses (OPEX) are costs related to the airport's functional and operational aspects (ACI, 2016). In 2013, the majority of operating expenses were personnel costs, which accounted for 35%, including salaries, and pensions and other employment costs relating to an airport's staff, followed by contracted services with 23% and communications, utilities, energy and waste with 8% (ACI, 2014). Readers can view the distribution of all operating costs in Fig. 12. In a report published in 2021 by Air Transport Action Group (ATAG), it was reported that 87.7 million jobs around the world are supported by the aviation industry, with around 44.8 million coming from the tourism sector. Tourism is one of the most important industries around the world, and the aviation sector is the cornerstone of carrying passengers around the world at any time. From an operational expenditure point of view, Serrano and Kazda (2020) indicate that the main short-term challenge will be to balance costs with an unstable developing demand and the reduction of staffing costs. For instance, UK airports face some of the highest total staff costs in Europe, only surpassed by Denmark and Switzerland, according to the Civil Aviation Authority (CAA, 2012).

The International Air Transport Association (IATA) (2022a) reported that the oil price has spiked to nearly $130 per barrel, and this is the airline's largest variable cost, absorbing such a massive price hike just as the industry is struggling to emerge from the pandemic crisis is a huge challenge. The COVID-19 pandemic and Ukraine's war are having a financial impact on airports and airlines due to limited infrastructural investments as traffic is lower than pre-pandemic at airports. Operating expenses are borne by airports, which should be accounted for to assess airports' efficiency of processes and optimise the economic available. Unfortunately, Ukraine's war is having an immediate negative impact on the tourism and aviation industries. The war is reducing economic benefits and driving up product and service prices in these sectors as a result of an increase in oil prices. The International Monetary Fund (IMF) reported that Russia and

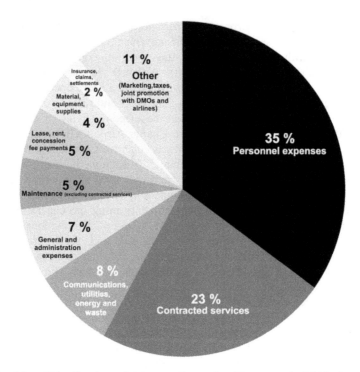

Fig. 12.   Distribution of Airport Operating Expenses in 2013. *Source:*
Adapted from ACI (2014).

Ukraine are major commodities producers, and the war has caused global prices to soar, especially for oil and natural gas (IMF, 2022). Airport operators need to effectively manage their financial returns. Hence, it is essential that they develop a clear understanding of their operating costs and how those costs align to their defined essential capabilities and strategic objectives to achieve operational excellence and deliver sustainable positive financial returns (Potter & Medeiros, 2015).

3.2 The Importance of Airport Revenues in the 21st Century

In the 21st century, the changing dynamics in the aviation industry have modified the role of airports within and outside their limits. Airport operators must increase aeronautical and non-aeronautical revenue streams, as well as the expansion of new products and services at airports. We must not forget how important it is to follow up on these revenues because an airport is part of an intermodal system, and its cost complex structure as well as its potential to generate income will depend on its importance and role inside a city, a tourist destination or a region. Aeronautical revenues like aeroplane landing charges for parking, mooring, baggage handling, boarding bridges, lighting, cargo and hangar charges and passenger facilities, among many others, are part of the income structure. These types of revenues are the cornerstone of airport revenues, and they are focused on the airport infrastructure, the category of airport and the type and quality of services offered by airport operators. Furthermore, airports earn income from financial activities like income from interest or even grants and subsidies from the government. Karanki et al. (2020) emphasise that US airports' aeronautical charges are spatially dependent, implying that they are in price competition with each other even though they are government-owned infrastructure.

Airport aeronautical charges are related to market structure, fares and the vertical relations between airports and airlines (Dender, 2007). Fig. 13 displays airport aeronautical revenue worldwide in 2017. Data reveal that passenger charges (43%) and aircraft-related charges (21.5%) are the main sources of revenue at airports (see Panel A in Fig. 13), followed by other aeronautical charges (15.5%) like fire department revenues, hangar charges, etc. terminal rentals with 12% and security charges with 8.1%. Regarding the structure of passenger charges by category shown in Panel B of Fig. 13, service charges per passenger category represent 80.9%, security about 15%, other passenger charges at 3.5% and transfer and transit charges at 0.7%. Nevertheless, in 2021, the COVID-19 pandemic provoked those revenues from passenger-related charges, which saw the largest declines of -65%, and revenues from landing charges plummeted as well by -42% (ACI, 2022; Airport World, 2022).

Landing and passenger charges are important sources of revenue at airports due to the increase in air traffic and passengers in the last 20 years (Florido-Benítez, 2016; Graham, 2004). Although it is a well-known fact that airports try to measure the impact of their aeronautical revenues, the results are of course strictly confidential (Fichert & Klophaus, 2011). After the September attacks, airport security activities are a priority in every airport in the world, and their security and cybersecurity levels are improving all the time. From a landing charge point of view, the main source of revenue at airports is the landing charge at 72.5%, followed by the parking charge (7.5%), the Navigation Aid (NAVAID) with 5%, boarding bridge (3.7%) and noise and environmental charges with 0.8% (see Panel C in Fig. 13). One of the main objectives of commercial and privatised airport operators is to maximise their own profit by determining their airport charges. For instance, aeronautical charges are higher for hubs and higher international traffic airports (Choo, 2014).

On the other hand, commercial activities are not related to air traffic, and these are not subject to International Civil Aviation Organization (ICAO) cost recovery policies. Non-aeronautical revenues are associated with parking fees, rentals, catering services, restaurants, cafeterias, bars, shops, rentals, duty-free establishments, among many others (Doganis, 2019; Florido-Benítez, 2022a; Graham, 2008; Wittmer et al., 2011). In the airport's commercial revenue context, duty-free shopping at an airport is a major part of these non-aeronautical commercial activities (Lin & Chen, 2013), and travellers' duty-free shopping as a non-aeronautical revenue is an important contributor to the revenue maximisation of airports (Han et al., 2018).

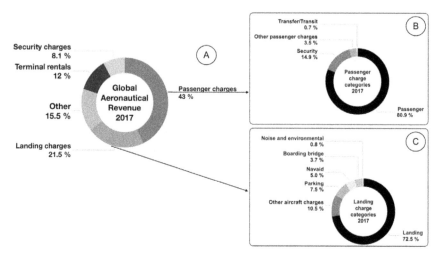

Fig. 13.   Airport Aeronautical Revenue Worldwide in 2017 (Panel A),
by Passenger Charge Categories (Panel B), and Landing Charge Categories
(Panel C). *Source:* Adapted from ACI (2019)

- Passenger charges include Airport Improvement Fee (AIF) Passenger Facility Charge (PFC).
- Terminal rentals are mainly limited to North America. The Federal Aviation Administration (FAA) classifies Other: miscellaneous passenger; aircraft; cargo-related charges. and all other unidentified charges of an aeronautical.

On the contrary, a comprehensive study undertaken by Shin and Roh (2021) revealed that an increase in the non-aeronautical revenue share has a statistically significant negative effect on airport charges, and these authors suggest that airport operators must be more active in promoting commercial activities to reduce airport charges. For example, Puls and Lents (2018) recommend the identification of personalised offerings and the inclusion of individual travellers' needs for a flexible approach by airports and shop locations regarding retail sales that have a direct impact on commercial revenues. Concessionaires apply individual customer and sales strategies that include a tailored product portfolio based on the needs and shopping preferences by passengers (Chien-Chang, 2012). Non-aeronautical revenue has therefore become a vital part of the airport business, but its growth has stagnated at many airports in the last 10 years.

In 2018, non-aeronautical revenue accounted for around half of the total operating revenue at 900 commercial airports around the world (ACI, 2020). The airport's commercial revenue worldwide by item is shown in Fig. 14. The two largest sources of non-aeronautical revenue are from retail concessions (30.2%) and car parking (20.1%) activities (see Panel A in Fig. 14). Airport operators choose the retail market structure by selecting the number of retail concessions to be awarded. Airports from

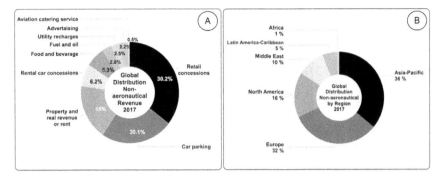

Fig. 14. Airport's Non-Aeronautical Revenue Worldwide (Panel A) and by Region in 2017 (Panel B). *Source:* Adapted from ACI (2019).

the Asia-Pacific region are the largest non-aeronautical revenue generators in the world, followed by European airports with 32%, American airports (16%), the Middle East (5%) and the network of African airports with 1% (see Panel B in Fig. 14). Many large Asian and Middle Eastern airports with high levels of international passenger traffic had more than 50% of their revenues attributed to non-aero revenues prior to the pandemic (Airport World, 2022).

Evidence of that fact is that the Middle East region gets the greatest percentage of retail concession revenues in the world with 52.9% and second was the Asia-Pacific region with 45.4% in 2017 (see Fig. 15). European airports improve their competitiveness through retail concession revenues (Puls & Lents, 2018); in fact, the profitability of an airport requires contracted concessionaires to generate sales to all customer groups and define retail strategies with a distinct customer focus (Freathy & O'Connell, 2012). Additionally, products like liquor shops, jewellery and cosmetics are placed in areas immediately after security and immigration checks to maximise passenger footfall and increase retail revenues at airports. As stated by Chen et al. (2020) as the airport retail industry continues to grow due to increasing travel demands, airport operators are increasingly developing their retail revenue potential to ensure financial viability.

Nevertheless, Fig. 15 also displays as that US airports are the ones that get the most revenue worldwide by car parking activities, with 40.7%, followed by Europe (16.1%) and Africa with 10.7%. Parking is a large source of revenue for airports and often the largest non-aviation-related source. For example, revenue from car parking at Los Angeles International airport (IATA: LAX) was $97.6 million in 2018, whereas revenue from transportation network companies' operations like Uber and Lyft at the airport was $44.3 million, where ride-hailing service drivers pay a $4 fee for every passenger picked up or dropped off at the airport curb (Martin, 2019; Wadud, 2020).

The convenience and flexibility of the private car mean that it is the principal method of accessing airports for passengers, employees and visitors (Aldridge et al., 2006).

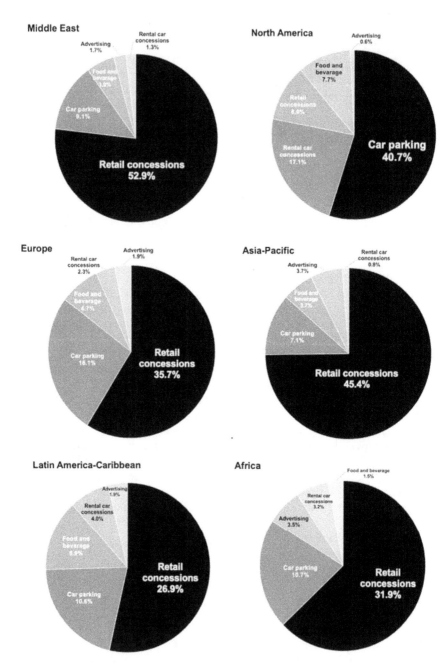

Fig. 15. Airport's Non-Aeronautical Revenue Categories by Region in 2017. *Source:* Adapted from ACI (2019).

From aircraft parking services, these are considered very important to airport operators because these charges are typically levied based on aircraft characteristics and are highly dependent on traffic at each airport. In addition, if the fees are attractive, the airline will decide to park its aircraft wherever it is most advantageous, which could be anywhere in the world. Some airports are used for long-term aircraft parking, like Teruel airport (IATA: TEV) in Spain or Upington airport (IATA: UTN) in South Africa. Obviously, their business models are completely different from those of other conventional airports.

Regarding food and beverage revenue, it is the third largest source of non-aeronautical revenue worldwide, especially in the North America region, where this type of income represents 7.7%, followed by Latin America and the Caribbean with 6.9% and Europe with 4.7%. The profitability of airports is largely based on commercial activities, particularly retail and food and beverage services. Large brands such as Burger King, McDonald's, Starbucks and Pizza Hut, among many others, operate in almost all of the world's airports.

Recently, airport operators are introducing new local brands to enhance the quality of food and beverage retailers in airport areas (Del Chiappa et al., 2017), with the aim of fulfilling the needs of consumers by providing an experience that reflects a sense of community and place (Assies, 2014). IATA (2018) reported that passenger numbers could double to 8.2 billion by 2037 and that, on average, 50% of passengers are eating and drinking at airports. For an increasing number of passengers, particularly the young, food provenance is key as they target produce sourced from local, sustainable supply chains (Airport Technology, 2020). For this reason, many airports want to increase the localisation of their local food and beverage offer on the high street to create a unique sense of place and differentiate the experience. Food and beverage service is fundamental to passengers' satisfaction and experience. In 2021, Tokyo Haneda airport won the Travel Retail Award in the category of the Best Food & Beverage Offer in the world by consumers (Florido-Benítez, 2022b; Travel Retail Awards, 2021).

The COVID-19 global health crisis resulted in a significant decline in demand for air transport. All sources of non-aeronautical revenues understandably decreased in 2020 compared with 2019. Sources directly affected by passenger volumes suffered the most, such as retail concessions (−65.2%), aviation catering services (−64.1%), food and beverage (−53.1%) and car parking (−48.9%) saw the most severe declines in revenues in 2020. Property and real estate revenues with −12% were the most resilient with the lowest decline (see Fig. 16). Non-aeronautical revenues, which usually serve as an additional cushion during economic downturns, are not able to play that role in the COVID-19 outbreak context. For example, passenger traffic from China and Eastern Asia tends to generate comparatively high revenue for retail concessions and other non-aeronautical services, but this typology of traffic is most affected by the outbreak and seriously challenges the ability of airports to continue generating much-needed commercial income (Lioutov, 2020).

Many airports provide a broad selection of product varieties and an augmented shopping experience. Airport retailers need to be a part of the overall airport design conversation by emphasising how crowding behaviour can inform layout planning for the benefit of all (Creed et al., 2021). Han et al. (2021) suggest that airport

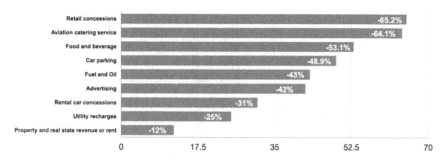

Fig. 16.   Non-Aeronautical Revenues Worldwide YoY% by
Categories in 2020–2019. *Source:* Adapted from ACI (2022). *Note:* Car
parking revenue includes revenue from airport-operated parking lots and car
parking concessions revenue.

operators and firms should enhance some attributes of retail stores, such as attractive physical environments and excellent employee and encounter services, to be superior to those of other alternative shopping locations like department stores, city shopping districts, etc. In 2020, aeronautical revenue worldwide continued to be the most important source of income for airports, representing 47.8% of the total, whereas non-aeronautical revenues made up 38.8% and non-operating revenue represented a smaller proportion of the total at 13.4% (ACI Insights, 2022).

3.3 Airport Pricing After the COVID-19 Pandemic

Airport pricing is divided into two factors: the point of view of the demand for airport services, which depends on airport charges, and, on the other hand, the congestion costs of both passengers and airlines due to demand for airport facilities measured by the number of flights and the airport's price and capacity. A study conducted by Basso and Zhang (2008) revealed that airport pricing is efficient if air carriers have no market power, that is, when airlines are atomistic or when they behave as price takers and have constant marginal operational costs. On the contrary, when there is market power at the airline level, this approach may generate deadweight losses for airport operators that may be large if the degree of competition between air carriers is low. Airport pricing decisions are often guided by the need to cover costs and raise money for investment, where cost-based principles are used to set and regulate aeronautical charges (Halpern & Graham, 2022). There is a positive relationship between pricing, promotion, location, product and service strategies, implying that the application of marketing strategies positively influences an organisation's performance (Amin, 2021).

Pricing is an integral component of marketing to create revenue at companies and airports. Lancioni (2005) indicates that price setting and implementation are multidimensional processes affecting customers, products, cost recovery efforts, produce margin levels, customer retention, market share and domestic and international sales. In the same vein, pricing should also be customer-value because the perceived value of a product or service is arguably more important to customers than price (Kotler et al., 2008). In Spain, the AENA operator manages 46 Spanish airports and 2 heliports, and this operator is always monitoring all prices from aeronautical and non-aeronautical revenues with the aim of responding to changes in demand, higher fuel prices, joint promotion strategies or emerging trends in the aviation sector. Airport operators consider commercial and aeronautical operations jointly to manage better airport pricing and design marketing strategies aligned with the market's needs, new business models, location and category of the airport itself. Major US airports set profit maximising prices for non-aeronautical services to passengers and Ramsey prices for aeronautical services to airlines (Ivaldi et al., 2015).

Fig. 17 presents factors affecting airport pricing decisions by operators. These factors affect pricing decisions to a great extent. Airport operators set the prices according to organisational goals. In airports, like any other responsible organisation, airport pricing decisions are affected by a range of factors. Some are internal to the airport, such as marketing strategic plans, goals of the airport operator, costs and revenue's structure, the way it is owned and operated, price

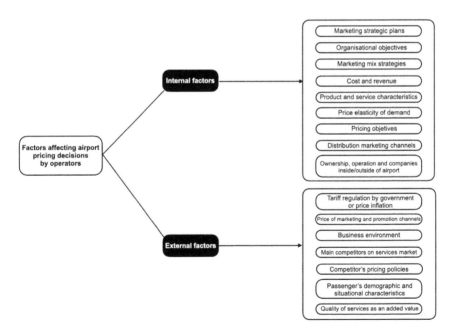

Fig. 17.   Factors Affecting Airport Pricing Decisions by Operators.
Source: Compiled by the author.

elasticity of demand or its marketing mix strategies. On the other hand, factors external to the airport, like tariff regulation by the government, price inflation, the business environment, the main competitors in the service market, passengers' demographic and situational characteristics or the quality of services as added value, must be considered by airport operators in the determination of airport pricing decisions.

For instance, an airport operator has set a goal to provide quality services like customised personal training sessions 'fitness or dance' for passengers and the airport's workers; thus, the prices will be set according to the quality of the services. Therefore, if the airport operator has a goal to increase revenue by 5% every year for this personalised service, then reasonable prices must be set to increase the demand for this attractive service. Customisation of services for passengers when they are inside the airport is a good opportunity for airport operators and companies that are operating inside the terminal.

The relationship between the airport operator and airlines is fundamental to the success of any airport business. The attractiveness of an airport is also determined by where planes depart from how often this is done and which airlines operate each route.

But travelling by air was very expensive in 2022. With the inflation across countries, most people had less money to spend on travel and leisure. Furthermore, we must add that jet fuel prices shot up to 175 dollars per barrel on 22 May 2022, due to Moscow's invasion of Ukraine (see Fig. 18), slamming low-cost and legacy carriers and travellers with steep cost increases just as air travel was starting to recover from the pandemic crisis (Koustav, 2022; IATA, 2022b; S&P Global Platts, 2022). The increase in the price of oil negatively affects the price elasticity of demand for flying by carriers and passengers, particularly when the jet

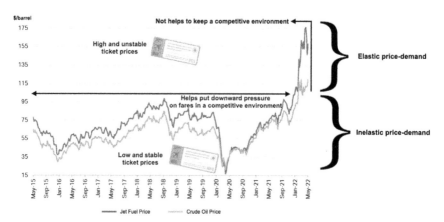

Fig. 18.   Jet Fuel Price Development and Crude Oil Price From May 2015 to May 2022. *Source:* Adapted from IATA (2022b, 2022c) and S&P Global Platts (2022).

fuel price is above $100 per barrel and air ticket prices are beginning to be prohibitive for most citizens. Thus, the price elasticity of demand is elastic due to the high air ticket prices by airline operators as a direct consequence of the increase in the jet fuel price (see IATA, 2022c). Moreover, evidence of directional (origin or destination) price discrimination in the aviation industry affects airlines' decisions to charge passengers different round-trip fares depending on trip origin. Dynamic pricing plays a crucial role in the implementation of revenue management in passenger airline reservation systems (Godwin, 2017; IATA, 2022c; Kelemen et al., 2019), due to most airlines modify the price and quantity of different fare classes offered in each flight using a variety of revenue management forecasting, un-constraining, and optimisation techniques (Fukushi et al., 2022).

On the contrary, when the jet fuel price is below $100 per barrel, the price elasticity of demand is inelastic because many airlines can propose some very attractive air ticket prices for tourists or passengers, so most people can pay reasonable prices for an air ticket. Abdella et al. (2021) suggest that customers are seeking to get the lowest price while airlines are trying to keep their overall revenue as high as possible and maximise their profit. The correlation between total jet fuel consumption (domestic and international) and passenger kilometres performed (PKP) is strong at 90%, indicating that passenger traffic is indeed one of the main determinants of jet fuel consumption (Mazraati & Faquih, 2008).

In July 2022, Ryanair boss Michael O'Leary warned that fares will rise for the next 5 years due to high oil prices and environmental charges, and flight tickets will average fare up from €40 to between €50 and €60 over the medium term at Ryanair's airlines because flying has become too cheap to make profits as industry costs spiral. O'Leary said that it absurd every time that he flies to Stansted airport, the train journey into central London is more expensive than the air fare (Georgiadis, 2022; Financial Times, 2022; MailOnline, 2022). In 2021, median fares from London to summer destinations in Portugal, Spain, Ireland and Greece have all jumped compared with the previous year, although they are significantly lower than 10 years ago. For example, prices from London to Athens have halved in the past decade (Kayak.com, 2022). In parallel with historical business-to-business (B2B) links within the pipeline with airlines, travel agents, tour operators, catering arms and car rentals, among others, airports are developing new innovative market strategies to contact end customers and then directly manage long-term relationships with them (Jarach, 2005).

The most fundamental impact of COVID-19 on aviation is the tremendous reduction in the number of flights, which is a non-trivial interaction between two elements: a reduction in demand and supply, maybe surprising inability of airlines to match hidden demand with supply downstream of the pandemic crisis. Management of non-aeronautical revenue, new airports' business models and commercial opportunities at airports have been affected by these negative impacts. In 2020, studies mainly provided quantitative descriptions of the reductions in supply, as measured by the number of flights for selected markets, often at an aggregated level. Studies published in 2021 were more concerned with seeking explanations and finding ways out of the demand–supply inconsistency (Sun et al., 2022). Airports' underperformance stemming from the low volume of passengers and flight traffic leads to a modest operational scale, which impacts average costs per unit (Chutiphongdech & Vongsaroj, 2022).

The main factors influencing airline pricing are oil prices, the perishability of services and exchange rates. These indicators, when properly combined, will drive airlines into implementing correct and fruitful pricing strategies. The impact of pricing can be critical for the success of new product and service launches, airport and airline brand image or the airport's short-and long-term success. For example, airport and airline pricing will affect pricing strategies, products and services, promotional campaigns and distribution strategies. For these reasons, airports and airlines' pricing must be in keeping with the organisation's vision and mission.

References

Abdella, J. A., Zaki, N.-M., Shuaib, K., & Khan, F. (2021). Airline ticket price and demand prediction: A survey. *Journal of King Saud University-Computer and Information Sciences, 33*(4), 375–391.

ACI. (2014). *State of airport economics.* https://www.icao.int/sustainability/airport_economics/state%20of%20airport%20economics.pdf. Accessed on April 2, 2022.

ACI. (2016). *ACI releases the 20th edition of the airport economics report and key performance indicators.* https://aci.aero/2016/03/07/aci-releases-the-20th-edition-of-the-airport-economics-report-and-key-performance-indicators/. Accessed on April 24, 2022.

ACI. (2019). State of the industry. 4 short stories in airport economics. In *Tampa 2019 ACI-NA Annual Conference Finance Workshop.* https://airportscouncil.org/wp-content/uploads/2019/09/Patrick_Lucas.pdf. Accessed on June 19, 2022.

ACI. (2020). *ACI report shows the importance of the airport industry to the global economy.* https://aci.aero/2020/04/22/aci-report-shows-the-importance-of-the-airport-industry-to-the-global-economy/. Accessed on May 4, 2022.

ACI. (2021). *Global outlook of airport capital expenditure.* https://store.aci.aero/product/global-outlook-of-airport-capital-expenditure/. Accessed on April 4, 2022.

ACI. (2022). *Airport economics report* (2022 edition). https://store.aci.aero/product/airport-economics-report-2022-edition/?_cldee=7uRU3zsqsSM0Gkwk_ohPmDV4tz6gLNKMDWqtHYTN1jSD1BuXeDCb3hS1efio9h-8&recipientid=lead-2894f0d8352bebl1a813000d3af3a14a-790e7e309e524382a6f08bd2876f614a&esid=8cac0eef-08d2-ec11-a7b5-0022483e24ad. Accessed on June 7, 2022.

ACI Insights. (2022). A glimpse into airports' financial activities during the first year of the pandemic. https://blog.aci.aero/a-first-in-depth-look-into-airports-financial-activities-during-the-first-year-of-the-pandemic/. Accessed on August 31, 2022.

Airport Technology. (2020). Are airports presenting a wide enough food and drink offering? https://www.airport-technology.com/analysis/food-and-drinks-offering-at-airports/. Accessed on June 8, 2022.

Airport World. (2022). Non-aeronautical revenues: Diversify and grow. https://airport-world.com/non-aeronautical-revenues-diversify-and-grow/. Accessed on June 22, 2022.

Aldridge, K., Carreno, M., Ison, I., Rye, T., & Straker, I. (2006). Car parking management at airports: A special case? *Transport Policy, 13*(6), 511–521.

Amin, H. J. (2021). Influence of marketing strategies on the performance of SMEs: Evidence from Abuja SMEs. *Journal of Economics and Business, 4*(1), 294–307.

Ashford, N. J., Martin-Stanton, H. P., Clifton, A. M., Pierre, C., & Beasley, J. R. (2013). *Airport operations* (3rd ed.). McGraw-Hill Education.

Assies, H. (2014). Local heroes on the move: How a growing number of local brands are gaining presence at airports. *Journal of Airport Management, 8*(4), 305–308.

ATAG. (2021). Employment. https://aviationbenefits.org/economic-growth/supporting-employment/. Accessed on April 18, 2022.

Basso, L. J., & Zhang, A. (2008). On the relationship between airport pricing models. *Transportation Research Part B: Methodological, 42*(9), 725–735.

CAA. (2012). *CAA airport operating expenditure benchmarking report 2012*. https://publicapps.caa.co.uk/docs/33/CAP%201060%20Airport%20Operating%20Expenditure%20Benchmarking%20Report%202012.pdf. Accessed on June 24, 2022.

Chen, Y., Wu, C.-L., Koo, T. R., & Douglas, I. (2020). Determinants of airport retail revenue: A review of literature. *Transport Reviews, 40*(4), 479–505.

Chien-Chang, C. (2012). Evaluating the quality of airport service using the fuzzy multi-criteria decision-making method: A case study of Taiwanese airports. *Expert Systems, 29*(3), 246–260.

Choo, Y. Y. (2014). Factors affecting aeronautical charges at major US airports. *Transportation Research Part A: Policy and Practice, 62*, 54–62.

Chutiphongdech, T., & Vongsaroj, R. (2022). Airport business model innovations for local and regional airports: A case of cultural entrepreneurship in Thailand. In V. Ratten (Ed.), *Cultural entrepreneurship* (pp. 53–66). Springer.

Creed, B., Shen, K. N., Ashill, N., & Wu, T. (2021). Retail shopping at airports: Making travellers buy again. *Journal of Business Research, 137*, 293–307.

Del Chiappa, G. D., Giménez, M. N. S., & Zapata-Aguirre, S. (2017). Travelers satisfaction with food and beverage services in airports. *Journal of Hospitality Marketing & Management, 26*(8), 829–845.

Dender, K. V. (2007). Determinants of fares and operating revenues at US airports. *Journal of Urban Economics, 62*, 317–336.

Doganis, R. (2019). *Flying off course. Airline economics and marketing*. Routledge.

Fichert, F., & Klophaus, R. (2011). Incentive schemes on airport charges, theoretical analysis, and empirical evidence from German airports. *Research in Transportation Business & Management, 1*(1), 71–79.

Financial Times. (2022). Ryanair chief warns fares will rise for 5 years because flying is 'too cheap'. https://www.ft.com/content/32108696-9ef5-49ad-8a07-fa30375702bf. Accessed on July 1, 2022.

Florido-Benítez, L. (2016). Airport mobile marketing as a channel to promote cross-selling. *Journal of Airline and Airport Management, 6*(2), 133–151.

Florido-Benítez, L. (2020). Seville airport: A success of good relationship management and interoperability in the improvement of air connectivity. *Revista de Turismo Estudos ePrácticas, 5*(2), 1–30.

Florido-Benítez, L. (2022a). The pre/on/post of low-cost carriers in Spanish tourist destinations. *Revista de Turismo Estudos & Prácticas, 11*(1), 1–26.

Florido-Benítez, L. (2022b). The world airport awards a quality distinctive and marketing tool for airports. *Journal of Airline Operations and Aviation Management, 1*(2), 54–81.

Florido-Benítez, L. (2023). The role of the top 50 US cargo airports and 25 air cargo airlines in the logistics of E-commerce companies. *Logistics, 7*(1), 8.

Freathy, P., & O'Connell, F. (2012). Planning for profit: The commercialization of European airports. *Long Range Planning, 32*(6), 587–597.

Fukushi, M., Delgado, F., Raveau, S., & Santos, B. (2022). CHAIRS: A choice-based air transport simulator applied to airline competition and revenue management. *Transportation Research Part A: Policy and Practice, 155*, 297–315.

Georgiadis, P. (2022). Ryanair chief warns fares will rise for 5 years because flying is 'too cheap'. https://www.ft.com/content/32108696-9ef5-49ad-8a07-fa30375702bf. Accessed on July 1, 2022.

Godwin, T. (2017). An empirical analysis of Delhi – Mumbai sector flight fares. *International Journal of Business Analytics, 4*(4), 60–78.

Graham, A. (2004). *The regulation of US airports* (pp. 63–72). University Westminster: Studies in Aviation Economics and Management.

Graham, A. (2008). *Managing airports – An international perspective* (3rd ed.). Elsevier.

Halpern, N., & Graham, A. (2022). *Airport marketing* (2nd ed.). Routlegde.

Han, H., Lee, M. J., & Kim, W. (2018). Role of shopping quality, hedonic/utilitarian shopping experiences, trust, satisfaction and perceived barriers in triggering customer post-purchase intentions at airports. *International Journal of Contemporary Hospitality Management, 30*(10), 3059–3082.

Han, H., Quan, W., Gil-Cordero, E., Cabrera-Sánchez, J.-P., & Yu, J. (2021). Performance of retail stores at airports and their role in boosting traveler satisfaction and willingness to repurchase. *Sustainability, 13*(2), 590.

IATA. (2018). IATA forecast predicts 8.2 billion air travelers in 2037. https://www.iata.org/en/pressroom/pr/2018-10-24-02/. Accessed on May 17, 2022.

IATA. (2022a). War in Ukraine and air transport. https://airlines.iata.org/analysis/war-in-ukraine-and-air-transport. Accessed on May 6, 2022.

IATA. (2022b). Jet fuel price monitor. https://www.iata.org/en/publications/economics/fuel-monitor/. Accessed on June 8, 2022.

IATA. (2022c). *Global outlook for air transport. Times of turbulence.* https://www.iata.org/en/iata-repository/publications/economic-reports/airline-industry-economic-performance—june-2022—report/. Accessed on September 1, 2022.

IMF. (2022). How war in Ukraine is reverberating across world's regions. https://blogs.imf.org/2022/03/15/how-war-in-ukraine-is-reverberating-across-worlds-regions/. Accessed on May 7, 2022.

Ivaldi, M., Sokullu, S., & Toru, T. (2015). Airport prices in a two-sided market setting: Major US airports. *Toulouse Scholl of Economics.* No TSE-587. https://ssrn.com/abstract=2619233

Jarach, D. (2005). *Airport marketing. Strategies to cope with the new millennium environment* (1st ed.). Routledge.

Karanki, F., Lim, S. H., & Choi, B. J. (2020). The determinants of aeronautical charges of U.S. airports: A spatial analysis. *Journal of Air Transport Management, 86*, 101825.

Kayak.com. (2022). When to book flights from London to Athens. https://www.kayak.com/flight-routes/London-LON/Athens-Eleftherios-V–ATH. Accessed on June 29, 2022.

Kelemen, M., Pilát, M., Makó, S., Rozenberg, R., & Tobisová, A. (2019). Pricing policy aspects in competitive fight between low-cost airlines on Kosice airport. *Journal of Konbin, 49*(1), 331–342.

Kotler, P., Wong, V., Saunders, J., & Armstrong, G. (2008). *Principles of marketing* (5th ed.). Pretince Hall-Pearson Education.

Koustav, S. (2022). Jet fuel price surge deals heavy blow to fragile air travel recovery. https://www.reuters.com/markets/europe/jet-fuel-price-surge-deals-heavy-blow-fragile-air-travel-recovery-2022-03-08/. Accessed on June 1, 2022.

Lancioni, R. (2005). Pricing issues in industrial marketing. *Industrial Marketing Management, 34*(2), 111–114.

Lin, W., & Chen, C. (2013). Shopping satisfaction at airport duty-free stores: A cross-cultural comparison. *Journal of Hospitality Marketing & Management, 22*(1), 47–66.

Lioutov, I. (2020). COVID-19: The importance of airport charges and revenue in a time of crisis. https://blog.aci.aero/covid-19-the-importance-of-airport-charges-and-revenue-in-a-time-of-crisis/. Accessed on July 7, 2022.

MailOnline. (2022). The age of cheap air travel is over! Ryanair boss Michael O'leary warns fares will rise for the next five years because tickets are 'to cheao'. https://www.dailymail.co.uk/news/article-10976529/Ryanair-boss-Michael-OLeary-warns-fares-rise-five-years.html. Accessed on July 4, 2022.

Martin, H. (2019). Airports feared losing revenue to Uber and Lyft. Here's what happened. https://www.latimes.com/business/la-fi-airport-uber-parking-revenue-20190301-story.html. Accessed on July 5, 2022.

Mazraati, M., & Faquih, Y. Y. O. (2008). Modelling aviation fuel demand: The case of the United States and China. *OPEC Energy Review, 32*(4), 323–342.

Potter, J., & Medeiros, A. (2015). *Airport operators' quest for efficiency. How airports can focus operational improvement efforts on their addressable drivers of cost.* https://www.strategyand.pwc.com/gx/en/insights/2015/airport-operators-quest-for-efficiency/airport-operators-quest-for-efficiency.pdf. Accessed on June 8, 2022.

Puls, R., & Lents, C. (2018). Retail concessions at European airports: Commercial strategies to improve non-aeronautical revenue from leisure travelers. *Journal of Air Transport Management, 71*, 243–249.

Reuters. (2014). Changi airport to invest $80 million to help airlines cut costs. https://www.reuters.com/article/uk-singapore-changi/changi-airport-to-invest-80-million-to-help-airlines-cut-costs-idUKKBN0EN0LJ20140612. Accessed on April 23, 2022.

S&P Global Platts. (2022). Russia losing OPEC+ clout as Ukraine war weakens oil market role. https://www.spglobal.com/commodityinsights/en/market-insights/latest-news/oil/050422-russia-losing-opec-clout-as-ukraine-war-weakens-oil-market-role. Accessed on June 10, 2022.

Serrano, F., & Kazda, A. (2020). The future of airports post COVID-19. *Journal of Air Transport Management, 89*, 101900.

Shin, T., & Roh, T. (2021). Impact of non-aeronautical revenues on airport landing charge in global airports. *Transportation Research Record, 2675*(10), 667–677.

Storto, C. L. (2018). The analysis of the cost-revenue production cycle efficiency of the Italian airports: A NSBM DEA approach. *Journal of Air Transport Management, 72*, 588–601.

Sun, X., Wandelt, S., & Zhang, A. (2022). Aviation under COVID-19 pandemic: Status quo and how to proceed further? *SSRN Electronic Journal, 1*, 1–31.

Tavassoli, M., Fathi, A., & Farzipoor Saen, R. (2021). Developing a new super-efficiency DEA model in the presence of both zero data and stochastic data: A case study in the Iranian airline industry. *Benchmarking: An International Journal, 28*(1), 42–65.

Travel Retail Awards. (2021). Best airport food and beverage offer. https://www. travelretailawards.com/fandb-award. Accessed on June 11, 2022.

Wadud, Z. (2020). An examination of the effects of ride-hailing services on airport parking demand. *Journal of Air Transport Management, 84*, 101783.

Wittmer, A., Bieger, T., & Müller, R. (2011). *Aviation systems. Management of the integrated aviation value chain.* Springer.

Chapter 4

Airport Business Portfolio

Abstract

This chapter discusses the importance of airport business portfolios in the digitalisation of aeronautical and non-aeronautical activities, particularly in this economy uncertainly period. Airports are in a transitional period of digitalisation, decarbonation and new business activities, with the aim of redefining their business models. A successful airport marketing strategy must take tangible and intangible items into account. For this reason, airport operators are developing modern business models to diversify income sources and optimise the available resources of the airport's infrastructure. The implementation of these new business models is influenced by competition levels between airports, destination attractiveness, airport reputation, a proactive value proposition, catchment area and the quality of service offered by airport operators.

4.1 Traditional Business at Airports

Large and regional airports have their own business portfolios based on sustainable economic development with potential for profitable growth over a 4-year period. Depending on the airport's characteristics (hub-and-spoke, medium, small, cargo and logistics, regional, touristic, or private and business aviation), market segment (domestic and international), location (large capitals, islands, coastal or urban zone), and business and professional sectors localised where the airport operates, like technological, tourism, industrial, agri-food, universities, logistics, and maritime industries, airport operators design their own business portfolios. However, the airport business portfolio cannot only be analysed from a marketing perspective. The CEO of the airport, the senior of the marketing department and their staff should consider their sources in input and output terms, for they adapt their products and services to the existing demand and the needs of passengers, airlines and companies in and outside of the airport. In a few

Airport Marketing Strategies, 55–66

Copyright © 2024 Lázaro Florido-Benítez

Published under exclusive licence by Emerald Publishing Limited

doi:10.1108/978-1-83608-082-420241004

words, the economic and business prosperity of airports is based on the premise that connects users and businesses with the airport's activities.

Fig. 19 presents airport traditional business and the main inputs and outputs at the airport to operate in different business modalities. The airport services are classified into airside and landside operations. Landside operations are aimed at serving passengers and maintenance terminal buildings, parking facilities and vehicular traffic circular drives. On the other side, airside operations include aircraft landing and navigation, airport traffic management, runway management and ground handling safety. For instance, conclusions from a study conducted by Karanki et al. (2020) demonstrated that US airports seek to increase aeronautical outputs through lower aeronautical fees, and they then cross-subsidise aeronautical operations or recoup the cost of operations through non-aeronautical services. This practice incentivises airlines to bring in more air travellers but the captive air travellers now paying for the non-aeronautical services they consume, and they are also subsidising aeronautical operations at the airport.

According to Jarach (2001), the traditional business of airports must identify a series of actors that interact with the airport to bundle service packages for final audiences. His approach allows for an analysis of multiple customers and airport competition. New dynamics appear in liberalised markets and strongly impact the airport industry: the opposition of airlines and regulators to increases in aeronautical fees, the trend towards airport privatisation or commercialisation, the pressure from governments for airport self-sufficiency and the emergence of multiple customers for the airport services are the main difficulties that airports face in a competitive environment nowadays (Jimenez et al., 2014). In this chapter, we try to show how the new business paradigms at airports are leaving without effects on the traditional business of the airport, with the aim of promoting new approaches to airport management by operators. Furthermore, they can develop innovative marketing strategies focused on the interaction among

Fig. 19.   Airport Traditional Business. *Source:* Own elaboration.

Destination Marketing Organizations (DMOs), airlines, passengers, stakeholders and the business approach selected by the operators.

Many airports promote and advertise as smart and innovative airports, and they are a safe alternative to traditional business airports but, contrary to their reports, show a continued dependence on airport traditional business (airlines and passengers). These myths are demystified by International Air Transport Association (IATA), ICAO and ACI's reports every year. Historically, the aviation industry has been fairly conservative in implementing new ideas. Many airport operators continue to have monopolistic management based on a lack of competition; airport business or even a vision of the airport focused only on safety and security measures without considering the need to explore new business models to increase aeronautical and commercial revenue. Fig. 20 shows that aeronautical revenues represented 55.9% of 936 airports around the world in 2018, followed by non-aeronautical revenue with 39.2% and non-operating with 4.9% (ACI, 2020). Non-operating revenues are passive income from sources not directly associated with airport operations, such as state grants, investments in reserve accounts, restricted capital funds and others. Moreover, this figure displays airports' revenue from 2005 to 2018. In 2005, non-aeronautical revenue represented 43.1%, and it has been reduced by 39.9% in 2018.

If airports worldwide want to continue to keep pace with this demand, airport operators must be able to invest, improve and grow. Charges for services rendered to airport users and non-aeronautical revenues are the major sources of funds for airports to invest in infrastructure and service improvements. Generating a positive economic return depends on sound strategic planning with appropriate

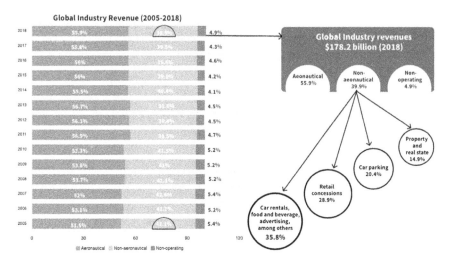

Fig. 20.   Global Aviation Industry Revenues (2005–2018). *Source:* Adapted from ACI (2020).

financing mechanisms. There is no one-size-fits-all approach, and airports must take a long-term perspective to their business and ensure capacity improvements (ACI, 2017). Airport operators need to maximise competitiveness by diversifying the revenues generated at their airports (Bel & Fageda, 2010). Airport facilities are gradually being modernised and expanded in response to technological advances in the aviation industry (Shin & Roh, 2021).

Whereby, the majority of airport business portfolios are focused on non-aeronautical activities related to concessions, food average, retail business, catering, parking, advertising, and rental cars. Although we must emphasise the introduction of new business models and partners in the airport business portfolios as a result of the e-commerce industry and the COVID-19 pandemic. Now is the time for airport operators to reassess their business models to become more resilient. For instance, in Spain, the Teruel airport (IATA code is TEV) is managed by the Government of Aragon and Teruel City Council, also known as PLATA Consortium; it does not belong to the Aeropuertos Españoles y Navegación Aérea (AENA) Group. Innovative management by this consortium has placed it as a world benchmark in airport applications for long-stay parking, aircraft maintenance and recycling, rocket engine testing, applications and drone testing, prototype testing, aircraft certification and flight tests. Today, this regional airport is the largest airpark in Europe, and according to Hosteltur (2021), this airport increased its income by 30% due to the pandemic in 2020. The COVID-19 pandemic has forced many airports to redefine and renew their business models in aeronautical and non-aeronautical activities. Airport operators must understand that new business models are outside of the airport's hinterland boundaries.

4.2 Tangible and Intangible Elements at the Airport

Many researchers and experts in the aviation industry continue to think that airlines and passengers are the only potential customers of an airport, but the reality is quite different. Logistics and cargo activities, a sustainable and well-planned tourism activity, e-commerce companies, new working and digital environments, pharmaceutical product dispatch, the ubiquitous transaction of purchase by consumers and products and services dispatched by online companies need a greater degree of connectivity and accessibility by airports and airlines. Particularly, the growth of services linked to the internet and internet of things (IoT) has accelerated the development of the marketing of services at airports. Doganis (2019) claims that e-commerce is now at the core of business-to-customer (B2C) products purchased to satisfy customer needs and business-to-business (B2B) relationships, and the internet-based technologies that underpin this commercial binomial are constantly evolving and offering new business opportunities at airports and airlines (i.e. products bought to use in a company's operations or to make other products or services).

The interrelation between the business interests of airport operators and external companies that operate inside and outside of airports is particularly complicated, due to the different factors and activities that are combined to serve airlines, passengers, e-commerce and logistics companies and cargo forwarders. Another special feature of the airport's operability in its business portfolio is the predominance of the intangibility of services at airport infrastructure. As stated by Berry (1980), services differ fundamentally from physical goods. A good is defined as an object, whereas a service is a deed, act or performance. Services have several characteristics, like intangibility, heterogeneity, inseparability of production and consumption and perishability (Grönroos, 1978). Services marketing is noted for the characteristics of services and interactions that occur during the service creation, delivery and consumption (Ambrose & Waguespack, 2021).

The airport product consists of a supply of services, both tangible and intangible, to meet the needs of different market segments. Urfer and Weinert (2011) classify the tangible features as the airside infrastructure like runways, navigational aids or taxiways. The landside infrastructure presents control towers, terminals or parking facilities. And last, airport support infrastructure shows aircraft maintenance, in-flight catering services or aircraft rescue and firefighting (ARFF). On the other hand, the intangible elements are defined as the organisational, structural and operational aspects such as state support, administration (airport planning and management), operations (air traffic control, airport safety-hygiene and security), airport maintenance and external factors like regulations and the environment (Halpern & Graham, 2022; Tłoczyński, 2018). As depicted in Fig. 21, each airport is therefore part of a complex system. A successful airport strategy must take these tangible and intangible items into account.

According to customer's satisfaction as an intangible attribute at 18 Taiwan airports, it is very important to include intangible elements and services in airport and airline productivity to the extent of airport terminals (Yu & Hsu, 2012). In 2003, at Chiayi airport in Taiwan, a plan to extend its main terminal building was carried out, along with several terminal facilities for passengers, such as passenger-moving corridors, and luggage control systems, according to the Civil Aeronautics Administration of Taiwan (CAA). After 4 years, the result was that customers' satisfaction increased thanks to the better service provided to customers by Chiayi airport (CAA, 2013; Yu & Hsu, 2012). The main challenges faced by airport operators are infrastructure's management and congruence with their wider environment (Efthymiou & Papatheodorou, 2018).

The future of airports will be based on how the quality of services and facility operations are provided. The differentiation through service quality in this competitive market by airport operators requires a proactive approach in the design and initiatives of marketing strategies to tackle today's demanding challenges that B2C and B2B activities demand. For this reason, airport marketing strategies based on service quality must be analysed from passengers and firms' databases collected to assess the interaction between customers, companies, service providers and services in the competitive landscape of airports. But the main challenge facing the aviation industry is to reduce CO_2 emissions through 'decarbonisation actions' and implement alternative sources of energy like bio-fuel, electric and hybrid engines.

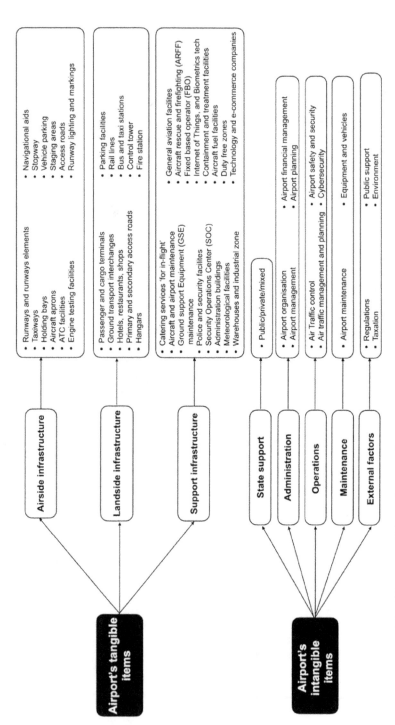

Fig. 21.   Tangible and Intangible Elements at Airport. *Source:* Compiled by the author.

4.3 Airport's Business Portfolio to Enhance Their Profitability

An airport expansion strategy across the globe is a complex undertaking that involves various factors that contribute to its profitability. For example, a well-executed airport's business portfolio can lead to increased aeronautical and commercial revenues, an improved passenger experience and enhanced opportunities for airport economic growth. Understanding market demand, enhancing infrastructure, fostering airline partnerships, diversifying revenue sources, optimising operations and gaining government support are all critical factors for successful and profitable airport growth and its business portfolio. A clear example of that is the Schiphol airport in Amsterdam (The Netherlands). This international airport has a diversified business portfolio around the world, and it includes equity participation, management contracts and strategic partnerships with different airports such as Reina Beatrix airport on the island of Aruba, Incheon airport in South Korea, Hobart airport in Australia and Beijing Capital airport in China. This disruptive strategy has attracted new partners, clients and foreign investors (Schiphol, 2024). Regularly managing, updating, optimising and assessing the airport's business portfolio is crucial to staying informed about the airport's progress and driving its success and growth.

Fig. 22 displays the new airport business portfolios in the digital era, how airport operators are developing modern business models in order to diversify income sources and optimise the available resources of the airport's infrastructure. The implementation of these new business models is influenced by competition levels between airports, destination attractiveness, a proactive value proposition, catchment area and the quality of service offered by airports. Business activities such as consultancy and managerial services at internationalisation of products and services are offered to companies by airport operators. The current pandemic crisis and war in Ukraine oblige the need for new services at airports, and it also capitalises on the potential of personalised service offers. By offering services, airport companies can improve their performance and be sustainable and competitive. This development, combined with innovative technologies, can open completely new business areas. In the same line, Lehman (2019) claims that airport operators need to ensure that they gain appropriate insight into the service process and actual performance to improve it and attract potential customers. For example, Brussels airport (IATA: BRU) in Belgium launched a new consultancy subsidiary called Airport Intelligence in 2021, to share its operational and commercial expertise with other companies globally (Airport Technology, 2021), or the international connectivity enlargement and infrastructures of regional airports, with the aim of ensuring sufficient capacity to meet the expected growth of air freight by local and regional territories (Florido-Benítez, 2023).

Another business model to be highlighted in Fig. 22 is to design and develop commercial activities based on customers' needs, customised products and services and monitoring of passengers' dwell time inside terminals through smartphones, supported by artificial intelligence (AI), virtual reality (VR), holograms, blockchain, the IoT and biometric tools. The purpose of these innovative business

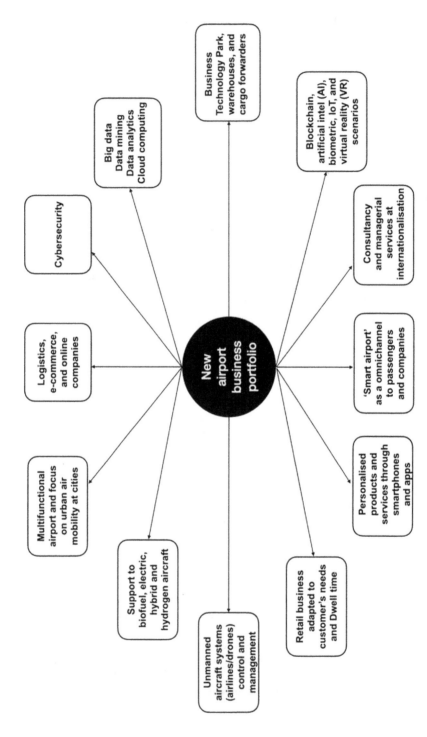

Fig. 22.   New Airport Business Portfolio. *Source:* Compiled by the author.

models is to improve passengers' experiences and satisfaction at airport terminals while increasing non-aeronautical revenues. As stated by Alabsi and Gill (2021), the massive pressure on existing airport facilities requires airport operators to rethink their traditional structures with a view to optimise their operations, increasing capacity, expanding revenues and improving passengers' experiences while ensuring physical safety and digital security due to the pandemic crisis. As such, digital technology enables cooperation between airport facilities, data and applications to help personalising customer experiences (Florido-Benítez, 2022a; Rotondo, 2019; SITA, 2022). These operational and technological strategies implemented by airports are highly valued by passenger surveys in the Skytrax World Airport Awards; these are the most prestigious qualities in air transport. For instance, in 2019, the Bush Intercontinental airport (IATA code, IAH) was awarded the 'Best Airport Website and Digital Services' by the Skytrax World Airport Awards (Florido-Benítez, 2022b). Skytrax is a consultancy firm based in London, United Kingdom (Skytrax, 2022).

Nonetheless, one of the fundamental principles underpinning the concept of a smart airport is the digitalisation of business, security-safety, cybersecurity, logistics, retail and smart service systems provided by airports. The European Union Agency for Network and Information Security (ENISA) defines smart airports as those 'airports making use of networked, data driven response capabilities that, on the one hand, provide travellers with a better and more seamless travel experience and, on the other hand, aim to guarantee higher levels of security for the safety of passengers and operators'.

These airports are implementing new smart components to offer travellers a portfolio of services that spans from self or automatic check-in, baggage and document check, flight booking management and way finding services to automated border control and security checks' (see Alabsi & Gill, 2021; ENISA, 2016; Göçmen, 2021; ICAO, 2020; Koroniotis et al., 2020; Narongou & Sun, 2022). Passengers in competition-heavy US markets like Los Angeles, Chicago, Dallas-Fort Worth, Houston and New York will gravitate towards airports that reduce hassle and create more satisfying travel experiences. Fasone and Scuderi (2012) indicate that the choice to invest in non-aeronautical activities can be attributed to the strategic orientation adopted by airport operators rather than the growth rates of passengers.

The smart airports sector is growing as airports in these markets try to position themselves as the providers of choice (ITB Business Travel, 2019). In 2016, the US Department of Transportation (USDOT) reported that aviation accounted for more than 5.2% of the gross domestic product (GDP), contributing $1.8 trillion in total economic activity and supporting nearly 11 million jobs with $488.2 billion in earnings that year. Considering only the direct sectors, the impact is 2.3% of GDP, $850 billion in economic activity and over 4 million jobs (USDOT, 2020). Designing the airport environment for passenger comfort can lead to commercial performance benefits, so airport design features that reduce passenger stress can increase retail revenue (Hedge et al., 2021).

An airport's business portfolio must be attractive to customers and strategically viable for airport operators. Finding a balance between these two aspects is not an easy task because the new airport business models imply a long process in which many different inputs and outputs must be taken into account. An airport's business portfolio is a living document, and this is subject to revision constantly as it evolves over time. Besides, the airport's own characteristics and the permanent monitoring of the market situation play an essential role in airport marketing strategies. Mahagaonkar (2010a, 2010b, 2010c) emphasises that the implementation of a new marketing method involves significant changes in product placement, promotion, distribution and communication.

From a sustainable point of view, airports must provide biofuel, electric, hybrid and hydrogen resources to airlines because the aviation industry is moving decisively towards 'decarbonisation' using biofuels, electro fuels and other alternatives to fuel technologies. For instance, Repsol and Iberia airlines have made the first flight using biofuel produced from waste in Spain with an Airbus A320neo aircraft of the Iberia airline (Repsol, 2021). The European Union Aviation Safety Agency (EASA) suggests that the last decade has seen considerable progress in developing Sustainable Aviation Fuels (SAFs) produced from bio-based feedstocks that have a lower carbon intensity, to mitigate the environmental impact of aviation (EASA, 2022). A report by KPMG consulting (2019) revealed that airport operators will face pressure to integrate sources including biofuel, hybrid-electric and fully electric into their existing fuel storage and distribution infrastructure. Airports managed by governments have more advantages in the role of creating business portfolios, which can generate more profits through non-aeronautical revenues (Shin & Roh, 2021). Airports are businesses in their own right, and diversifying their portfolios of businesses is a key axiom in this endeavour to maximise the benefits and minimise the risk of investment for operators.

References

ACI. (2017). Non-aeronautical revenues are vital to airport success, says ACI world. https://aci-lac.aero/news/non-aeronautical-revenues-are-vital-to-airport-success-says-aci-world/. Accessed on February 11, 2022.

ACI. (2020). *2020 airport key performance indicators.* https://store.aci.aero/product/2020-airport-key-performance-indicators/. Accessed on February 13, 2022.

Airport Technology. (2021). Brussels airport launches new subsidiary to organize consultancy services. https://www.airport-technology.com/news/brussels-airport-consultancy-services/. Accessed on March 1, 2022.

Alabsi, M.-I., & Gill, A. Q. (2021). A review of passenger digital information privacy concerns in smart airports. *IEEE Access, 9*, 33769–33781.

Ambrose, S., & Waguespack, B. (2021). *Fundamentals of airlines marketing.* Routledge.

Bel, G., & Fageda, X. (2010). Privatization, regulation and airport pricing: An empirical analysis for Europe. *Journal of Regulatory Economics, 37*(2), 142–161.

Berry, L. L. (1980, May–June). Services marketing is different. *Business Week,* 24–29.

CAA. (2013). *Annual report 2013*. https://www.google.com/url?sa=t&rct=j&q=&esrc=s&source=web&cd=&ved=2ahUKEwi9lsG4hYn2AhVOgs4BHQX6BxkQFnoECAcQAQ&url=https%3A%2F%2Fwww.caa.gov.tw%2FFileAtt.ashx%3Flang%3D2%26id%3D7577&usg=AOvVaw2edKZPEJHWgSZ7-AM6xAKP. Accessed on February 13, 2022.

Doganis, R. (2019). *Flying off course. Airline economics and marketing*. Routledge.

EASA. (2022). *Sustainable aviation fuels*. https://www.easa.europa.eu/eaer/climate-change/sustainable-aviation-fuels. Accessed on February 21, 2022.

Efthymiou, M., & Papatheodorou, A. (2018). Evolving airline and airport business models. In N. Halpern & A. Graham (Eds.), *The Routledge companion to air transport management* (pp. 122–136). Routledge.

ENISA (2016). *Securing smart airports*. https://doi.org/10.2824/865081

Fasone, V., & Scuderi, R. (2012). Non-aviation revenues and growth in passengers' traffic: Clustering Italian airports. *International Journal of Aviation Management*, *1*(4), 304–317.

Florido-Benítez, L. (2022a). International mobile marketing: A satisfactory concept for companies and users in times of pandemic. *Benchmarking: An International Journal*, *29*(6), 1826–1856.

Florido-Benítez, L. (2022b). The world airport awards a quality distinctive and marketing tool for airports. *Journal of Airline Operations and Aviation Management*, *1*(2), 54–81.

Florido-Benítez, L. (2023). The role of the top 50 US cargo airports and 25 air cargo airlines in the logistics of E-commerce companies. *Logistics*, *7*(1), 8.

Göçmen, E. (2021). Smart airport: Evaluation of performance standards and technologies for a smart logistics zone. *Transportation Research Record*, *2675*(7), 480–490.

Grönroos, C. (1978). A service-oriented approach to marketing of services. *European Journal of Marketing*, *12*(8), 588–601.

Halpern, N., & Graham, A. (2022). *Airport marketing* (2nd ed.). Routledge.

Hedge, A., MacNaughton, P., Woo, M., Guglielmetti, R., & Tinianov, B. (2021). Airport passenger experiences in concourses with either electrochromic or low-e glass windows. *International Journal of Aviation Management*, *5*(1), 1–16.

Hosteltur. (2021). *The largest air parking in Europe, the Teruel airport remains small*. https://www.hosteltur.com/143644_teruel-tiene-el-mayor-parking-de-aviones-de-europa-y-se-queda-pequeno.html. Accessed on February 12, 2022.

ICAO. (2020). *Smart airports*. https://www.icao.int/safety/iStars/Documents/IUG%20Meeting%201/Presentations/Smart%20Airports%20-%20Vijay%20Narula.pdf. Accessed on February 1, 2022.

ITB Business Travel. (2019). *Coming soon: Smart airports around the world*. https://jtbbusinesstravel.com/smart-airports/. Accessed on February 22, 2022.

Jarach, D. (2001). The evolution of airport management practices: Towards a multi-point, multi-service, marketing-driven firm. *Journal of Air Transport Management*, *7*(2), 119–125.

Jimenez, E., Claro, J., & de Sousa, J. P. (2014). The airports business in a competitive environment. *Procedia–Social and Behavioral Sciences*, *111*, 947–954.

Karanki, F., Lim, S. H., & Choi, B. J. (2020). The determinants of aeronautical charges of U.S. airports: A spatial analysis. *Journal of Air Transport Management*, *86*, 101825.

Koroniotis, N., Moustafa, N., Schiliro, F., Gauravaram, P., & Janicke, H. (2020). A holistic review of cybersecurity and reliability perspectives in smart airports. *IEEE Access, 8*, 209802–209834.

KPMG. (2019). *Aviation 2030. Disruption and its implications for the aviation sector.* https://assets.kpmg/content/dam/kpmg/xx/pdf/2019/12/aviation-2030.pdf. Accessed on February 24, 2022.

Lehman, C. (2019). *Exploring service productivity: Studies in the German airport industry.* Springer Gabler.

Mahagaonkar, P. (2010a). What do scientists want: Money or fame? In *Money and ideas. International studies in entrepreneurship* (Vol. 25). Springer.

Mahagaonkar, P. (2010b). *Money and ideas. Four studies on finance, innovation and the business life cycle.* Springer Science+Business Media.

Mahagaonkar, P. (2010c). Regional financial system and the financial structure of small firms. In *Money and ideas. International studies in entrepreneurship* (Vol. 25). Springer.

Narongou, D., & Sun, Z. (2022). Applying intelligent big data analytics in a smart airport business: Value, adoption, and challenges. In Z. Sun & Z. Wu (Eds.), *Handbook of research on foundations and applications of intelligent business analytics* (pp. 216–237). IGI Global.

Repsol. (2021). Repsol and Iberia make the first flight with biofuel produced from waste in Spain. https://www.repsol.com/en/press-room/press-releases/2021/repsol-iberia-first-flight-with-biofuel-produced-from-waste-in-spain/index.cshtml. Accessed on February 22, 2022.

Rotondo, F. (2019). An explorative analysis to identify airport business models. *Research in Transportation Business & Management, 33*, 100417.

Schiphol. (2024). Portfolio. https://www.schiphol.nl/en/schiphol-group/page/schiphol-international-portfolio/. Accessed on February 7, 2024.

Shin, T., & Roh, T. (2021). Impact of non-aeronautical revenues on airport landing charge in global airports. *Transportation Research Record, 2675*(10), 667–677.

SITA. (2022). Smart technology, smarter airports. https://www.sita.aero/resources/videos/smart-technology-smarter-airports/. Accessed on February 18, 2022.

Skytrax. (2022). About the world airport awards. https://www.worldairportawards.com/about-us/. Accessed on February 28, 2022.

Tłoczyński, D. (2018). The quality of the airport's product. *European Journal of Service Management, 2*(26), 273–282.

Urfer, B., & Weinert, R. (2011). Managing airport infrastructure. In A. Wittmer, T. Bieger, & R. Muller (Eds.), *Aviations systems: Management of the integrated aviation value chain.* Springer.

USDOT. (2020, November). *The economic impact of civil aviation on the U.S. economy. State supplement.* https://www.faa.gov/about/plans_reports/media/2020_nov_economic_impact_report.pdf. Accessed on August 30, 2022.

Yu, M.-M., & Hsu, C.-C. (2012). Service productivity and biased technological change of domestic airports in Taiwan. *International Journal of Sustainable Transportation, 6*(1), 1–25.

Chapter 5

Airport Marketing Strategy

Abstract

This chapter focuses on strategy, marketing strategy and airport marketing strategy concepts from an aviation and marketing point of view. Furthermore, in this chapter, we introduced a new and innovative airport marketing strategy concept and how this can influence tourism, financials, business, consumers' behaviour, sustainability and aviation activities. This chapter also analyses how operators implement new airport strategies to improve their operability, sustainability, governance and customer satisfaction. When selling an innovative product or service, the airport operator needs to examine the underlying factors that drive passengers' purchasing decisions. Airport marketing strategies are changing in the aviation and tourism sectors due to the pandemic crisis and Ukraine's war, and operators subsequently need to consider these new factors when they develop new marketing plans and goals.

5.1 The Concept of Strategy as a Business and Marketing Tool at Airports

The development of innovative strategies by airport operators may increase new opportunities in a globalised marketplace, as is the case in the aviation industry, to gain competitive advantages. Strategy is what you will do to reach your objective, which is driven by your vision and mission statement. A strategy requires the design of actions or tactics that tackle the price, place, product and promotion components of marketing, planning, organising, directing and management (Randazzo, 2014). In business management, the concept of strategy means looking at the long-term future to determine what the company wants to become and putting in place a plan for how to get there. A strategy helps the airport operator meet uncertain situations with due diligence. For example, a strategy of internationalisation of airports requires visualisation of the future of the airport, proactiveness, creativity and imagination to encourage those who will

Airport Marketing Strategies, 67–86

Copyright © 2024 Lázaro Florido-Benítez

Published under exclusive licence by Emerald Publishing Limited

doi:10.1108/978-1-83608-082-420241005

apply the strategy and connect with your target audience or, in a nutshell, 'positioning'.

Establish and conduct a good strategy by the airport operator or company, which provides a road map for managers and indicates what must be done to survive, be profitable and grow as an organisation in an industry as competitive as the aviation sector. A good strategy must be based on clearly identified and framed challenges by airport operators. Strategy is science because it requires analytical skills, the ability to organise and analyse information and the ability of make well-informed decisions.

The origin of strategy is found in the ancient Greek military lexicon. Heuser (2010, p. 4), tracing the evolution of the use of the concept of strategy, states: The Greek word strategy (either strategia or strategiké) was used in antiquity for the art or skills of the general (the strategós). The general is the one who practises strategy. Nevertheless, the history and evolution of the concept of strategy have changed very considerably over time; this has been implemented in business, the marketing sector, human interactions, economics and political activities, among many others. Nowadays, a strategy is a cohesive core of guiding decisions and is an entity's evolving theory of winning high-stake challenges through power creating use of resources and opportunities in uncertain environments (Khalifa, 2020). The definition of strategy covers several usually paired concepts like governance and performance, strategy and structure, control and learning, intention and action, planning and emergence and formulation and execution (Freedman, 2013; Heuser, 2010; Khalifa, 2020; Strachan, 2013).

From a competitive point of view, the concept of strategy is the way in which a corporation endeavours to differentiate itself positively from its competitors, using its relative strengths to better satisfy customer needs (Ohmae, 1982). Ohmae's definition highlights the competitive aspect of strategy and the strengths required to satisfy customer needs. This definition thus aims at customer satisfaction as the driver of the strategy. In terms of achieving a company's objectives, Andrews (1997) defines strategy as the pattern of major objectives, purposes or goals and essential policies or plans for achieving the goals, stated in such a way as to define what business the company is in or is to be in and the kind of company it is or is to be. For example, in 2020, Singapore Changi airport (IATA: SIN) closed terminal two for 18 months, while Heathrow airport in London (IATA: LHR) closed one runway. Both established survival strategies to ensure the operability of airports during the COVID-19 pandemic, and their goals were to keep airports open to domestic and international air traffic but with limited services to reduce overall cost (ACI, 2020).

In addition, this concept of strategy emphasises purpose and how purpose will be achieved. It also emphasises the values and cultures that the company stands for. According to previous definitions of strategy used by scholars, in this chapter, we propose to introduce a new definition of strategy aligned with marketing activity that could better reflect the complex nature of the strategy concept in the commercial sector: A strategy is a set of decision-making processes oriented towards achieving the established objectives of an organisation and aligned with the company's values and business culture. For example, real estate development centred on airports arises as a strategy to maximise non-aeronautical revenues and as a response to a need for revenue diversification due to globalisation and liberalisation processes (Peneda et al., 2011).

As a service platform, the main airport customers are airlines (e.g. legacy, low-cost carriers, freight carriers and integrators) in the aeronautical area. Airport operators provide them with runways, refuelling and handling, aircraft aprons, etc. But passengers are also direct customers of airports from a commercial perspective; airport operators provide them with restaurants, shops, play areas for children, Wi-Fi, parking facilities and very important person (VIP) services, among many others. As previously mentioned about airport revenues in Chapter 4, the revenues of airports are separated into aeronautical and commercial revenues, and airport operators develop strategies dependent on the airport's category, type, size, capacity, demand and air traffic flows. They lay out strategies and options in their marketing plans to generate more income. Badanik et al. (2010) indicate that there are two types of strategies adopted by airport operators: first, the strategies of specialisation will aim at developing aeronautical revenues, and second, the strategies of diversification will have the goal of increasing commercial revenues (see Fig. 23). The identification of overarching and specific objectives in aeronautical and commercial activities should be aligned with the existing strategies and priorities of airport operators and marketers over a 4-to-8-year time horizon.

Airports continue to focus on the health and welfare of their passengers and staff, cost reductions in line with decreased traffic levels and planning. For this reason, airport operators and governments are constantly designing strategies focused on technology priorities (e.g. biometric ID services, cybersecurity, cloud services, business intelligence or customer care via digital channels like the official website, airport apps or social media) to make airports as safe as possible with the aim of regaining passenger confidence as well as remaining agile in uncertain times (Shallow, 2021).

Airport strategies adopted by operators should be understood within the context of a dynamic industry where consumer change, legislative provision and government policy upheaval continue to reconfigure the sector (Freathy, 2004). Spanish airports of the *Aeropuertos Españoles y Navegación Aérea* (AENA) network ended in 2019 with more than 275.2 million passengers, which was 4.4% more than the previous year and the best performance in their history. This was possible thanks to two pillars based on AENA's strategic plan: leadership consolidation worldwide and fulfilment of objectives established (AENA, 2018, 2020). The airport marketing tool is prepared to provide pricing incentives, funding of activities, market research and promotional campaigns to design future marketing strategies (Graham, 2008). Indeed, airport strategic planning requires partnering with other companies (e.g. Duty Free, FedEx, Menzies, WHSmith or American Airlines) carefully planning for the actions of others, like competitors or supply sources.

Developing and executing strategies are central to the practice of marketing activities. Airport operators need to combine commercial strategies with digital commerce solutions inside and outside of airports to promote new business

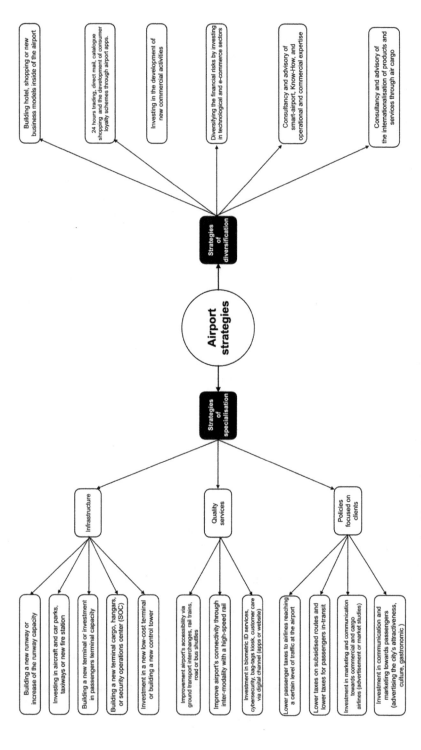

Fig. 23.   Airport Strategies. *Source:* Compiled by the author.

models, so all stakeholders must be involved: airport operators, concessionaires, airlines and passengers, with the aim of increasing revenue from the synergies between them. A good strategy not only increases profitability but also increases passenger satisfaction. Schiphol airport (IATA: AMS) in Amsterdam, Heathrow (IATA: LHR) in the United Kingdom, Düsseldorf airport in Germany (IATA: DUS) and Dallas Fort-Worth airport (IATA: DFW) in the United States are pioneers in the development of airport apps focused on improving the passenger's experience and satisfaction, and this type of commercial strategy results in increased commercial revenues for airport operators and the rest of the companies that are operating at airports (Florido-Benítez & del Alcázar, 2015).

5.2 An Overview of the Marketing Strategy Definition in the Aviation Sector

The proliferation of marketing strategies combined with databases has made airports and airlines better manage passengers' relationships and enhance decision-making in business in a more efficient and effective manner. When an airport operator is going to plan a marketing strategy, it is necessary to document a situation analysis with a gathering of data and updated information that details the current state of the airport, its main competitors, its customers and its immediate surroundings in economic and operational terms. An airport operator must have a high understanding of the aviation sector on which the airport will tackle its economic and operative efforts in an industry in constant technological, security and migration policy changes (e.g. the COVID-19 pandemic crisis). Disruptive companies like Uber, Expedia or Airbnb use new technologies and strategies to change how tourists travel, shop for daily needs (Amazon or Tesco) and even how users book airline tickets (Google flights, Kayak, or Skyscanner). At the end, the cornerstone of airport marketing strategy must be focused on the customers' satisfaction and experience and the achievement of the airport's goals through its marketing plan by the airport operator.

This is one of the reasons why airport operators and marketers may be able to design innovative marketing strategies that can take competitive advantage of the new paradigm of the aviation industry in a globalised world. In 2022, Heathrow airport (IATA: LHR) launched an advocacy campaign called 'Heathrow 2.0: Connecting people and planet'. This is a sustainability strategy for the next decade, with the aim of reducing carbon dioxide emissions and pollution around its facilities. The FGP Topco Limited consortium is the airport's operator at Heathrow airport, and it is committed to reducing up to 15% of the carbon emitted by the flights operating in this airport and to reducing at least 45% of the emissions produced on the ground by 2030 (Heathrow airport, 2022).

Since developing and executing marketing strategy is central to what marketers do in practice, research relevant to understanding these activities is key to establishing the relevance of the academic discipline of marketing (Morgan et al., 2019). Marketing strategy defines how to properly shape the marketing structure to attract and satisfy target markets and achieve the goals of the organisation.

The main task of a marketing strategy is to correctly plan products, distribution channels, promotion and pricing policy. Many researchers define the concept of marketing strategy in different ways.

The conceptualisation of marketing strategy was originally created by Oxenfeldt (1958) which consists of two parts: first, the definition of the target market, the selection of the market segment (the group of consumers) to whom the company wishes to appeal. And second, the development of a marketing mix, the choice of the tools that the company intends to combine to satisfy this target group. In this same vein, Varadarajan (2010) defines a marketing strategy as an integrated set of decisions that helps the firm make critical choices regarding marketing activities in selected markets and segments, with the aim to create, communicate and deliver value to customers in exchange for accomplishing its specific financial, market and other objectives. The passenger or user as customer pays for a service in advance, hoping for an orderly performance (Schmitt & Gollnick, 2016). Stated another way, marketing strategy is a plan for how the organisation will use its strengths and capabilities to match the needs and requirements of the market (Ferrell et al., 2021).

A marketing strategy can be composed of one or more marketing mixes known as the 4Ps: product, price, place and promotion. To develop a marketing strategy, an organisation must select the right combination of target market and marketing mix to create distinct competitive advantages over its rivals (Ferrell et al., 2021; Florido-Benítez, 2016a; Kotler & Keller, 2009). On the contrary, Ye (2022) suggests that the 4Ps model is less useful in the airport context, as the product cycle is much longer. Ye (2022) recommends the 4Cs model (customer value, cost, convenience and communication) focused on customers, airlines, companies and authorities inside and outside of airports, and satisfying them through a tailor-made approach. This marketing strategy helped to increase by 26% non-aeronautical revenue at FlyBalaton airport (Tiboldi, 2008). The 4Cs elements of this model are shown in Fig. 24.

An interesting study carried out by Chiu et al. (2016) revealed that airline marketing strategies are effective in predicting tourist consumption behaviour and tourists' expectations on purchase intention. For instance, Singapore Airlines has achieved its outstanding competitive advantage by effectively implementing marketing strategies based on brand image and product and service differentiation through service excellence and innovation in its business mode. This has been a good strategic choice, giving priority to profitability over size (Heracleous & Wirtz, 2012). The young generation is very efficient at navigating the internet and quickly noticing a price difference. They may get discouraged very quickly and not take advantage of the offers provided by airlines' websites, which may result in a decline in revenues due to a bad marketing strategy or promotion campaign by operators and marketers of airlines (Walczack, 2022).

Sometimes marketing strategies may be wrongly focused. A real example is when a customer buys flight tickets on the app or official website of EasyJet, Vueling or Ryanair airlines. It is possible to book a car rental or hotel in cooperation with the AVIS's or Booking.com website or apps. The issue here is that the offers provided by these airlines are often not as attractive as when a user

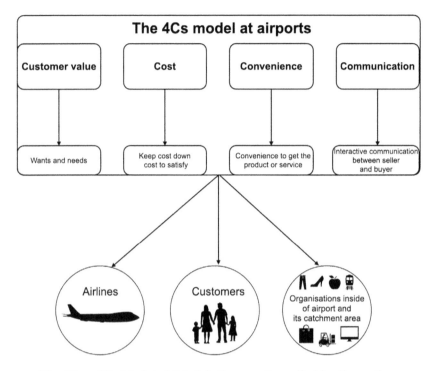

Fig. 24. 4Cs Updated Model. *Source:* Compiled by the author.

orders directly from AVIS or Booking.com's official website or apps, especially with young people who know all the tricks of airlines' marketing strategies and are willing to travel on these airlines for very little money. We should not forget that airports and airline marketing strategies must fulfil the needs and wants of their passengers.

From the airport operator's point of view, digital marketing strategies are very important for airports because marketing strategies through mobile marketing in retail shopping and customer satisfaction terms are considered vital and niche areas of an airport business to generate income to allow maintenance of the airport's operability. Regarding the security and control supplied by the mobile marketing tool to passengers at the airport, it has been demonstrated that it favours an increase in cross-selling (Florido-Benítez, 2016b). In addition, the security/control provided by mobile marketing to users increases sales. One of the main keys to the success of the correlation between security and cross-selling is the fact that mobile marketing is both customised and non-intrusive (Florido-Benítez, 2016c, 2016d, 2016e, 2016f).

As stated by Wu and Ma (2022), there are two tactics for forming effective mobile marketing strategies: first, the customisation of mobile coupons by passengers, and second, location-based mobile coupon push notifications through airport apps by airport operators and marketers. Normally, airport operators design marketing strategies depending on air passengers and shoppers of retail shopping inside the airport terminal. This is commonly done by two strategies: shaping passenger flows in the terminal by special layout designs and maximising retail exposure to passengers in the terminal environment (Hubregtse, 2016). For instance, some Italian airports, like Rome Fiumicino (IATA: FCO) in Italy, or Milan Malpensa (IATA: MXP) airports have adopted a differentiation strategy for passengers, offering unique features to fulfil the demands of the market of luxury consumers (Giovanelli & Rotondo, 2022).

With the aim of creating long-term value for Munich airport (IATA: MCU), the surrounding region, Bavaria and Germany, the airport operator of Munich Airport International GmbH (MAI) has developed five strategies based on the principle of sustainable development called 'Strategy 2030' (see Fig. 25). These five strategies describe five fields of action: airside traffic development, landside access and traffic development, seamless travel, expansion of non-aviation businesses and off-campus growth of the airport (Munich airport, 2024). These marketing strategies help the airport of Munich develop a holistic strategy that incorporates all the drivers of value, both financial and sustainability related. When the airport's strategy is set, airport operators and sales and marketing staff define the impact on the airport's workforce, economic budget, operating procedures, capital equipment requirements and a contingency plan to prevent possible errors.

Airport operators must provide products and services characterised by high levels of quality; this helps to make travel more pleasant for air passengers, with the ultimate objective of attracting more users. Allen et al. (2021) pointed out that marketing strategies focused on airport service quality are fundamental both for users and airport management companies because travellers will be delighted by a comfortable and well-functioning airport.

5.3 Airport Marketing Strategy: Role and Scope of Business Activity

Airports play a strategic role for the cities where they are localised and serve. Airports have the power to encourage the pace of growth of a city's economic and brand visibility worldwide, especially at this age of globalisation and digitalisation in the production of inputs and outputs, efficient and optimised work carried out in that region. The importance of the airport marketing strategy and its location in relation to large cities is vital for local development. Destination Marketing Organizations (DMOs) emphasise that airports are the city's strong point, that they provide a better prospect of increased air traffic in the city and that they help to create jobs and attract investors. The airport's positioning and branding worldwide is the main attractive asset of a city's tourism and business portfolio, thus a relevant driver in the development of the destination's value proposition. Indeed, large cities like New York, Paris, Shanghai, London, Amsterdam, Málaga, Hong Kong or Dubai depend on economic and logistic opportunities provided by airports. The airport's infrastructure is a significant

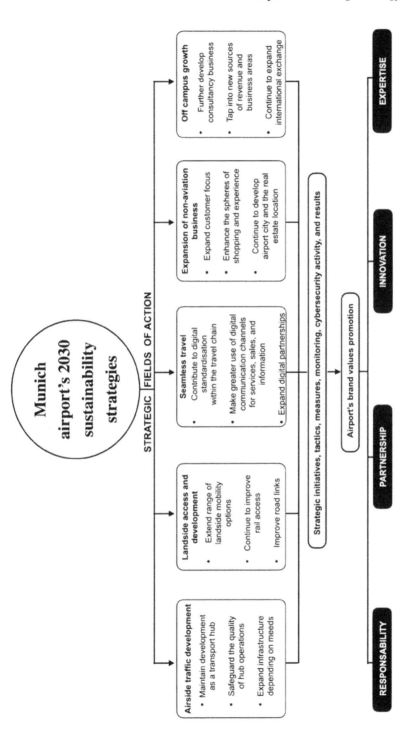

Fig. 25. Munich Airport's 2030 Sustainability Strategies. *Source:* Adapted from Munich airport (2024).

logistic support in the movement of both passengers and goods to and from a specific geographic area, acting as gateways of inbound and outbound business and tourist traffic for great multinationals and tourist destinations.

An airport with its commercial and cargo airlines has a direct and indirect impact on logistic efficiency and effectiveness between airport–companies–stakeholders, and its international development of business activities depends on large multinationals and small and medium-sized enterprises, also known as SMEs. This is also known as trade reciprocity. The airport is a symbol of the economic and urban development of the region, which enables large companies and SMEs to exploit both local comparative advantages and reinforce the firm's own international competitive supremacy. For cities, airports are able to improve the rate of employment of residents by means of third-party job creation in their catchment area (Florido-Benítez, 2021a, 2021b; Jarach, 2005; Morrison & Coca-Stefaniak, 2020).

In 2021, a good airport strategy was developed by Incheon airport (IATA: ICN) in South Korea; Incheon International Airport Corporation operator established three airport marketing strategies for the systematic environment, social and governance (ESG), based on management tactics (see Fig. 26), to promote human-oriented management based on the ESG happiness platform and through innovation and growth, achieve a 100% transition to renewable energies in 2040. The creation of 120,000 jobs in 2030 and improve the anti-corruption and

Fig. 26.   Three Airport Marketing Strategies Focused on Tactics Management by Incheon Airport. *Source:* Adapted from Incheon airport (2017, 2022).

corporate ethics systems in 2025 (Incheon airport, 2022). It is no coincidence that this airport has been among the four best airports in the world for 10 consecutive years by Skytrax (2021); it requires commitment and involves hard work in all senses.

Nevertheless, airport operators should pay attention to what their customers are talking about or what apps, websites or payment methods they are using, with the aim of designing good marketing strategies and capturing their target market's attention. Sometimes, you can be your best friend or your own worst enemy, depending on how you view it. Bad marketing is something many companies suffer from. If airport operators and marketing staff are not able to identify and rectify signs of failure or weak points in their marketing strategies and promotion campaigns, they are likely heading for an utter fiasco. There is nothing worse than seeing your prospective customers turn to your competitors for their products and services. For instance, in 1987, American Airlines was going through a rough patch and looking for quick ways to raise capital. Instead of securing bank loans, the company introduced an 'AAirpass' that offered unlimited first-class air travel for a flat rate of $250,000. This marketing strategy was a commercial flop by the operator and marketing staff of American Airlines to make quick money, which backfired, resulting in financial losses and angry customers. The problem was that the AAirpass was truly limitless, and membership was lifelong. At the end, the result of this bad strategy was that American Airlines lost millions of dollars due to the high volume of flights taken by AAirpass holders (The Guardian, 2019).

Although all the vicissitudes of marketing strategies have been previously shown to readers, an airport marketing strategy definition is yet not available for researchers and marketers in business and marketing literature and field reports. From now on, this new concept must be empowered by marketing scholars and practitioners to identify and understand companies and customers' needs in the aviation and tourism industries, particularly when new business models have been introduced at airports to create new solutions for tourists, passengers, organisations, e-commerce and logistics sectors and commercial and cargo carriers. Airport marketing strategies face new challenges that did not exist in the past in aviation and tourism activities (e.g. processes of digitalisation, joint business strategies, pandemic crisis or cyberattacks). While marketing strategies trends continue to change, trying different approaches and techniques will allow airport operators and marketers to experiment and find what works best for their airport's operability and their customers. Digital technology is indispensable today, thanks to the technology, life is made easier, opportunities for creativity are widely opened for companies and users, the ubiquity of information is available at hand and interconnection knows no boundaries. In this context, joint collaborations optimise possibilities to solve borderless complex issues or existential threats such as financial crises, climate change, the COVID-19 pandemic or wars (Harari, 2019).

In consequence, we define airport marketing strategy as an ongoing process of developing marketing and promotion tactics and actions by airport operators to reach established goals with the aim of satisfying airline, customer and organisation needs inside and outside of the airport. When airport operators and their marketing team lay out airport marketing strategies, these can have different goals (together or individually), purposes and preferences of actors (e.g. airlines, passengers, cities, tourists, museums, theme parks, among many others), depending on disciplines (e.g. tourism, travel and leisure, financial, safety and hygiene standards, political and economic activities or even international positioning), which airport operators have agreed with other organisations or airports, large multinationals, commercial and airline carriers, e-commerce and logistics companies and DMOs. Fig. 27 shows us the development of airport marketing strategies depending on actors and disciplines for which these have been directed to reach objectives and target audiences through diverse marketing channels. Airport marketing strategies are always developed and included in a strategic marketing plan by operators.

Some airport marketing strategies developed through digital marketing channels by Dallas-Fort Worth International airport (IATA: DFW) have been driven by the United States' regulatory conservation priorities and DFW Airport Board operators; their overall objectives are focused on the Clean Water Act (CWA) to return the United States' waters to standards that are fishable and swimmable. Dallas-Fort Worth airport is committed to operating the airport in a manner that encourages environmental stewardship, social responsibility and demonstrates performance by exceeding regulatory compliance standards through sustainability, resiliency and innovation. Airport marketing strategies by DFW airport embrace sustainability as a way to protect the environment in its catchment area, support its neighbours and develop its new business models (Dallas-Fort Worth airport, 2021).

5.4 How Important Are Airport Marketing Strategies for the Tourism Sector?

The aviation industry is the cornerstone of tourism activity because airports open the tourist market for large cities and tourist destinations, promote the development of the city's infrastructure and encourage the creation of new tourist products and services in the territory. Airports are the gates of cities where tourists enjoy and satisfy their dreams in the desired tourist destination, and they are an internal part of the tourism service system. Thus, an airport is an ambassador of a destination or city, which exhibits the positive characteristics of a city (Florido-Benítez & del Alcázar, 2020). If we analyse the impact of the airport on the tourism industry, it would be necessary to see which city this is going to. As stated by Florido-Benítez (2020), the value chain in tourism activity and the need for integration and coordination by the three main actors: airports, DMOs and airlines are fundamental to improving the existing tourism offer and the development of new products in the cities. The interoperability between regional authorities, airports and airlines was evidenced in 2018 at Seville airport (IATA: SQV) in Spain, increasing the operations from 5 to 10 million passengers in Europe since relating the city of Seville as a tourism destination brand image for the 2030 airport strategy.

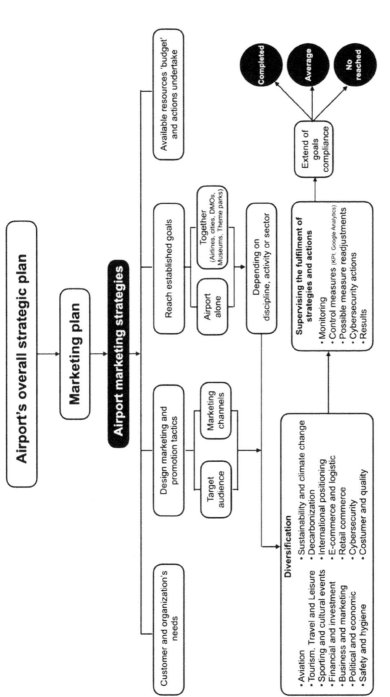

Fig. 27. Development of Airport Marketing Strategies Depending on Actors and Disciplines. *Source:* Compiled by the author.

The aviation and tourism industries complement each other. Tourism activity depends on transportation through commercial airlines to bring visitors (e.g. joint promotion strategies between airlines and tourist destinations), while the transportation industry depends on tourism to generate demand for its services. For instance, a 2021 report by the China Tourism Academy contends that China's booming tourism is bringing vigour to Shanghai Disneyland, which has increased the numbers of international tourist arrivals at this theme park and the city of Shanghai (China Travel News, 2021). The growth in the tourism sector directly reflects on air transportation. Airports are required to be more attractive to airlines and passengers with relevant investments in commercial policies. Airports Council International (ACI) (2017) affirms that airports are vital economic generators, providing a gateway to their region or country. In a competitive environment, airports require expanding and enhancing their appeal to increase their share of air travel and tourism.

DMOs, airports, airlines and stakeholders must participate actively in the air transport planning projects to improve the connectivity of destinations (Yang et al., 2019) because air transport connectivity has a great influence on tourist flows; thus, airports will always give wings to the tourism industry (Florido-Benítez, 2021c). Air transport plays an important role in facilitating increased destination access and paves the way for entirely new routes to operate (Koo et al., 2017). This interdependency between tourism and aviation, along with the increase in competition, has transformed airports (Prentice & Kadam, 2019) and their marketing strategies globally in terms of creativity, innovation, diversification, sustainability and corporate image.

International and domestic air connectivity systems provided by airports and airlines are essential for a country's and a tourist destination's economic development, as they facilitate the movement of tourists in the territory, an important increase in passenger arrivals at airports and the exchange of goods and services between different countries and regions. On the contrary, Florido-Benítez (2021d) indicates that airports are essential infrastructures in the strategic and marketing plans of Spanish destinations because $\frac{3}{4}$ of tourists arrived in Spain through airports in the last 10 years, but we are aware that every tool has a mathematical and social divergence. In the case of Spanish airports, these have been the gateways of the Spanish tourist destinations, but at the same time, they have become the controllers of the future of many Spanish tourist destinations, in which they condition the economy, urban planning and the labour and social scenario of the natives of that territory.

The COVID-19 pandemic has been a disruptive factor with a direct negative impact on aviation, tourism and leisure sectors that is changing the future of airports, DMOs and airlines in terms of operations, security, connectivity, promotion and quality of service. It is clear that airport and airline operators and DMOs need to formulate innovative marketing strategies to improve international and domestic air connectivity in cities. The short- and long-term effects of the pandemic crisis, Russia's invasion of Ukraine and high oil prices are causing many tourist destinations and DMOs to implement new alliances with low-cost and legacy carriers, airports and stakeholders in planning the future for their marketing and promotion strategies with the aim of increasing the numbers of passengers at airports and airlines, and, hence, more tourists at destinations.

Conversely, Papatheodorou et al. (2019) indicate that airlines' property (aircraft) is spatially transferable, whereas airports and destinations' infrastructure is fixed in location. A badly handled conflict may lead an airline to move away from an airport and its served destination, resulting in a loss of business at the local level. Airlines constantly struggle to change the economic terms of the contracts and agreements they sign with airports. A research project carried out by Malina et al. (2012) showed that from a sample of 200 European airports, one-third adopted incentive programmes providing lower aeronautical charges and promotional payments when negotiating with airlines (66 of the 200). Moreover, 33 bilateral agreements in the form of fixed payment guarantees were detected among airports and airlines and 26 among destination authorities and airports.

Cheung et al. (2020) claim that well-developed international air connectivity can accelerate the growth of air traffic, improve the competitiveness of airports and increase their influence over other cities. International air connectivity is related to flight frequency, number of seats and flying distance (Zhang, Hou, et al., 2022). Indeed, air connectivity is a determinant factor in European regions, local economic growth and firms that require good air connectivity to move shipments rapidly (Antunes et al., 2020). UNWTO (2023) reported that international arrivals reached 80% of pre-pandemic levels in the first quarter of 2023, with destinations worldwide welcoming an estimated 235 million international arrivals, more than double the same period in 2022. Data from 2022 present over 960 million tourists travelling internationally last year, meaning two-thirds (66%) of pre-pandemic numbers were recovered. Improving air transport connectivity is one of the major elements of increasing economic growth in a country. Law et al. (2022) indicate that there is bidirectional causality between air passenger traffic and economic growth in the long run. Inbound tourism has a significant impact on air transport demand in the long run, but no significant relationship exists between the two in the short run.

Air connectivity is one of the most important aspects of tourism development, especially for island state destinations that rely on air travel for accessibility. The complexity of the tourism industry necessitates close interaction among involved stakeholders to ensure successful policy implementation of air transportation operations that facilitate tourism mobility in cities and islands around the world. This underpins the argument that airports, DMOs and the government's role in coordinating tourism as a phenomenon of interlinked sectors with a plethora of businesses is not easy. Liasidou et al. (2022) found that air transportation and connectivity are not fully integrated with tourism policy and strategy planning. Yet it is crucial that a stakeholder approach be adopted that accounts for the needs of diverse stakeholders and airline strategies, along with diversified tourism policies and strategies that can establish tourist flows in tourist destinations year round, especially in the island of Cyprus, the Canary Islands or the Balearic Islands (Florido-Benítez & Dogra, 2022).

A notable study of air connectivity in cities is Zhang, Wang, et al. (2022) who provide evidence that air connectivity in the China and Oceania markets increased through transfer flights in the past two decades. While the mainland China and Oceanian hubs expand their capabilities of offering transfer flights, Hong Kong and other Asian hubs are facing various challenges. The leadership of Hong Kong has been challenged and eventually replaced by Guangzhou and Sydney. The hubs, such as Seoul, Tokyo and Singapore, started to play less important roles. Lenaerts et al. (2022) suggest that two elements are needed to apply the effects of air transport and to estimate aviation's spatial economic impact. First, mapping airports to their impacted regions is needed, which would enable the analysis of the spatial scope of airports' economic impact and potential shadow effects. This is particularly important in Europe's dense airport network, where airports can serve multiple regions and have impacts beyond the region they are located in. Second, air market access needs to be calculated, considering connecting flights generated through air networks. Lenaerts et al. (2021) captured market access generated by aviation in the form of air connectivity, and this provides the quality of air transport services as a means to overcome distances and the quality of the destination market.

In the area of tourism, there has always been a great debate between quantity and quality. Many experts and organisations in this area of knowledge defend the annual increase of tourists in the destinations since they generate employment and wealth in the territory. But this correlation is not always feasible and acceptable in tourist destinations since tourism is a very seasonal, changing and capricious activity, especially in Spain and Italy, given their geographical locations close to the European tourist issuing countries. Tourism experts defend the quality of the offer and the tourist spending before the number of visitors (Florido-Benítez & Dogra, 2022). For these reasons, it is important that airport operators and DMOs design joint marketing strategies based on digital channels and new technologies to pool efforts and initiatives in the framework of tourism strategies. If the tourism sector can boast of anything, it is the speed and integration of digitalisation in the companies that make up this activity, from airports, tour operators and airlines to hotels. This subject will be covered in Chapters 6 and 7 through the tools and strategies of marketing.

References

ACI. (2017). Airport digital transformation. https://aci.aero/Media/98748da4-556a-468d-b6e4-2cb36778bc71/gjg-8A/About%20ACI/Priorities/IT%20-%20New/Documentation/Airport%20Digital%20Transformation%20V1.0.pdf. Accessed on May 2, 2022.

ACI. (2020). The seven pillars of an airport survival strategy during and post COVID-19. https://blog.aci.aero/the-seven-pillars-of-an-airport-survival-strategy-during-and-post-covid-19/. Accessed on July 27, 2022.

AENA. (2018). The company's 2018–2021 strategic plan. https://www.aena.es/en/shareholders-and-investors/general-information/companys-strategic-plan.html. Accessed on July 11, 2022.

AENA. (2020). AENA network airports have closed 2019 at more than 275.2 million passengers. https://www.aena.es/en/press/aena-network-airports-have-closed-2019-at-more-than-275.2-million—passengers.html&p=1575086693589. Accessed on July 10, 2022.

Allen, J., Bellizzi, M. G., Eboli, L., Forciniti, C., & Mazzulla, G. (2021). Identifying strategies for improving airport services: Introduction of the gap-IPA to an Italian airport case study. *Transportation Letters, 13*(3), 243–253.

Andrews, K. (1997). The concept of corporate strategy. In N. J. Foss (Ed.), *Resources firms and strategies: A reader in the resource based perspective* (pp. 52–60). Oxford University Press.

Antunes, A., Martini, G., Porta, F., & Scotti, D. (2020). Air connectivity and spatial effects: Regional differences in Europe. *Regional Studies, 54*(12), 1748–1760.

Badanik, B., Laplace, I., Lenoir, N., Malavolti, E., Tomova, A., & Kazda, A. (2010). Future strategies for airports. In *WCTR 2010, 12th World Conference on Transport Research*, Nice, France (pp. 1–10).

Cheung, T. K., Wong, C. W., & Zhang, A. (2020). The evolution of aviation network: Global airport connectivity index 2006–2016. *Transportation Research Part E: Logistics and Transportation Review, 133*, 101826.

China Travel News. (2021). Shanghai Disneyland sees rising revisit numbers, boosted by recovering tourism, report says. https://www.chinatravelnews.com/article/145517. Accessed on July 28, 2022.

Chiu, S.-C., Liu, C.-H., & Tu, J.-H. (2016). The influence of tourists' expectations on purchase intention: Linking marketing strategy for low-cost airlines. *Journal of Air Transport Management, 53*, 226–234.

Dallas-Fort Worth airport. (2021). Sustainability-environmental. https://www.dfwairport.com/business/community/sustainability/. Accessed on July 9, 2022.

Ferrell, O. C., Hartline, M. D., & Hochstein, B. W. (2021). *Marketing strategy. Text and cases*. Cengage Learning.

Florido-Benítez, L. (2016a). *The implementation of mobile marketing as a multidisciplinary tool in the tourism and airport sector*. Editorial Académica Española.

Florido-Benítez, L. (2016b). Mobile payment security favors airports' cross-selling and word of mouth communication across mobile marketing. *Gran Tour, 13*, 26–47.

Florido-Benítez, L. (2016c). The impact of mobile marketing in airports. *Journal of Airline and Airport Management, 6*(1), 1–18.

Florido-Benítez, L. (2016d). Airport mobile marketing as a channel to promote cross-selling. *Journal of Airline and Airport Management, 6*(2), 133–151.

Florido-Benítez, L. (2016e). New marketing strategy: Mobile applications as a marketing tool in airports. *Indian Journal of Computer Science, 1*(2), 13–22.

Florido-Benítez, L. (2016f). Las aplicaciones móviles contribuyen a mejorar los niveles de satisfacción del pasajero. *Revista de Turismo Estudos e Prácticas, 5*(2), 122–148.

Florido-Benítez, L. (2020). Seville airport: A success of good relationship management and interoperability in the improvement of air connectivity. *Revista de Turismo Estudos e Prácticas, 5*(2), 1–30.

Florido-Benítez, L. (2021a). Málaga Costa del Sol airport and its new conceptualization of hinterland. *Tourism Critiques, 2*(2), 195–221.

Florido-Benítez, L. (2021b). How Málaga's airport contributes to promotes the establishment of companies in its hinterland and improves the local economy. *International Journal of Tourism Cities, 8*(2), 393–411.

Florido-Benítez, L. (2021c). The effects of COVID-19 on Andalusian tourism and aviation sector. *Tourism Review, 76*(4), 829–857.

Florido-Benítez, L. (2021d). The supremacy of airports generates a high dependence on the tourist destination Spain. *Revista de Turismo Estudos e Prácticas, 5*(2), 1–30.

Florido-Benítez, L., & del Alcázar, B. (2015). The effects of apps as a marketing tool in airport infrastructure and airlines. *International Journal of Leisure and Tourism Marketing, 4*(3/4), 222–240.

Florido-Benítez, L., & del Alcázar, B. (2020). Airports as ambassadors of the marketing strategies of Spanish tourist destination. *Gran Tour, 21*, 47–78.

Florido-Benítez, L., & Dogra, J. (2022). Study of relationship between Spanish airport and destination marketing: Insights for destination management organizations. *Journal of Tourism and Development, 8*(4), 844–882.

Freathy, P. (2004). The commercialization of European airports: Successful strategies in a decade of turbulence? *Journal of Air Transport Management, 10*(3), 191–197.

Freedman, L. (2013). *Strategy: A history*. Oxford University Press.

Giovanelli, L., & Rotondo, F. (2022). Determinants and strategies behind commercial airports' performance in general aviation. *Research in Transportation Business & Management, 43*, 100795.

Graham, A. (2008). *Managing airports: An international perspective*. Elsevier.

Harari, Y. N. (2019). *21 lessons for the 21st century*. Spiegel & Grau.

Heathrow airport. (2022). *Heathrow 2.0: Connecting people and planet. Our sustainability strategy*. https://www.heathrow.com/content/dam/heathrow/web/common/documents/company/heathrow-2-0-sustainability/futher-reading/Heathrow%202.0%20Connecting%20People%20and%20Planet%20FINAL.pdf. Accessed on July 30, 2022.

Heracleous, L., & Wirtz, J. (2012). Strategy and organisation at Singapore airlines: Achieving sustainable advantage through dual strategy. In O. Inderwildi & S. King (Eds.), *Energy, transport, & the environment*. Springer.

Heuser, B. (2010). *The evolution of strategy: Thinking war from antiquity to the present*. Cambridge University Press.

Hubregtse, H. (2016). Passenger movement and air terminal design: Artworks, wayfinding, commerce, and kinaesthesia. *Interiors, 7*(3), 155–179.

Incheon airport. (2022). *Incheon airport's ESG management innovation strategy*. https://www.airport.kr/esg_main/en/index.do. Accessed on July 30, 2022.

Incheon airport. (2017). *The initiatives for our better future*. https://www.airport.kr/co_file/ko/file01/SR_2017_eng.pdf. Accessed on December 30, 2023.

Jarach, D. (2005). *Airport marketing. Strategies to cope with the new millennium environment* (1st ed.). Routledge.

Khalifa, A. S. (2020). Strategy: Restoring the lost meaning. *Journal of Strategy and Management, 13*(1), 128–143.

Koo, T. T. R., Rashidi, T. H., Park, J. W., Wu, C. L., & Tseng, W. C. (2017). The effect of enhanced international air access on the demand for peripheral tourism destinations: Evidence from air itinerary choice behaviour of Korean visitors to Australia. *Transportation Research Part A: Policy and Practice, 106*, 116–129.

Kotler, P., & Keller, K. L. (2009). *Marketing management*. Pearson Education.

Law, C. C. H., Zhang, Y., Gow, J., & Xuan-Binh, V. B. (2022). Dynamic relationship between air transport, economic growth and inbound tourism in Cambodia, Laos, Myanmar and Vietnam. *Journal of Air Transport Management, 98*, 102161.

Lenaerts, B., Allroggen, F., & Malina, R. (2021). The economic impact of aviation: A review on the role of market access. *Journal of Air Transport Management, 91*, 102000.

Lenaerts, B., Allroggen, F., & Malina, R. (2022). Air connectivity and regional employment: A spatial econometrics approach. *Regional Studies, 57*, 1–16.

Liasidou, S., Garanti, Z., & Pipyros, K. (2022). Air transportation and tourism interactions and actions for competitive destinations: The case of Cyprus. *Worldwide Hospitality and Tourism Themes, 15*(5), 470–480.

Malina, R., Albers, S., & Kroll, N. (2012). Airport incentive programmes: A European perspective. *Transport Reviews, 32*(4), 435–453.

Morgan, N. A., Whitler, K. A., & Feng, H. (2019). Research in marketing strategy. *Journal of the Academy of Marketing Science, 47*(1), 4–29.

Morrison, A. M., & Coca-Stefaniak, A. J. (2020). *Routledge handbook of tourism cities.* Routledge.

Munich airport. (2024). Strategy 2030. https://www.munich-airport.com/strategy-2025-263402. Accessed on January 30, 2024.

Ohmae, K. (1982). The strategic triangle: A new perspective on business unit strategy. *European Management Journal, 1*(1), 38–48.

Oxenfeldt, A. R. (1958). The formulation of a market strategy. In E. J. Kelley & W. Lazer (Eds.), *Managerial marketing: Perspectives and viewpoints* (pp. 264–272). Richard D. Irwin, Inc.

Papatheodorou, A., Vlassi, E., Gaki, D., Papadopoulou-Kelidou, L., Efthymiou, M., Pappas, D., & Parashi, P. (2019). The airline–airport–destination authority relationship: The case of Greece. In N. Kozak & M. Kozak (Eds.), *Tourist destination management. Tourism, hospitality & event management.* Springer.

Peneda, M. J. A., Reis, V. D., & Macário, M. D. R. M. R. (2011). Critical factors for development of airport cities. *Transportation Research Record, 2214*(1), 1–9.

Prentice, C., & Kadam, M. (2019). The role of airport service quality in airport and destination choice. *Journal of Retailing and Consumer Services, 47*, 40–48.

Randazzo, G. W. (2014). *Developing successful marketing strategies.* Business Expert Press.

Schmitt, D., & Gollnick, V. (2016). *Air transport system.* Springer.

Shallow, B. (2021). Airport technology priorities in a time of pandemic. https://blog.aci.aero/airport-technology-priorities-in-a-time-of-pandemic/. Accessed on July 28, 2022.

Skytrax. (2021). World's top 100 airport 2021. https://www.worldairportawards.com/worlds-top-100-airports-2021/. Accessed on July 15, 2022.

Strachan, H. (2013). *The direction of war: Contemporary strategy in historical perspective.* Cambridge University Press.

The Guardian. (2019). My father had a lifelong ticket to fly anywhere. Then they took it away. https://www.theguardian.com/lifeandstyle/2019/sep/19/american-airlines-aairpass-golden-ticket. Accessed on May 21, 2022.

Tiboldi, T. (2008). Marketing strategy and airport revenue at FlyBalaton airport. *Journal of Airport Management, 2*(2), 153–157.

UNWTO. (2023). World tourism barometer. https://www.unwto.org/news/tourism-on-track-for-full-recovery-as-new-data-shows-strong-start-to-2023. Accessed on July 20, 2023.

Varadarajan, R. (2010). Strategic marketing and marketing strategy: Domain, definition, fundamental issues, and foundational premises. *Journal of the Academy of Marketing Science, 38*(2), 119–140.

Walczack, W. (2022). Marketing instrument of competition in low-cost airlines. In *Ekonomia I miedzynarodowe stosunki gospodarcze* (pp. 40–54). Wydawnictwo Uniwersytetu Ekonomicznego we Wroclawiu.

Wu, C.-L., & Ma, N. K. (2022). The impact of customised mobile marketing on passenger shopping behavior in the airport terminal. *Journal of Retailing and Consumer Services, 66*, 102941.

Yang, Y., Li, D., & Li, X. (2019). Public transport connectivity and intercity tourist flows. *Journal of Travel Research, 58*(1), 25–41.

Ye, Q. (2022). The best strategy for Chinese airlines to achieve optimal allocation of resources. Analysis of name your own price strategy. Proceedings of the 2022 7th international conference on social sciences and economic development (ICSSED 2022). *Advances in Economics, Business and Management Research, 652*, 363–369.

Zhang, L., Hou, M., Liu, Y., Wang, K., & Yang, H. (2022). Measuring Beijing's international air connectivity and suggestions for improvement post COVID-19. *Transport Policy, 116*, 132–143.

Zhang, Q., Wang, B., & Xue, D. (2022). The hub competition in delivering air connectivity between China and Oceania. *Sustainability, 14*(11), 6482.

Chapter 6

Diversification of Airport Marketing Strategies

Abstract

The study and analysis of airport marketing strategies and the diversification of its activities through strategic alliances are essential for airports, and these should be a priority to plan and develop marketing plans in these times of uncertain economic and pandemic, because the future of the aviation and tourism industries lies in stressing the value of unity between the two sectors. This chapter shows real examples of airport marketing strategies around the world to help airport and airline operators, marketers and destination marketing organisations (DMOs) improve their marketing strategies in a competitive and environmentally sustainable market, as is the case with aviation and tourism activities. Opportunities to develop mutually beneficial relationships in cities between DMOs and airports are plentiful but often largely untapped by both parties due to miscommunication and the common interests of business operators. The marketing strategy of diversification is critical to reviving in times of economic downturn.

6.1 Airport's Own Marketing Strategies

There are many books and articles on marketing and airport marketing, but there is not one yet that speaks directly about airport marketing strategies. This book will substantiate the academic literature regarding the role of airports and their marketing strategies in the aviation and tourism industries. One of the purposes of this book is to understand and document the nature of the airport's management and business through marketing strategies, the distinct challenges that airport and airline operators and destination marketing organisations (DMOs) currently face during these difficult times of economic, social and pandemic periods and how airport operators should try to cope with a global crisis in a coherent, well-planned, coordinated and comprehensive manner. Alone or together? Can airport and airline

Airport Marketing Strategies, 87–108
Copyright © 2024 Lázaro Florido-Benítez
Published under exclusive licence by Emerald Publishing Limited
doi:10.1108/978-1-83608-082-420241006

operators work to address this pronounced fall in passenger and freight volumes for 5 or 6 years more? As we saw earlier in Chapter 5, what are the marketing strategies used in aviation and tourism activities?

Are airport and airline operators, politicians, firms and DMOs aware that this is the best time to guarantee a global paradigm shift towards sustainable and green development (Aviation decarbonisation), offer domestic and international flights at an economically viable rate for airlines and customers, design personalised trips for each individual or family or even give every customer the opportunity to create and book his/her own trips (flights, hotels, tourist attractions, restaurants, train tickets and museums, among many others) in consonance with his/her needs and budget through DMO official websites in this technological and pandemic transitional period. In that way, everybody plays, and everybody wins. These questions are needed to tackle these adversities with different airport marketing strategies to boost the airport's economy and operability in its catchment area, including the city where the airport is localised and all the businesses related to the airport's activities.

Marketing strategies help companies to differentiate themselves from their competitors, cultivate and keep clients and create competitive advantages (Pettinger, 1998) because the structure, breadth and depth of marketing strategies remain based on consumers' needs and the differentiation of products and services (Assael, 1993). Much of the initial stimulus for airport marketing strategies emerged from the tourism marketing area, which provided the foundations for the development of tourism literature focused on marketing destinations and the creation of DMO by government bodies to plan and develop the strategies of marketing and promotion at tourist destinations. A study carried out by Thaker et al. (2022) analysed the impact of Kuala Lumpur International airport branding strategies on passengers' experiences, and they found that the Kuala Lumpur airport (IATA: KUL) is an important part of the overall tourist experience. These branding and marketing strategies encourage a more diversified collection of customers and products and services, thus attracting new investments and companies, creating employment and increasing tourist flow into Malaysia.

Each airport has its own marketing and communication strategies, its own objectives, its own needs and its own limitations. It is not the same to develop airport marketing strategies in a hub and spoke airport like Los Angeles airport (IATA: LAX) in the United States or Hamad International airport (IATA: HIA) in Qatar as to develop airport marketing strategies in a tourist airport like Son Sant Joan airport (IATA: PMI) in the Balearic Islands, Spain, or a regional airport like Belfast airport (IATA: BFS) in Northen Ireland. Hub and spoke airports have great budgets for marketing and communication investment because they represent the best examples of airport infrastructure and air transport in a country.

For instance, Amsterdam Airport Schiphol (IATA: AMS) in the Netherlands is a hub and spoke airport, and it is managed by the Schiphol Group operator. This airport included three significant marketing strategies to overcome the threats from its main competitors in 2013. The first strategy was to improve customer service and experience through customised products and services. As a second marketing strategy, Schiphol airport introduced dynamic pricing to attract more low-cost airlines and, thereby, more passengers and shoppers passing through the airport's terminal. And the third international strategy was to continue growing cargo volumes (cargo carriers) in the next 5 years due to cargo flows from countries such as China being routed through several main European gateways like Schiphol airport. Evidently, these three marketing strategies improved non-aeronautical and commercial revenues in the income statement of Schiphol airport. In 2013, this airport won the World Airport Awards for Europe's Best Airport by Skytrax (Schiphol Group, 2013, 2014; Skytrax, 2013).

Dubai International airport (IATA: DXB) in the United Arab Emirates is a great example of an airport's own marketing strategies. This airport has not stopped growing in passenger and air cargo volumes since it was opened in 1960. As a result of their airport marketing strategies focused on increasing the number of passenger arrivals and air cargo movements over the last 11 years (excluding 2020 and 2021 by the pandemic crisis); these data are shown in Fig. 28. In 2021, Dubai airport was the world's busiest international hub for the eighth consecutive year, with 29.1 million passengers (ACI, 2022), as shown in Table 1. According to the annual ceremony for the Business Traveller Middle East Awards (BTME), Dubai airport was awarded as the Best Airport in the Middle East in 2022, the Best Customer Service, the Best airport in the world and the Best Airport Hotel in the Middle East 'Dubai International Hotel'. In fact, this airport won for the 21st consecutive year the Best Airport for Duty Free Shopping in the Middle East (BTME, 2022).

Hamad International airport is another example of how an airport plays an international ambassador role in a country or city through the airport's own marketing strategies. Qatar has one of the fastest-growing economies in the world, and Hamad airport is positioning itself as the gateway to Qatar, the Gulf and the world. In 2022, Hamad airport (IATA: HIA) was appointed as the World's Best Airport for the second year is a row. The main airport marketing strategy is positioning itself as a cosmopolitan airport open to the world, where the airport's strategic partnership

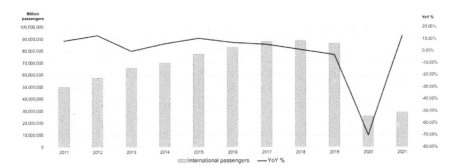

Fig. 28. Evolution of International Passenger at Dubai International Airport From 2011 to 2021. *Source:* Adapted from ACI (2022) and Wikipedia (2024).

Table 1. Dubai International Airport's Position in the World's Busiest
International Airports.

Year	Dubai Airport's Position In the World's Busiest International Airport	International Passengers	YoY%
2021	1	29,110,609	12.70%
2020	1	25,831,363	−70.10%
2019	1	86,328,896	−2.90%
2018	1	88,885,367	1.30%
2017	1	87,722,023	5.60%
2016	1	83,105,798	7.30%
2015	1	77,453,466	10.70%
2014	1	69,954,392	6.20%
2013	2	65,872,250	15.3%
2012	3	57,684,550	13.20%
2011	4	50,192,013	8.40%
Total Pax		*722,140,727*	

Source: Adapted from ACI (2022) and (Skytrax, 2023).

Note: International passengers enplaned and deplaned.

with the Qatar Tourism Authority has boosted tourism through visa-free entry for nationals from a total of 80 countries. 'Badr Mohammed Al Meer' CEO of Hamad International airport said that they are also preparing for Qatar's hosting of the 2022 FIFA World Cup, when it is expecting to serve 96,000 passengers per day. The World Cup will also bring significant economic value by providing an opportunity to create lasting business relations and a climate for investments and tourism growth (Airport Business, 2018). Airport marketing strategies through digital channels like official websites, airport apps, mobile marketing or digital television help to promote airports' competitive advantages in quality, connectivity, value added or security and safety terms; thus, airports are positioning their strengths against their major competitors. For example, Hamad airport promotes itself globally as the first airport in the Middle East to receive the 5-star COVID-19 airport safety rating in 2020 (Skytrax, 2020a, 2020b).

Moreover, readers can see how Hammad International airport advertises the video's safety and hygiene promotion campaigns as a competitive advantage through the YouTube digital communication tool at this link: (https://youtube.com/shorts/1kScNR7abTA?feature=share). As content marketing becomes a viable approach to building brands and connecting with consumers through the YouTube channel, organisations and marketers must analyse consumers' engagement and participation, interactivity between user and company, attention, emotion and cognition aspects with digital channels. Consumers' engagement through social media content marketing is highly contextual and platform dependent. YouTube capabilities, financial resources and product category play an important role in strategy differentiation (Wang & Chan-Olmsted, 2020).

It is very important to mention that airport operators will design their own categories of marketing strategies and tactics (e.g. international positioning, promotion, operations, pricing, distribution, product/market, financial, corporate) and objectives depending on their target audience, and which digital or physical channels are the best to communicate their messages in a timely and effective manner. Tactics are the means by which a chosen strategy is implemented. To accomplish this, operators need to understand what strategic priorities airports have for digital marketing, and why the internet is the best communication platform to implement digital airport marketing strategies. Accordingly, airport operators and marketing staff should review their airport business portfolios periodically and ensure that they are visible on the airport's official websites and apps, digital newspapers, the World ATM Congress, IATA's events, the AIAA Aviation Forum and Exposition and the National Civil Aviation Work Conference, among many others.

A digital marketing tool is not new, but it helps to improve and empower airports' corporate image internationally. With its strategic positioning, Beijing Capital International airport (IATA: PEK) is one of the major gateways to China and an established hub for both Chinese and foreign travellers. The airport is owned and operated by the Beijing Capital International Airport Company Limited, a state-controlled company. In 2012 and 2013, this airport obtained fifth place in the World's Best Airport (Skytrax, 2013). During 2008, this airport operator planed and developed two marketing strategies based on different promotion and communication campaigns to stimulate retail sales on the new terminal 3 of the airport (known as the Dragon terminal) during the 2008 Summer Olympics and promote its airport retail competitiveness against its main competitors. In order to do so, the airport operator and marketing staff performed six tactics to reach the objectives established (LEK, 2022):

(1) Development of a marketing communication plan based on case studies and stakeholder analysis.
(2) The design of three promotional and communication campaigns focused on Terminal 3 launch promotion, Beijing Summer Olympics promotion and Chinese New Year promotion.
(3) Internal diagnosis through interviews and surveys with various stakeholders, including management teams, airlines, airport retailers and passengers.
(4) Introduce a roadmap with the aim of effectively guiding third-party public relations, developing Key Performance Indicators (KPIs) to measure promotion executions and their possible changes and encouraging advertising agencies to develop and execute various marketing communications for 6-months preceding the Summer Olympics.
(5) Benchmarking review of Singapore Changi Airport and Sydney Airport for their retail practices.
(6) Provide recommendations on website improvement, terminal walk-through observation and shopping brand strategy.

Fig. 29 displays the results of these two marketing strategies, and how these enhanced passengers' experience and satisfaction levels in retail and food & beverage, boosted total revenues (a 14.5% increase in total revenues to $338 million) and encouraged new commercial revenue opportunities for the airport as China Duty Free Group in 2009. Furthermore, Beijing airport handled over 100 million passengers in 2019, with Terminal 3 playing a crucial role in handling the bulk of the gateway's international traffic operated by foreign airlines (Airport World, 2020; CAPA, 2009). These results demonstrate the potential of airport marketing strategies in terms of commercial revenues, the airport's positioning, promotion and communication activities and the constant improvement of passengers' experiences and satisfaction at airports by operators. The main objective of a marketing strategy is to create a product or service that can be perceived as unique in the aviation industry.

This book seeks to help airport and airline operators, marketers and DMOs improve their marketing strategies in a competitive and environmentally sustainable market, as is the case in the aviation and tourism sectors. It is extremely interesting and challenges us to think about our marketing strategies in a holistic way, as we must ask ourselves how customers and competitors see us to identify our own business strategies. A complex study of research carried out by Olson et al. (2021) suggest that managers and marketing and communication experts must ask themselves four questions related to their firms, to plan and develop the most appropriate marketing strategies and digital marketing tactics:

(1) Identify your business strategy. Is your firm more inclined to defend existing products/markets or to pursue new products/markets aggressively?
(2) If you identify more as a defender, do your customers purchase from you because you offer the lowest overall delivery costs (as a low-cost defender) or because you provide premium service, quality or brand image (as a differentiated defender)?
(3) If you identify more as an innovator, are you typically the first to market original products/services (as a prospector), or are you a quick follower that provides additional features or lower prices (as an analyst)?
(4) Pair your digital strategy with your business strategy. What is your firm's top marketing objective? Immediate sales? Building long-term relationships? New product awareness and trials?

In the context of aviation and tourism activities, airport operators and DMOs need to respond to these questions to plan and design the most appropriate marketing strategies, objectives and innovative tactics to achieve the proposed goals by operators. Airport marketing strategies need to satisfy the needs of customers and actively support those companies that are operating inside the airport and its catchment area, like logistic and e-commerce firms, agri-food and technology companies, hotels, restaurants, museums, theme parks and national natural parks, among others. From a strategic point of view, most airport operators will select a combination of the above questions because these decisions will depend on the category of airport, such as hub and spoke, regional, medium, small, cargo, private, reliever or general aviation airports.

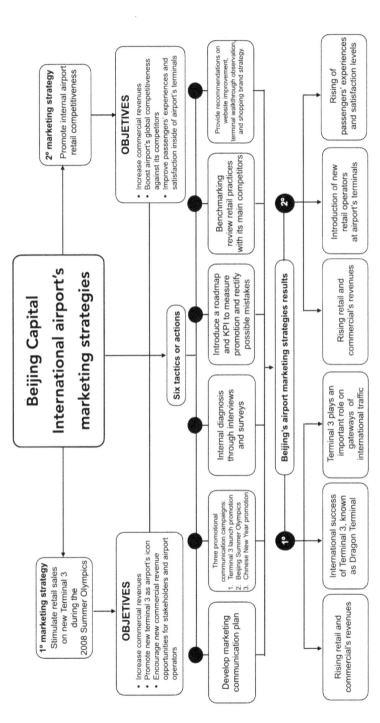

Fig. 29.   Beijing Capital International Airport's Marketing Strategies. *Source:* Compiled by author.

The marketing strategy of airports relies on the socio-economic profile of passengers, airlines and firms operating inside airports. While there is no single combination of marketing strategies and tactics that will prove optimal for all airports, operators, marketers and DMOs should be able to learn from the insights shared in this book. For that simple reason, this book can help decide which marketing strategies are most appropriate to promote and communicate in digital channels, manage more efficiently the budget lines of a marketing plan, improve the effectiveness rate of each marketing strategy implemented and facilitate the fulfilment of established objectives by airport operators and marketing managers. As stated, by marketing and promotion strategies it's critical to reviving the tourism and aviation industries in the viral world (Seyitoğlu et al., 2022).

6.2 Airport Strategic Alliances

To determine the marketing strategies and marketing mix are part and parcel of every business opportunity that airport and airline operators, stakeholders and DMOs venture into. Joint marketing strategies are a critical aspect in ensuring business and operational growth in the aviation and tourism industries. The success of an airport relies on the competitiveness of the city in which it is located, and the city's success is highly dependent on the airport's category and competitiveness. Government policies, challenges and constraints facing tourist destinations, DMO managers and their marketing teams are quite different from those faced by airports and low-cost and legacy carriers where they are located and operating. Air mobility will always be embedded in our socio-economic fabric. An understanding of such issues enables stakeholders to take advantage of opportunities in promotion, distribution and new product development, thereby enhancing their own success as well as contributing to the effectiveness of their DMOs and airports through marketing strategies and promotion and communication campaigns at digital channels. In differentiation of products and services, an airport must be able to associate a brand image, design, technology, features and customer service with an aligned marketing strategy of the tourist destination where this is located.

From this moment on, it is a question of developing the different foreseen strategic alliances to reach each joint goal defined and examining their implementation processes. We are saying that the airport operator is diversifying its marketing strategies with the support of DMOs, local governments, commercial and cargo airlines and all the businesses related to aviation, tourism and technological industries in its catchment area. Strategic alliances through marketing strategies are essential for airports, and these should be a priority to plan and develop marketing plans in these times of uncertain economic and pandemic conditions because the future of the aviation and tourism industries lies in stressing the value of unity between the two sectors. While I am writing these lines on Saturday, 16 July 2022, airlines all over the world have cancelled more than 25,000 flights from their flight schedules for August, with around 60% (15,788 flights) of them in Europe. The problems caused by staff shortages at airlines, airports and ground-handling companies have made headline news worldwide in the world's largest digital newspapers (Financial Times, 2022; Schengen Visa News, 2022; The Guardian, 2022).

These problems are seriously affecting the world's great and medium airports, like Heathrow (IATA: LHR), Paris Charles de Gaulle (IATA: CDG), Frankfurt (IATA: FRA), Dublin (IATA: DUB), Málaga Costa del Sol (IATA: AGP), Manchester (IATA: MAN) airports or even Amsterdam's Schiphol (IATA: AMS) airport, which set a cap of 70,000 passengers per day during the summer travel season due to labour shortages. Thus, 13,500 seats per day were fewer than airlines had planned, which means that airlines including KLM, the Dutch subsidiary of Air France-KLM, had to cancel an unspecified number of flights (Reuters, 2022). The question is what is going to happen in the next 4 or 5 years in the aviation industry? Where is the aviation sector headed? How can mobility be reinvigorated for it to be sustainable and support the 2030 Agenda for Sustainable Development and its 17 Sustainable Development Goals? and how airports and airlines will face this new economic, business and sustainable paradigm?

For a start, the ICAO (2022) and the World Bank, which leads Sustainable Mobility for All (SuM4All), encourage that mobility actors should come together in a shared vision. These two organisations suggest jointly unpacking a roadmap of actions that is tailored to countries and cities to implement a plan for continuous improvement of the system's security and efficiency levels. This should be a legally binding obligation for all countries and not an arbitrary decision by a power centre that provides how countries must comply with the regulations governing sustainability, safety and efficiency terms because alternative fuels are going to significantly change the current scenario of aviation in support of environmental protection. The vast investment in artificial intelligence (AI) and big data could be seen as a promising way of increasing safety, efficiency and sustainability. These technologies can help improve aviation infrastructure and airspace utilisation. If we want the aviation and tourism industries to become more sustainable and efficient soon, we need to ensure that everyone communicates and collaborates to make effective use of these innovations. In today's world, mobility by air, road and water is all about efficiencies, speed, interconnectivity and accessibility for all (ICAO, 2022).

The priority and most urgent matter for the aviation and tourism sectors in this economic and energy efficiency transition period is to reach proper commercial agreements among airports, tourist operators and local and national governments, where all stakeholders actively participate, share and develop innovative business ideas under a strategy that is clearly oriented to accelerate the process of decarbonisation in the air sector, safeguard the environment, improve work-related benefits for employees, improve the well-being and quality of life of the members of the community and increase the profit margins of organisations that are operating in the aviation and tourism industries. Conversely, Hübel et al. (2022) revealed that research on strategic alliances between large and small firms is complicated due to differences in resource portfolios, compatibility of objectives, market experience and cultures. Such alliances can involve unequal processes to the detriment of the smaller firm. Some studies even claim that strategic alliances have negative impacts on business operations (Hamel et al., 1989; Robinson, 1988).

We cannot overlook, but on the contrary, we must emphasise the context of airports within the tourism industry. The proximity of an airport to a large city in the region, with good access to road and rail communications, means its favourable location, and it represents a development opportunity for cities and tourist attractions. Local economic entities servicing the airport are also developing, cooperating with companies in the zones and benefiting from the improved income situation of residents (Piotrowska-Trybull & Sirko, 2022). In 2017, BMW and IBM firms announced that they were jointly developing a cloud computing project that could help up to 8.5 million drivers diagnose and repair problems, save on auto insurance and benefit from other third-party services. Through this alliance, the BMW CarData network was integrated with the IBM Bluemix platform to access Watson Internet of Things (IoT) capacity, while drivers using the BMW ConnectedDrive app were able to access services as data was collected (Ferrigno et al., 2022).

Much of the interest in strategic alliances comes from the fact that airports and airlines are implementing them to spread the costs and benefits of innovation, maximise common interests and mitigate risks. Global aviation deregulation made the aviation industry more competitive and led to increased strategic airline alliances, which increased aviation efficiency and productivity. Li et al. (2021) examined the three main global airline alliances: Star Alliance, SkyTeam and Oneworld to explore the efficiency of business performances in 22 individual Asian airlines from 2014 to 2016 using the Data Envelopment Analysis (DEA) model, in which labour, the number of airports and the number of aircraft were the inputs. The output's indicators were total revenue, passenger load rate and delay rate. Their results were that:

In 2014, the most efficient airlines were Qantas Airways, Aeroflot Aviation, Royal Jordanian, Air New Zealand, All Nippon, Japan Airlines, Siberia Airlines and Singapore Airlines. From 2015 to 2016, the most efficient airlines were Qantas Airways, Royal Jordanian, Air New Zealand, All Nippon, Japan Airlines, Siberia Airlines, Singapore Airlines and Vietnam Airlines, all of which had excellent efficiency in business performances. The airline with the poorest overall efficiency was China Eastern Airlines. By joining an alliance with other airlines, a company can take advantage of economies of scale and improve bargaining power through their investment funds and purchases (Wang, 2014). Typically, one airline sells the flight with fares determined by their pricing team through digital marketing channels, whereas the second airline operator charges the marketing airline for all or part of the combined course (Doganis, 2019; Soomro et al., 2022).

In the context of the passenger air transport sector, collaboration and value creation through strategic alliances have been fostered by airlines and airports to provide a point of differentiation, improving the overall passenger experience, and ultimately leading to increased loyalty and commercial revenue streams. Moreover, by using collaborations, the aviation and tourism sectors can open new ways of doing business and provide sustainable growth (Pereira et al., 2021). Strategic alliances involve analysing a system of indicators and futures scenarios (see Table 2) with the aim of examining all possible options to achieve the objectives established, taking into consideration strengths, weaknesses, opportunities and

Table 2. Analysis System of Indicators at Strategic Alliances.

Number	Indicators
1	Networking and partner choice
2	Cultural context
3	Behaviour and compatibilities
4	Collaboration configuration
5	Issues and risks shared
6	Skills and knowledge transfer
7	Capacities and experience
8	Infrastructure and resources available (budget)
9	Engagement activities and quality of services
10	Knowledge of new rules and legislation
11	Absorption and appropriation
12	Collaboration management
13	Communication flows
14	External environment and demand
15	High level of interoperability
16	Great creativity and imagination in promotion and communication campaigns
17	Compatibility of niche markets
18	Compatibility of objectives established
19	Total empathy towards the client
20	Evaluation and selection of digital marketing channels to implement promotion and communications campaigns
21	Social media reach and engagement
22	Key performance indicators (KPIs) metrics
23	Outcome measures and rectify possible mistakes and weak points
24	Cybersecurity control of processes and protocols
25	Expectations and outcomes in return on investment (ROI) and return on invested capital (ROIC) terms

Source: Compiled by the author.

threats (SWOT), which will help operators make better decisions regarding how to use available company funds. Airport operators must negotiate all the conditions laid down before entering a strategic alliance to prevent risks and ensure smooth operation in the future.

For instance, cybersecurity is a sociotechnical phenomenon, which heavily influences the interaction between costumers and companies through e-commerce's processes, promotions and communication campaigns. Florido-Benítez (2021) detected an interoperability deficit between public and private organisations in aviation activity. Cybersecurity protocols facilitate the internationalisation of the aviation and tourism industries. In this same vein, Raimundo and Rosário (2022) note that cybersecurity is concerned with the protection of electronics, software and data, along with the procedures by which systems are accessed on. In general, security objectives comprise privacy, in terms of information not inappropriately disclosed to unauthorised devices or individuals to be modified or destroyed. A greater understanding of these processes will enable us to develop more informed prevention and mitigation strategies to address the increasing challenges we face within cybersecurity (McAlaney & Benson, 2020).

Strategic alliances are assuming prominence in the strategies of leading airports and airlines. Schiphol International airport (IATA: AMS) in the Netherlands and Frankfurt airport (IATA: FRA) in Germany formed a strategic alliance in 2008 to reduce their operational costs, increase the market shares of the two hub airports and become a powerful logistics developer providing value-added products (Jiang et al., 2019). In 2009, strategic alliances like the East Asia Airport Alliance and North-eastern Hinterland and Bohai Rim Region Aviation Market Strategic Airport Alliance in China were founded to provide a platform for airlines and airports to negotiate air routes, but in 2021, the entry of Heze airport (IATA: HZA) made it the largest airport alliance in China. The entire alliance airport passenger throughput has increased from 43.31 million passenger-times in 2009 to 243 million passenger-times in 2020, and the flight movements have increased from 47.8 ten thousand flights to 235 ten thousand flights (Bai, 2021).

According to Varadarajan (2010), two issues are fundamental to marketing strategies: first, what explains differences in the marketing behaviour of competing businesses in the marketplace? And second, what explains the differences in the marketplace and financial performance of competing brands, product lines and businesses? At the end, strategic alliances are indispensable for airport and airline operators in terms of marketing activities, international brand positioning, promotion and communication campaigns, efficiency in business performances, cost reduction, interoperability, logistics development, new flight connections, maximising benefits in retail sales, reducing competition or increasing aeronautical and commercial revenues. These strategic alliance forms need to be applied through diversification of strategies at promotion and communication campaigns with key business partners such as DMOs, hotels, rental car firms, theme parks, museums, logistics and distribution companies, e-commerce and retail firms, tour operators, and online travel agents (OTAs) because together they are able to overcome this difficult moment of pandemic, economic and war crisis.

We must not overlook this fact during our debate of companies and their strategic alliances because companies are managed by people. Every day, in every organisation, people need to socialise by collaborating, communicating and sharing information (these are the basic principles on which social networks have been created). To have a sense of belonging, recognition, legitimacy and shared values is an unavoidable necessity of any human society, but all these feelings are also common human emotions and a vehicle for attracting people to consume more products and services in the consumer society model, in which globalisation is dissolving national boundaries and changing people's consumption behaviour.

We need to look at Disney's promotion and communication around the world on television, digital newspapers, social media, smartphones, etc., so that the whole world wants to catch a flight to Florida in the United States and enjoy a few wonderful days in Walt Disney World (e.g. Magic Kingdom, EPCOT, Disney's Hollywood Studios, Disney's Animal Kingdom, Disney's Blizzard Beach or Disney's Typhoon Lagoon). These marketing strategies handle the emotional and physical needs of customers in a globalised market where people need to socialise and enjoy pleasant holidays. The Disney Company's marketing mix is a deciding factor in the company's competitive performance in different industries like tourism, travel, leisure and aviation. Indeed, marketing mix is the combination of strategies and tactics used to access the company's target market: product, price, place and promotion (4Ps) through digital marketing channels. As stated by Harari (2014) the invention of new imagined realities and human innovations has established social order and culture.

6.3 Diversification of Strategies and Alliances in the Aviation and Tourism Industries

In today's aviation dynamic and turbulent business environment, diversification of marketing activities through strategic alliances has become a catalyst for achieving competitive advantages and the creation of synergy at international and domestic market operations. This is because airports and airlines operate in a highly competitive environment, particularly among companies that produce similar perishable intangible services. With the continuous improvement of marketisation, the diversification of strategic alliances through digital marketing channels has become one of the main means for airport and airline operators to gain competitive advantages, empower the quality of their business portfolios and promote their products and services in the aviation and tourism markets. From an airport operator's point of view, the diversification of airport marketing strategies (short/medium/long-terms) in other market activities like tourism, logistics, air cargo and technological industries creates new dynamic synergies in brand image positioning, increasing profitability, the airport's international expansion and improving the performance of promotion and communication campaigns.

Let me take the Fort Worth Alliance airport (IATA: AFW) in Texas, US, as an example. This is a public airport, owned by the City of Fort Worth and managed by Alliance Air Services. The operability of this airport is focused primarily on cargo airlines, integrators and logistics companies such as Cargolux, Asiana Cargo, Qatar Cargo, Korean Cargo, FedEx Express, UPS and DHL, among many others. In 2019, Fort Worth Alliance Airport received $5.5 million from the Federal Aviation Administration (FAA) with the aim of becoming a regional air hub for Amazon (Kezar, 2019). The strategic alliance between this airport and Amazon Air has consolidated this airport worldwide as an innovation cargo hub for new surface and air transportation technologies. This business alliance is empowered to attract more companies related to logistics, e-commerce, air cargo and agri-food activities to Fort Worth Alliance airport. In response to the pandemic's effects on the aviation industry, airports are applying a variety of strategies to enhance air cargo and logistics activities and reduce expenditures.

The World Bank (2022) reported that freight carried by carriers and managed by airports and organisations is helping the progress of aviation development worldwide because cargo carriers are withstanding the pandemic significantly better than commercial airlines (see Fig. 30). Global cargo ton-kilometres (CTKs) were down −25.8% compared to 2019 levels in April 2020 but then rose steadily until the end of the year to reach full recovery. Global CTKs continued to climb and has since mostly held above the 2019 level (IATA, 2022). If we compare with the 1.8 billion passengers who flew in 2020, this decreased by −60.2% compared to the 4.5 billion who flew in 2019.

Extensive competition exists among airports in the United States and Canada to become intermodal logistics and distribution centres (Kramer, 2010) because the COVID-19 pandemic has accelerated the global transition in the e-commerce and logistics industries. Especially for freighter planes dedicated to carrying cargo, the surge in e-commerce and the reduction in passenger aircraft cargo volumes due to a significant reduction in passenger flights are huge positives for the accelerated transition to e-commerce (IATA, 2022; Lyu & Zhang, 2022).

The role played by governments to support the air transport industry through the pandemic crisis has been critical to the survival of many airlines and airports. It has prevented widespread airline and airport failures and the broader, long-term adverse impacts that this would deliver throughout the global economy. The COVID-19 crisis is provoking a massive loss of income at airports and airline companies. In these times of difficulty and uncertainty (pandemic crisis, Brexit and Russia–Ukraine war), the future of the tourism and aviation industries lies in stressing the value of unified 'joint strategies' (Florido-Benítez, 2022a). Consequently, if not properly planned and implemented, diversification of marketing strategies may lead to the retrogressive performance of airports and companies that are operating inside the catchment area. Nevertheless, diversification of strategies by airport and airline operators cannot be seen as a panacea that will meet every single one of the various challenges faced by these organisations in today's aviation and tourism environment.

Diversification is not a very efficient strategy to increase an organisation's profit, and a higher level of diversification is retrogressive in terms of overall performance (Oladimeji & Udosen, 2019; Sahu, 2017; Santarelli & Tran, 2015). Diversification refers to a firm's entry into new lines of business activities through internal business development or acquisition because organisations need to consistently engage in exploratory and exploitative activities simultaneously in order to achieve superior outcomes (Lin et al., 2020; Ramanujam & Varadarajan, 1989).

In practice, many successful companies like Apple, Amazon, Disney, Warner Bros, Universal Studios Hollywood, Coca-Cola, Pepsi, Volkswagen, Mercedes, Schiphol Amsterdam airport (IATA: AMS), Marco Polo Venezia's airport

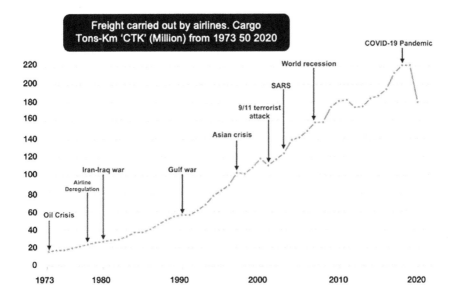

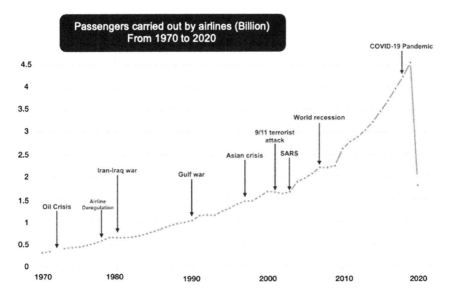

Fig. 30.   Evolution Air Cargo vs Passengers Carried by Airlines Worldwide. *Data Source:* Adapted from the World Bank (2022).

(IATA: VCE), Air Canada and American Airlines undertake simultaneously diversification strategies and strategic alliances when they are in complex economic contexts or vice versa 'economic boom' to internationalise their new lines of products and services. In 2013, Disney and American Airlines designed a marketing strategic alliance to promote Disney's Planes movie through digital channels like social media, TV and digital newspapers, as well as physical marketing tools like billboards. Furthermore, this marketing alliance included traditional media buys, promotions and inflight entertainment and gave the airline the exclusive rights to offer 'Planes' to its customers (American Airlines, 2013; Variety, 2013). Readers can see YouTube's Plane movie promotion campaigns at this link (https://youtu.be/0VFaT8J79sg).

Casino di Venezia and Marco Polo Venezia airport (IATA: VCE) in Italy are yet another example of the marketing strategic alliance and its action effectiveness. In 2007, two baggage conveyors at Venezia's airport were dressed to look like roulette. The passengers claiming their baggage received one free entry at the casino. The results showed that the number of guests at the casino rose to 60%, and their revenues increased by 16% compared to the previous year (AdmCom, 2008). Readers can see YouTube's Casino di Venezia and Venezia airport's promotion campaigns at this link (https://youtu.be/mP9_B9Qkky8). As I mentioned previously, many companies are focusing on achieving high efficiency around the world by launching the production of new types of products and services driven by the diversification of strategic alliances (Shaturaev, 2022).

Most airports are defining the future organisations and business models for their future operations focused on joint strategic alliances, energy efficiency and sustainability to improve cost efficiencies and sustainability advantages through operational optimisation (Cirig, 2021; Florido-Benítez, 2023a). Marketing management of business activities in the context of international diversification involves the construction of an appropriate system of information gathering, study of foreign markets, planning, implementation and control of the marketing programme, risk and profit assessment and effectiveness of marketing decisions (Tanasiichuk et al., 2020). If we come together and walk together in one step, we can make a difference. Air connectivity and the proximity of airports provide added value for tourist attractions and cities (Florido-Benítez, 2024).

The airport's atmosphere and characteristics of luxury products and services provided by companies that are working inside the airport's terminal affect the development of luxury brands' strategies on the airport's website. Teixeira et al. (2022) point out that digital channels affect the development of luxury brands' strategies on several levels. Digital channels are an asset for luxury fashion brands, as online interactions between consumers, brands, bloggers and sellers allow the brand to create social status associations through the easy sharing of information about what is trendy and stylish and through the dissemination of word-of-mouth (WoM) communication about new trends.

Passengers or tourists' experience and satisfaction are an excellent indicator when organisations must plan for and execute substantial changes. A bad inflight or airport's terminal experience by passengers may be positive if we know how to draw conclusions from it, or vice versa, a good experience of diversity and quality of products and services tourist-oriented at destinations and airports can enable airport and DMO managers to elevate the levels of excellence in efficiency and service quality. For example, a key focus of enhancing the passenger experience at

Singapore Changi airport (IATA: SIN) has been to grow the air hub and connect passengers to more destinations around the world. Changi Airport Group (CAG) operates closely with more than 100 airline partners to tap on opportunities in the region and strengthen the airport's position. For eight consecutive years (2013–2020), Changi airport has been awarded the Best Airport Award in the world, according to Skytrax (2020c). For instance, when an airport wins the Skytrax's prize or is positioned very well in the Skytrax's ranking, this airport cites the achievement on its official's app and website with the aim of advertising and promoting quality services and brand image worldwide (Florido-Benítez, 2023b).

In May 2019, Changi Airport Group operator announced a marketing strategic alliance with Busan Metropolitan city, Korea Airports Corporation, Eastar Jet, Jeju Air and SilkAir to jointly promote trade, business and tourism flows between Singapore and Busan. The strategic partnership resulted in the opening of a new non-stop route between Singapore and Busan, offering greater convenience and low-cost carrier options to South Korea for travellers. CAG operator also worked with the Wonderful Indonesia Tourism Organization to organise an in-airport Indonesian appreciation event, encouraging Singaporean families to learn more about Indonesia's culture through a plethora of activities (Changi airport, 2019). Recognised for its efforts in supporting airlines, trade partners and the overall aviation community, Changi Airport was awarded the Best Airport Marketing Award in the category of 'Over 50 million passengers' for the fourth consecutive year running at the World Routes Awards (2019).

In 2019, the airport operator promoted the brand's 'Win with Changi' shopping campaign, which rewards shoppers and diners with a $1 million top prize. This promotion campaign is a big driver of awareness about the shopping and dining offers at Changi Airport. The latest draw received more than 1.4 million entries from 212 countries, with Singapore, China and Indonesia being the top three participant nationalities (Changi airport, 2022a). Another advertising campaign was promoting the airport's Butterfly Garden through online banners, a website and airport billboards. 'We expect every airport to be the same', one ad reads. 'Until we experience one that raises the bar', The tagline, 'Rethink travel at changiairport.com', requests travellers to put aside their preconceived notions of what an airport should be and arrive early for their flight to experience the airport (Changi airport, 2022b).

These real examples of marketing strategic alliances through digital channels (particularly smartphones) illustrate the huge changes that airports, airlines and DMOs are experiencing, which call for revisiting the theoretical and practical perspectives of joint strategies by operators and academics. Marketing and strategy innovation is a tool with which airports and airlines can and should use external ideas as well as internal to cover the needs of customers and firms in this complex industry.

New modes of interfirm collaboration for strategic alliances will emerge, driven by new business models moving towards digitalisation and decentralisation of information processing (Cong, 2018), because changing customer expectations of firms in terms of sustainability and social responsibility, while providing products and services at lower cost, greater speed and with better customisation, mean that firms need to collaborate more widely to secure better profit margins (He et al., 2020). Business and trade events are a significant source of tourists and visitors for major cities and airports, as well as a key focus for city destination marketing and branding (Morrison & Coca-Stefaniak, 2020). This Chapter has contributed to make better future decisions in the international digital expansion of airports, airlines and DMOs by operators, executives and marketing experts.

References

ACI. (2022). The top 10 busiest airports in the world revealed. https://aci.aero/2022/04/11/the-top-10-busiest-airports-in-the-world-revealed/. Accessed on July 12, 2022.

AdmCom. (2008). Casino di Venezia 'keep playing'. https://www.admcom.net/en/portfolio/casino-di-venezia-keep-playing/

Airport Business. (2018). Hamad international airport offering a highly personalized, connected, and hassle-free passenger experience. http://www.airport-business.com/2018/06/hamad-international-airport-offering-highly-personalised-connected-hassle-free-passenger-experience/. Accessed on July 7, 2022.

Airport World. (2020). Beijing capital to revamp terminal 3's retail offerings. https://airport-world.com/beijing-capital-to-revamp-terminal-3s-retail-offerings/. Accessed on July 26, 2022.

American Airlines. (2013). American airlines and Disney launch high-flying collaboration with 'Disney's planes'. https://news.aa.com/news/news-details/2013/American-Airlines-And-Disney-Launch-High-Flying-Collaboration-With-Disneys-Planes/default.aspx. Accessed on July 19, 2022.

Assael, H. (1993). *Marketing principles and strategy*. Dryden Press.

Bai, B. (2021). Strategic business management for airport alliance: A complex network approach to simulation robustness analysis. *Physica A: Statistical Mechanics and Its Applications*, 607, 126682.

BTME. (2022). Business traveller awards 2022. https://btme.ae/2022-winners/. Accessed on July 6, 2022.

CAPA. (2009). *Beijing capital – Easily the busiest airport in China in 2009*. https://centreforaviation.com/analysis/reports/beijing-capital–easily-the-largest-airport-in-china-in-2009-19422. Accessed on July 30, 2022.

Changi airport. (2019). Growing the air hub with partners. https://www.changiairport.com/corporate/media-centre/changijourneys/the-airport-never-sleeps/growing-the-air-hub-with-partners.html. Accessed on July 29, 2022.

Changi airport. (2022a). Time to #WINWITHCHANGI. https://www.changiairport.com/en/shop/promotions/win-with-changi.html. Accessed on July 30, 2022.

Changi airport. (2022b). Butterfly garden. https://www.changiairport.com/en/discover/attractions/butterfly-garden.html. Accessed on July 30, 2022.

Cirig, T. (2021). The airport of the future is on the horizon. https://blog.aci.aero/the-airport-of-the-future-is-on-the-horizon/. Accessed on July 28, 2022.

Cong, L. W. (2018). Navigating the next wave of blockchain innovation: Smart contracts. *MIT Sloan Management Review*, 1. https://sloanreview.mit.edu/article/navigating-the-next-wave-of-blockchain-innovation-smart-contracts/. Accessed on July 29, 2022.

Doganis, R. (2019). *Flying off course. Airline economics and marketing.* Routledge.
Ferrigno, G., Del Sarto, N., Cucino, V., & Piccaluga, A. (2022). Connecting organizational learning and open innovation research: An integrative framework and insights from case studies of strategic alliances. *The Learning Organization, 29*(6), 615–634.
Financial Times. (2022). Delays, shortages and strikes: Can the aviation industry get airborne by summer? https://www.ft.com/content/8bdb785a-4770-416c-b453-dbfcb1c21d68. Accessed on July 16, 2022.
Florido-Benítez, L. (2021). Identifying cybersecurity risks in Spanish airports. *Cyber Security, 4*(3), 267–291.
Florido-Benítez, L. (2022a). The safety-hygiene air corridor between UK and Spain will coexist with COVID-19. *Logistics, 6*(52), 1–22.
Florido-Benítez, L. (2023a). The location of airport an added value to improve the number of visitors at US museums. *Case of Studies on Transport Policy, 11*, 100961.
Florido-Benítez, L. (2023b). The role of the top 50 US cargo airports and 25 air cargo airlines in the logistics of E-commerce companies. *Logistics, 7*(1), 8.
Florido-Benítez, L. (2024). Analysis of Latin American theme parks in a tourism context. *Tourism and Hospitality, 5*(1), 124–147.
Hamad International airport. (2022). Hamad international airport COVID-19 measures. https://dohahamadairport.com/airport-guide/at-the-airport/covid-measures. Accessed on July 3, 2022.
Hamel, G., Doz, Y., & Prahalad, C. K. (1989). Collaborate with your competitors and win. *Harvard Business Review, 67*(1), 133–139.
Harari, Y. N. (2014). *Sapiens: A brief history of humankind.* Vintage Books.
He, Q., Meadows, M., Angwin, D., Gomes, E., & Child, J. (2020). Strategic alliance research in the era of digital transformation: Perspectives on future research. *British Journal of Management, 31*, 589–617.
Hübel, C., Weissbrod, I., & Schaltegger, S. (2022). Strategic alliances for corporate sustainability innovation: The 'how' and 'when' of learning processes. *Long Range Planning, 55*, 102200.
IATA. (2022). *Global outlook for air transport. Times of turbulence.* https://www.iata.org/en/iata-repository/publications/economic-reports/airline-industry-economic-performance—june-2022—report/. Accessed on July 23, 2022.
ICAO. (2022). Future of aviation. https://www.icao.int/Meetings/FutureOfAviation/Pages/default.aspx. Accessed on July 23, 2022.
Jiang, Y., Liao, F., Xu, Q., & Yang, Z. (2019). Identification of technology spillover among airport alliance from efficiency evaluation: The case of China. *Transport Policy, 80*, 49–58.
Kezar, K. (2019). Fort worth alliance airport receives $5.5 million grant as it prepares to become Amazon Air hub. https://communityimpact.com/dallas-fort-worth/development-construction/2019/07/03/fort-worth-alliance-airport-receives-5-5-million-grant-as-it-prepares-to-become-amazon-air-hub/. Accessed on July 28, 2022.
Kramer, L. S. (2010). *Airport revenues diversification.* ACRP Synthesis 19, Transportation Research Board of the National Academies.
LEK. (2022). Marketing program stimulates new airport terminal visibility and retail sales [BCIA]. https://www.lek.com/insights/cs/marketing-program-stimulates-new-airport-terminal-visibility-and-retail-sales-bcia. Accessed on July 23, 2022.

Li, Y., Lin, T.-Y., Chiu, Y., Lin, S.-N., & Chang, T.-H. (2021). Impact of alliances and delay rate on airline performance. *Managerial and Decision Economics, 42,* 1607–1618.

Lin, H.-E., Hsu, I.-C., Hsu, A. W., & Chung, H.-M. (2020). Creating competitive advantages: Interactions between ambidextrous diversification strategy and contextual factors from a dynamic capability perspective. *Technological Forecasting and Social Change, 154,* 119952.

Lyu, J., & Zhang, L. (2022). Covid-19: A disaster while also an opportunity for the U.S. airline industry. Proceedings of the 2022 2nd international conference on enterprise management and economic development (ICEMED 2022). *Advances in Economics, Business and Management Research, 656,* 1181–1187.

McAlaney, J., & Benson, V. (2020). Cybersecurity as a social phenomenon. In *Cyber influence and cognitive threats* (pp. 1–8). Academic Press.

Morrison, A., & Coca-Stefaniak, J. A. (2020). *Routledge handbook of tourism cities.* Routledge.

Oladimeji, M. S., & Udosen, I. (2019). The effect of diversification strategy on organizational performance. *Journal of Competitiveness, 11*(4), 120–131.

Olson, E. M., Olson, K. M., Czaplewski, A. J., & Key, T. M. (2021). Business strategy and the management of digital marketing. *Business Horizons, 64*(2), 285–293.

Pereira, B., Lohmann, G., & Houghton, L. (2021). The role of collaboration in innovation and value creation in the aviation industry. *Journal of Creating Value, 7*(1), 44–59.

Pettinger, T. (1998). *Construction marketing strategies for success.* Macmillan Press.

Piotrowska-Trybull, M., & Sirko, S. (2022). Airports in communes before and during the COVID-19 pandemic. *Sustainability, 14*(12), 7315.

Raimundo, R. J., & Rosário, A. T. (2022). Cybersecurity on the internet of things in industrial management. *Applied Sciences, 12,* 1598.

Ramanujam, V., & Varadarajan, P. (1989). Research on corporate diversification: A synthesis. *Strategic Management Journal, 10*(6), 523–551.

Reuters. (2022). Amsterdam's Schiphol airport limits number of summer passengers. https://www.reuters.com/business/aerospace-defense/amsterdams-schiphol-airport-limits-number-summer-passengers-2022-06-16/. Accessed on July 16, 2022.

Robinson, W. T. (1988). Sources of market pioneer advantages: The case of industrial goods industries. *Journal of Marketing Research, 25,* 87–94.

Sahu, S. K. (2017). Firm performance and diversification: An empirical investigation of chemical sector in India. *International Journal of Sustainable Economy, 9*(1), 56–71.

Santarelli, E., & Tran, H. (2015). Diversification strategies and firm performance in Vietnam. *The Economics of Transition, 24*(1), 31–68.

Schengen Visa News. (2022). Europe: Airlines cancel over 15,700 flights scheduled to fly in August. https://www.schengenvisainfo.com/news/europe-airlines-cancel-over-15700-flights-scheduled-to-fly-in-august/. Accessed on July 16, 2022.

Schiphol Group. (2013). *Schiphol Group Annual Report 2013.* https://www.schiphol.nl/en/schiphol-group/page/annual-reports/. Accessed on July 1, 2022.

Schiphol Group. (2014). *Schiphol Group Annual Report 2014.* https://www.schiphol.nl/en/schiphol-group/page/annual-reports/. Accessed on July 2, 2022.

Seyitoğlu, F., Costa, C., & Malta, A. M. (2022). Dimensions of (post-)viral tourism revival: Actions and strategies from the perspectives of policymakers in Portugal. *European Planning Studies*, *30*(4), 608–626.

Shaturaev, J. (2022). Company modernization and diversification processes. *ASEAN Journal of Economic and Economic Education*, *1*(1), 47–60.

Skytrax. (2013). The world's top 100 airports for 2012. https://www.worldairportawards.com/the-worlds-top-100-airports-2012/. Accessed on July 2, 2022.

Skytrax. (2020a). The world's top 100 airports for 2012. https://www.world airportawards.com/worlds-top-100-airports-2020/. Accessed on July 22, 2022.

Skytrax. (2020b). Hamad international airport is the first airport in the middle east to receive the 5-star COVID-19 airport safety rating. https://skytraxratings.com/hamad-international-airport-is-the-first-airport-in-the-middle-east-to-receive-the-5-star-covid-19-safety-rating. Accessed on July 12, 2022.

Skytrax. (2020c). The world's top 100 airports for 2020. https://www.world airportawards.com/worlds-top-100-airports-2020/. Accessed on September 2, 2022.

Skytrax. (2023). The world's top 100 airports for 2023. https://www.world airlineawards.com/worlds-top-10-airlines-2023/. Accessed on February 28, 2024.

Soomro, Y. A., Bhutto, M. Y., Ertz, M., Shaikh, A. H., Baeshen, Y., & Al Batati, B. (2022). Does brand love precede brand loyalty? Empirical evidence from Saudi airline customers in strategic alliance setting. *The Journal of Asian Finance, Economics and Business*, *9*(6), 81–93.

Tanasiichuk, A., Hromova, O., Kovalchuk, S., Perevozova, I., & Khmelevskyi, O. (2020). Scientific and methodological approaches to the evaluation of marketing management of enterprises in the context of international diversification. *European Journal of Sustainable Development*, *9*(3), 349–375.

Teixeira, S., Barbosa, B., Ferreira, C., & Reis, J. L. (2022). Luxury fashion brands' website strategies: A study with Portuguese designers. In J. L. Reis, E. P. López, L. Moutinho, & J. P. M. d. Santos (Eds.), *Marketing and smart technologies. Smart innovation, systems and technologies* (Vol. 279). Springer.

Thaker, H. M. T., Mand, A. A., Leong, C. H., Khaliq, A., Thaker, M. A. T., & Pitchay, A. A. (2022). International passenger perception on airport branding strategy: Evidence from Malaysia. *International Journal of Economics, Management and Accounting*, *30*(1), 1–25.

The Guardian. (2022). Heathrow asks airlines to stop selling summer flights as it caps passengers. https://www.theguardian.com/uk-news/2022/jul/12/heathrow-airlines-stop-selling-summer-flights-airport-staff. Accessed on July 16, 2022.

The World Bank. (2022). Air transport, freight (million ton-km). https://data.worldbank.org/indicator/IS.AIR.GOOD.MT.K1?end=2020&start=1973&view=chart. Accessed on January 8, 2022.

Varadarajan, R. (2010). Strategic marketing and marketing strategy: Domain, definition, fundamental issues, and foundational premises. *Journal of the Academy of Marketing Science*, *38*(2), 119–140.

Variety. (2013). Smart promo: American airlines flies with Disney's 'planes'. https://variety.com/2013/film/news/smart-promo-american-airlines-flies-with-disneys-planes-1200562686/. Accessed on July 16, 2022.

Wang, S. W. (2014). Do global airline alliances influence the passenger's purchase decision? *Journal of Air Transport Management*, *37*, 53–59.

Wang, R., & Chan-Olmsted, S. (2020). Content marketing strategy of branded YouTube channels. *Journal of Media Business Studies, 17*(3–4), 294–316.

Wikipedia. (2024). Dubai international airport. https://en.wikipedia.org/wiki/Dubai_International_Airport. Accessed on February 27, 2024.

World Routes Awards. (2019). World routes 2019. https://www.routesonline.com/awards/95/world-routes-2019/. Accessed on July 29, 2022.

Chapter 7

Digital Channels Improve Promotion and Communication Campaigns

Abstract

The use of digital channels to promote products and services is experimenting with an unprecedented boom in promotion and communication
marketing campaigns; airports such as Los Angeles (IATA: LAX) in the
United States, Orlando International (IATA: MCO) in the United States,
Schiphol Amsterdam (IATA: AMS) in the Netherlands or Changi airport
(IATA: SIN) in Singapore are pioneers and recognised experts in marketing
communication and technical aspects of promotion campaigns. The brand
image of airports is a great opportunity to universalise loyalty marketing and
price promotion for airport business portfolios. For this reason, in this
chapter, we speak about neuromarketing science, which is a marketing
discipline that uses medical techniques to understand how our central nervous system reacts to marketing stimuli. This is helping companies and
airports get more consumer insights through digital channels.

7.1 Digital Channels: An Improvement Tool for Marketing Activities for Airports and Companies

The use of digital channels like firms' official websites and apps, social media
platforms, tutorials, emails, digital magazines, WhatsApp and customised messages to promote aviation and tourism products and services worldwide is
considered a cost–benefit way of attracting new tourists and passengers at tourist
destinations and airports (Florido-Benítez, 2016a). Airport operators and Destination Marketing Organizations (DMOs) should use digital channels to promote
and improve positioning of brand image, new lines of products and services, new
international and domestic flight connections, the expansion of existing connections (greater frequency), provide updated information about new services or
government regulations (e.g. safety and hygiene rules, COVID certificate or

Airport Marketing Strategies, 109–154
Copyright © 2024 Lázaro Florido-Benítez
Published under exclusive licence by Emerald Publishing Limited
doi:10.1108/978-1-83608-082-420241007

showing the Reverse Transcription Polymerase Chain Reaction [RT PCR] test at airport departure or arrival) and encourage interoperability's internal business processes (see Florido-Benítez, 2020; Florido-Benítez & del Alcázar, 2020).

This implies that management's attitude and commitment to the use of digital channels by operators are important for the extent of usage of this marketing tool. All of us, both researchers and airport managers, need to have a forward-looking and globalised vision of the intrinsic relationships among aviation-tourism-marketing activities because we and our readers will never understand the content and scope of this book. As stated by Camilleri (2018), there is a positive and significant relationship between the perceived ease of use and the perceived usefulness of digital channels for promotion and communication campaigns. This author suggests that tourism communication and promotion campaigns are more effective when they are offered through interactive channels. It provides that there are opportunities for tourist businesses to enhance their reputation and image as they engage in interactive communications with different stakeholders. Digital promotion and communication create a ripple effect that grows as it has the potential to reach wider audiences (Buhalis & O'Connor, 2005). A world's air transport report presented by the International Air Transport Association (IATA) (2022a) indicated that the aviation sector enabled $3.5 trillion in global gross domestic product (GDP) and supported 87.7 million jobs around the world.

Indeed, 58% of international tourists reached their destinations by air. Fig. 31 displays the map of the top 21 countries by number of passengers, with the United States being the first country with 22.7%, followed by China with 15.2%, Spain with 3.8%, India (3.8%), Russia (3.6%) and Mexico with 3% in 2021. The rest of the airports are below 3%, although all these countries are part of the network of airport connections in the world, which provides accessibility and connectivity at all destinations. These countries accounted for 78.3% of global passengers. Europe is the first region in terms of number of global passengers, with 30.5%. The aviation industry is the great strength of the tourism, travel and leisure sectors, which has allowed these activities to flourish and succeed in the last 60 years.

The economic and commercial growth of tourism, aviation, travel and leisure activities cannot be understood without promotion and communication campaigns, particularly in the 21st century, where costumer and company and vice versa both communicate and interact mainly through digital channels like mobile marketing, social media, content marketing, a firm's official website and apps, holographic advertising, banners and Telegram, among others. Airport and airline operators must adopt proactive tactics and strategies in digital media and devices to diversify and expand their products and services, and so they will increase their revenues, profits and competitiveness. An airport operator can push communication messages to passengers through its official airport apps and websites while creating more visually appealing advertisements and trade marketing materials in their physical stores at the airport's terminal.

Digital channels are the cornerstone of promotion and communication campaigns by airports and airlines due to the ubiquity of information and their omnichannel presence in all digital media. For example, Frankfurt airport (IATA: FRA) in Germany offers 'at the gate delivery' for major brands that are

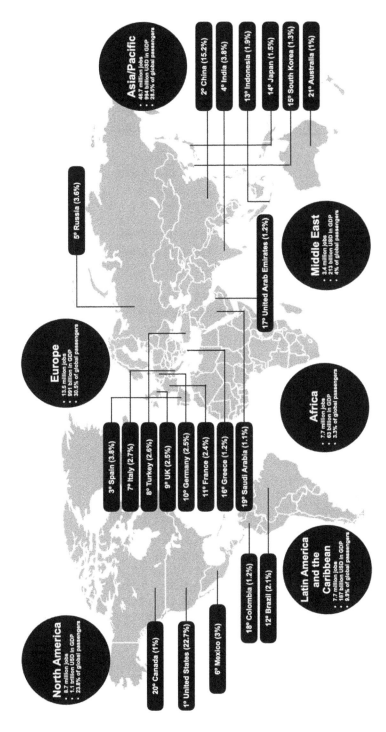

Fig. 31.   Regional Global Passenger Shares in 2021. *Source:* Adapted from IATA (2022a).

available from an airport shopping mall when ordered through the Frankfurt airport app or even through Lufthansa's in-air entertainment system (Gould, 2019; Shahriar et al., 2021).

One salient advantage of airport advertising is it fits in with different kinds of digital channels and can be applied in terminals, gates, corridors and other places inside and outside of airports. Because people tend to stay in airports for a long time due to the long waiting and dwelling time before boarding the plane, this increases the probability for visitors to notice and pay attention to these advertisements (CAPA, 2015; Gu, 2019). In 2013, a survey showed that a large proportion of visitors to airports noticed airport advertisements and took the time to read the message, especially those frequent flyers who normally take three or four round-trip flights in a year (Ruane, 2013).

In this same line, Straker and Wrigley (2018) analysed the role of digital channels at 100 airports worldwide, and they found that the growth in digital channel adoption has allowed airports to gain a competitive advantage through innovative offerings to passengers. In addition, providing information and recommendations on current digital channel use enables airports to benchmark their performance across digital channel platforms. In the digital marketing age, airports have embraced digital platforms to alter and add value to existing processes and functions in quality and efficiency terms (Halpern et al., 2021). To create a digital airport commerce ecosystem and an online platform, airport operators should embrace digitalisation and view it as an enormous opportunity to find new ways to generate commercial revenues inside and outside of the airport (Gould, 2019).

To be aware of the significant role of promotion, communication and strategic activities in digital channels and their existing new business opportunities in quantitative and qualitative terms, Insider Intelligence (2021) reported that worldwide, total digital ad spending reached $455.30 billion in 2020, which increased by 13.6% compared to the previous year. Of that, 55.2% went to display advertising, and 40.2% will go to search. In 2017, the gap between display and search was only around 10 percentage points, but in 2020, it will be 15, equating to $68.12 billion more in spending for display than for search. Consumer shifts towards social media and digital video are accelerating the rise of display. There are three improvement indicators related to the connection of digital channels for customer communication: internal efficiency, marketing and competition and financial benefit. Having a qualified marketing team working with digital marketing channels increases the perceived benefits and decreases barriers related to information and communication use between user and companies (Styvén & Wallström, 2019). Digital channels provide opportunities to connect and engage with passengers, building relationships before, during and after passengers visit the airport. Digital channels must provide information, entertainment, connect people and contribute to a passenger's emotions like joy and trust (Straker & Wrigley, 2016).

The Digital Economy Outlook report carried out by the Organisation for Economic Co-operation and Development (OECD) showed the average daily time users spent using the internet, mobile internet and social media worldwide in 2019 (OECD, 2020a). Fig. 32 displays the importance of developing mobile marketing strategies by international companies depending on their target

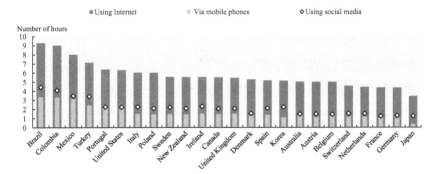

Fig. 32.   Average Daily Time Spent Using Internet, Mobile Internet and Social Media in 2019. *Source:* Adapted from OECD (2020a).

countries and the number of hours the population spends on mobiles. Users increasingly use smartphones in their daily lives, and airport and airline operators need to know the business opportunities generated by the interaction between users' smartphones and firms. Florido-Benítez (2022a) found that the average growth of all apps continues to increase, which demonstrates that customers demand products and services from companies through mobile devices. This author suggests universalising the firm's brand app, with the aim of increasing the number of users in direct contact and promoting products and services internationally in a more immediate way.

There is no doubt that tourists and passengers today have much more control over the buying process than airport operators and DMOs do. Thanks to the proliferation of available digital channels, users have more choices than ever when it comes to how they want to get information. When airport operators design promotion and communication campaigns through digital channels, they must not be limited to the aviation industry. Tourism, travel and leisure, e-commerce, technology, agri-food and logistics are sectors very lucrative in the context of international trade, and airport operators may also find partners willing to share their business model in order to smooth the commercial process transition in other countries.

The promotion and communication campaigns designed by operators and airlines must be appropriate to the characteristics of the digital channels. Users' ability to utilise the digital channel through devices (smartphones, PC, tablet or even Android or iOS operating systems) must also be fully considered, as well as the user's demographic and situational characteristics (e.g. Muslin citizens cannot eat pork and drink alcohol). It is precisely for that reason that it is so important to plan and develop marketing strategies. Operators, DMOs and stakeholders must consider and analyse consumers' needs, to guarantee the aptness and quality of their products and services offered through digital channels. In the perceived website quality on willingness to use online travel agencies by users, Florido-Benítez (2023c) found that ease of use of website was the most important dimension in determining willingness to use, followed by information-content, responsiveness, fulfilment, security and privacy.

7.2 Neuromarketing for a Better Understanding Between Consumers' Needs and Organisations

Human beings are an amalgam of perceptions, emotions, feelings and generators of thoughts. Sometimes, emotions tend to prevail over reason in most humans. Customers' emotions and feelings play a key role in the promotion and communication campaigns designed by companies, especially in the technologies, tourism, food, aviation, travel and leisure industries. Schuller and Schuller (2018) indicate that humans can be quite emotional about technology and computing systems. Nowadays, neuromarketing science is helping companies get more consumer insights through digital channels. Orzan et al. (2012) note that neuromarketing is a marketing discipline that uses medical techniques to understand how our central nervous system reacts to marketing stimuli. The term neuromarketing was initially used by Nobel Prize winner Ale Smidts in 2002 and defines this term as the study of the cerebral mechanism to understand the consumer's behaviour to improve marketing strategies (Fisher et al., 2010; Lim, 2018). Neuromarketing describes how changes in stimulation influence the decisions of the consumer. One of the major goals of the firm is to position their products in such a way that they generate the desired consumer response (Mashrur et al., 2022). Torres et al. (2019) showed that the arrival experience is critical in generating positive customer emotions at theme parks and tourist destinations.

Renvoise and Morin (2005) revealed that 'The three brains of humans: the thinking brain (neocortex), the emotional brain (limbic system), and the old brain (reptilian brain) have major implications of consumer decisions' because emotions dominate the decision-making process of the products and services consumers consume. For example, Renvoise and Morin (2005) observed that when watching a TV advertising or seeing a product on a smartphone, all three brains participate in the purchasing process. Based on the information received from the thinking brain and emotional brain, our reptilian brain makes the final decision: to buy or not buy that product. It is part of the subconscious mind. Furthermore, companies should consider consumers' demographics and situational characteristics to prevent possible errors in marketing campaigns like ignorance of the culture, religion, behaviours or language of countries, translation of the message by languages, and the economic context of the country concerned (see Fig. 33). To understand the buying process, neuromarketers consider it essential to comprehend both the conscious and unconscious minds (Orzan et al., 2012). Emotional control, fear, aggression, sexuality, and surviving instincts amongst many others, are strictly related to human's evolution (Luisetto et al., 2018). We must think that the urge to buy impulsively is an emotional state enabling consumers to purchase impulsively. As customers increasingly use digital channels, sellers must reconsider marketing strategic investments in at least two areas: the salesperson channel, which faces the threat of substitution, and customer-specific discounts, which may be more precisely targeted (Lawrence et al., 2019).

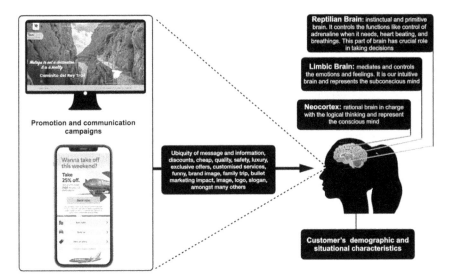

Fig. 33.   The Three Parts of the Brain and the Customer's
Demographic and Situational Characteristics That Influence Consumer
Decision-Making. *Source:* Compiled by the author.

Consumers' demographics, preferences, context and advertising contents are
important for personalised digital and mobile advertising because they influence the
degree of customer approval of mobile marketing messages, global customer satisfaction and sales proposals (see Fig. 34). Age is an individual characteristic that has
been found to influence impulse buying, whereby younger people tend to be more
impulsive than older people (Florido-Benítez, 2016a). For instance, tourists manifest
their behaviour through the products and services that they consume and buy. This
behaviour is determined by their needs, attitudes or personal motivations, which
have been previously thought of and adopted until they become true. In this regard, a
person's attitude is very important since it is composed of their individual values, like
how they think about situations, products, brands, tourist destinations, gastronomy,
etc. based on their values. To illustrate this point, a week-long trip to Málaga Costa
del Sol in Spain, where one can rest and enjoy the idyllic beaches, Caminito del Rey
hiking path, restaurants and luxury hotels, is a dream for many people. However,
most of the Chinese population does not enjoy the beach, and many of them find
sunbathing uncomfortable as it is seen as more culturally acceptable to keep skin as
fair as possible. These kinds of attitudes influence human's behaviour, purchase
intentions, frequency and repetition (Florido-Benítez, 2016b). A positive attitude is
vital to be able to predict the intention to purchase (Duarte & Silva, 2018). As shown
in Fig. 34, customers' characteristics have moderating effects on the elements and
evaluation of mobile marketing; this combination will have a positive or negative
impact on the customer's satisfaction and experience.

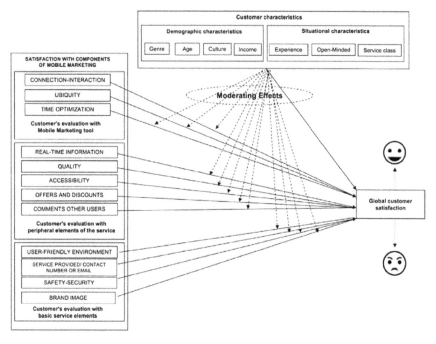

Fig. 34.   Variables to Consider in Mobile Marketing Strategies.
Source: Adapted from Florido-Benítez (2016b).

Torres et al. (2019) found that the arrival experience is critical in generating positive customer emotions at theme parks and tourist destinations. These authors recommend improving customers' retail experiences by adding more experiential elements to the retail shopping environment. Companies and community managers of marketing departments should add video short stories, interactive displays through digital channels, schedule theme park characters to walk around retail districts and more for customers to relate the theme park experiences with merchandise items purchased in store. It is important that retail store management display information about customer reviews of the goods or customer testimonials to reduce cognitive dissonance. In fact, to realise that the interaction between visitors themselves also plays a significant role in creating immersive experiences and being able to evaluate visitors' satisfaction levels (Wei et al., 2022).

By using neuromarketing techniques, marketers and airport and airline operators can discover the emotions, expectations, feelings and even hidden restraints of the passenger/user/visitor or tourist to design promotion and communication strategies that have more influence and persuasion on consumers' purchasing decisions through digital channels. Depending on the advertising, message that firms want to get across, each consumer has their own emotions and feelings when they are watching TV or mobile advertising, and they will make their own decisions regarding their needs, budget, time and to be able to cover their future expectations of the selected product or service.

Although some academics and marketers think neuromarketing is just another word for sales, they consider that these commercial activities should be forbidden due to their intrusive and persuading role in this consumer and impulsive society (Lee et al., 2018; Ulman et al., 2015). As seen in Chapter 1, the digital generation of the 21st century is called (HuMobAp) Human-Mobile-App humans move-mobile phones according to their needs and incentives that apps report to them (Florido-Benítez, 2022a). The duality of the ubiquity of information and smartphones in the hands of users has achieved a high degree of brands' international recognition and positioning. This powerful symbiosis has globalised the brands' products and survives in the hands of the user named 'brand in the hand'. Many business-to-business (B2B) companies expect their salespeople to promote e-commerce through digital channels to customers as an alternative way to purchase (Habel et al., 2021). However, when customers become accustomed to purchasing online, a salesperson's opportunity to cultivate the customer relationship through personal contact might become limited (Lawrence et al., 2021).

Authors such as Lindstrom (2010) and Plassmann et al. (2015) indicate that products and services and promotion and communication campaigns based on neuromarketing technologies will assist customers rather than influence them by simplifying their decision-making. Companies and marketing staff can ensure that they will save a significant portion of their money, which is now being spent on unproductive and costly advertising initiatives. El Kssaimi and Develi (2022) suggest that whatever we do is filtered by our emotions because what we see and pay attention to is filtered by the emotional situation we find ourselves in. Neuromarketing allows firms to achieve outcomes that would be impossible through any other type of study.

A short advertisement through smartphones or even an advertisement poster in the airport terminal can change passengers' minds in a few seconds. In today's digital environment, any company's success depends on paying attention to client behaviour and understanding the true causes of buying decisions, with the aim of ensuring that when someone thinks of a product or service, the firm's brand image comes to mind first.

7.3 Joint Promotion and Communication Campaigns

A joint promotion and communication marketing campaign is very common in the tourism and aviation industries. This symbiotic marketing activity is an alliance of tactics and resources between two or more companies laid out to improve and increase the international and domestic market potential of each through digital channels. The relationship between legacy carriers and low-cost carriers is illustrative of joint promotion campaigns through a close working relationship. Joint flight scheduling, price promotions and advertising are quite pervasive. For instance, a passenger can fly by Vueling Airlines from cities like Málaga, Seville,

Menorca or Granada in Spain to New York city/John Fitzgerald Kennedy International Airport (IATA: JFK) at a price that is considerably lower than the regular fare if the passenger chooses to fly by British Airways/London Gatwick airport (IATA: LGW) to their final destination. British Airways and Vueling Airlines work together under the Oneworld airline alliance. To conduct effective joint promotion campaigns, firms need to select suitable partners. For example, Fly Emirates Airlines is not likely to cooperate with a cheap beverage distribution firm; they probably work with prestigious firms like Chardonnay, Moët & Chandon, Ron Zacapa Centenario XO, among many others. Adler (1966) uses the term symbiotic marketing that refers to cooperation between companies other than those linked by traditional marketer–marketing intermediary relations. Nevertheless, sometimes, joint promotion campaigns differ with respect to lead strategy variables, goals and the choice of communication digital channels to promote their products and services (Varadarajan & Rajaratnam, 1986).

Nowadays, joint marketing, promotion and communication campaigns must be both feasible and desirable for airports and airlines to establish multiple joint relationships with firms offering a specific complementary good or service. Los Angeles International Airport (IATA: LAX) in the United States is a good example of joint promotion and communication campaigns through digital channels. LAX airport is the fourth busiest in the world. Travellers come from all over the world and pass through on their way to or from far-flung destinations, and this is a thriving market for airport hotels where travellers catch a few hours of shut eye before moving on with their travels. Los Angeles airport has commercial alliances with Hilton, Sheraton, Marriott, Sonesta and Regency hotels, mainly focused on internet search engines like Google, Baidu, Yahoo, Microsoft Bing, or Firefox. In addition, Los Angeles International Airport (2022) participates in price promotions through 'VIP QR Codes2' on the airport's official website with other firms and marketers of products and services such as green transportation buses (Antelope Express and Central Coast Shuttle), ground transportation (Flyaway Buses, Inner Curbside, Shared Rides and Free LAX Shuttles), rental cars for customers (Alamo, Avis, Dollar, Herts, Budget, among others), companies (Able Car Rental, Airport Van rental, Avail, Green Motion Car Rental, among others) and airlines (Air Canada, Air France, Air Lingus, Alaska Airlines, Air China, among others). Yan et al. (2022) revealed that when the effect of the coupon is relatively large, firms prefer the coupon as they can have higher prices, demands and profits, and their promotional strategies change with the denomination and effect of the coupon.

To enhance market competitiveness, many promotional methods are employed in practice, like promotional pricing, flash sales, probabilistic selling, joint promotion, etc. but promotional pricing is the major sales strategy for firms to attract prospective customers. To seek more business opportunities, firms pursue horizontal joint promotion to promote their products together (Yan et al., 2022). Chen et al. (2021) suggest that if a store wants to narrow the gap between them and their competitors, their promotional strategies may be aimed at attracting the customers of their competitors.

Regarding the scope of the relationship in joint marketing campaigns. Concerning the promotion and communication activities, the cooperating companies may either choose to develop a joint marketing strategy encompassing all of the relevant marketing mix (4Ps or 7Ps) variables through digital channels to reach joint goals or limit their cooperation to specific marketing actions or even communication channels that may constitute a part of the separate marketing strategies formulated by companies for their respective product and service offerings, with the aim of achieving particular objectives or targets in their established areas.

Joint promotion and communication campaigns managed by Orlando International Airport (IATA: MCO) are a good example of how an airport should establish joint marketing strategies with its main partners, such as airlines, DMOs, hotels, restaurants, OTAs, theme parks and other stakeholders; thus, everybody plays, and everybody wins. The most important airport in the city of Orlando in the US state of Florida is the Orlando International Airport in terms of proximity and passenger because this airport is approximately 21 minutes by car from the airport to Disney and Universal's theme parks and hotels. Fig. 35 presents how airports can design future joint promotion and communication campaigns with their main partners to achieve established joint goals. When Orlando International Airport establishes a joint marketing campaign with airlines, VisitOrlando and VisitFlorida DMOs, to attract more passengers at commercial airlines, more passengers and visitors at the airport and more tourists in Orlando city, the rest of the firms inside of the airport and its catchment area benefit because they also increase the number of visitors at theme parks and museums, restaurant and hotel reservations and package trips at OTAs.

Moreover, commercial airlines may also agree to design joint promotion campaigns with theme parks and museums or vice versa, to increase the number of passengers or visitors and revenues at organisations in these uncertain times. By the same token, the design of a joint communication campaign by the airport and its partners is a powerful source of innovation in the promotional landscape and firms' brand image positioning to drive loyalty programmes through apps, cards and rewards. The brand image of airports is a great opportunity to universalise loyalty marketing and price promotion for airport business portfolios.

Recent studies on vertical and horizontal joint promotion programmes are fruitful, and many important results have been reported in the marketing and business literature (see Chen et al., 2021; Yan et al., 2022; Yu et al., 2018). Yu et al. (2018) and Yu and Chen (2019) investigated the joint promotion strategies in the distribution channels, and they found that the brand image of firms is influenced by vertical and horizontal joint promotion campaigns. Brands are experimenting with tactical innovation in promotion through loyalty, payments and app tools, enabled by new digital channels, customer information and new intermediaries (Florido-Benítez, 2016a). Airports, airlines and DMOs must be effective in their promotion and communications campaigns to their customers, to create, interact with, maintain relationships and pursue their marketing purposes.

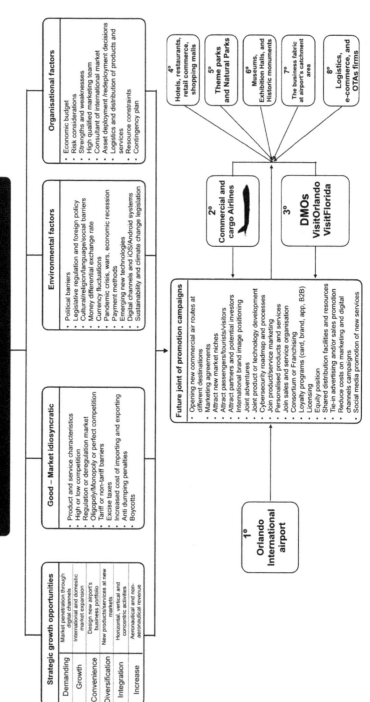

Fig. 35.   Airport Joint Promotion and Communication Campaigns. *Source:* Compiled by the author. Screenshots courtesy of Orlando International Airport and VisitOrlando and VisitFlorida DMOs.

7.4 Examples of Airports and Airlines Joint Promotion Campaigns With Other Partners

The aviation industry has been a very restricted and rather endogamic sector for aeronautical engineers, operators and governments. They monopolised the aeronautical and safety activities from 1970 to 2000, and for them, the non-aeronautical and marketing operations were only residual income for airports. Fortunately, this trend is positively changing thanks to tourism and marketing experts, who have provided a joint vision and a clearer of the interrelationship between the aviation and tourism industries to increase commercial revenue and passenger arrivals at airports worldwide. The management of marketing campaigns through digital channels by airport operators, marketing departments, airlines and DMOs has to be targeted with a clear, relevant and attractive message of products and services offered to users/passengers/tourists to reach a high conversion rate and return on investment of marketing campaigns. This is one of the reasons why airport operators and the rest of their partners are turning to a range of evaluation measures for aviation and tourism promotion campaigns.

Greater knowledge about the effectiveness of diversification promotion and communication campaigns through digital channels and online marketing tools could help airport operators and their partners adapt their marketing campaigns, identify relevant target markets, tailor their products, reduce costs and increase benefits. Darmawan et al. (2018) expose that the marketing team coordinates the timing and level of promotion to maximise revenues, while the production department focuses on production plans satisfying target sales and minimising total production-related costs. Pratt et al. (2010) revealed that there are five key indicators or factors determining a good return on DMOs' promotion and communication campaign investment, of which destination marketers can influence most factors (see Fig. 36).

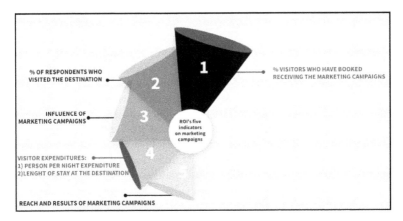

Fig. 36.   ROI's Five Indicators on Marketing Campaigns. *Source:* Adapted from Pratt et al. (2010).

For example, there are many tactics that airport operators can use to influence higher passenger expenditures at the airport's terminal. Passenger or visitor expenditures can be increased through vouchers, discounts and special offers from duty-free shops, Burger King, Pizza Hut, Calvin Klein, BOSS, Channel, Hamleys, JD Sports and WHSmith companies through the airport's app or websites.

From a tourism marketing point of view, DMOs and theme parks should increase the length of stays at theme parks' resorts or hotels in the city with incentives of extra nights' accommodation promotion and communication campaigns at their official's website and apps, or even DMOs can work together with international and domestic airlines and national parks (e.g. Yosemite, Yellowstone, Grand Canyon and Great Smoky Mountains National Park) to attract more tourists, visitors and passengers at airports, airlines, national parks and tourist destinations. So, all of them will build a brighter future for the United States' aviation and tourism industries, where citizens and firms obtain economic and social benefits, always from quality, sustainability, climate change actions, efficiency, protecting and preserving natural and heritage resources and landscape perspectives.

The greatest challenge facing societies and firms will be utilising the benefits of utilising artificial intelligence (AI) technologies, providing vast opportunities for both new products and services in marketing campaigns and achieving immense productivity improvements (Makridakis, 2017). Google, Zara, Netflix, Expedia, American Airlines, Apple, Samsung and Amazon, among many others, could process our behaviour to know what we want before we know it ourselves (Harari, 2016). Tourist, travel and leisure and supermarket products through digital devices are seen as actors that have influence on consumers (Savin-Baden, 2021).

Operators of airports and airlines should analyse the digital marketing tools and potential of utilising digital channels in their choice of digital platforms and improve their effectiveness in marketing strategies and campaigns. Social networks have become an active part of airport's marketing campaigns; it is a real example of how airports need to be actively and continuously interacting with social media users to increase their number of users and the quality of information they provide. Dublin Airport (IATA: DUB) in Ireland won the three Major Social Media Awards in 2019. This airport has been named the world's best airport Twitter feed in an international digital media awards competition by The Moodie's Award, the best airport Twitter account, which is the fourth time it has picked up this award in the past 6 years. It uses its Twitter account for news, passenger information, sharing engaging content, answering customer queries and rewarding its followers with regular competitions (Dublin Airport, 2019).

Dublin Airport was rewarded for best practices in social and digital media among airports and airport retailers globally. The major reason airports and tourism companies are so successful at adapting digital marketing strategies is because they carefully analyse how people interact with their surrounding while travelling. These insights help them recognise existing customers' needs and give travellers what they want to create electronic word-of-mouth (EWOM) marketing effects and ensure repeat sales. The ever-increasing volume of comments and

reviews on the internet offers new opportunities to capture passengers' perceptions and expectations of airport branding on a global scale (Florido-Benítez &
del Alcázar, 2020).

An interesting study carried out by Masa'deh et al. (2021) examined the impact
of social media activities on brand equity (brand awareness and brand image),
with a convenience sample of 362 participants who used one or more forms of the
Royal Jordanian Airline's social media. According to the analysis results, entertainment, customisation, interaction and EWOM were all significant predictors of
Royal Jordanian Airline's brand image. Airlines and airports are increasingly
using social media to deliver key messages associated with the brand to create a
solid and favourable brand image and brand awareness in the minds of
consumers.

Social media has given users the opportunity to show their complaints to a wider
audience, thereby threatening the image and reputation of the company (see Obembe
et al., 2021; Triantafillidou & Yannas, 2020). The reputation of airports and airlines
is very important through digital channels due to its intangibility as a resource that is
shaped by internal performance and collective external perceptions.

But sometimes airports and airlines make mistakes in promotion and
communication campaigns, and in the execution and transmission of messages. In
October 2011, Australia's Qantas Airlines launched a contest that invited its
customers to describe their 'dream luxury in-flight experience' in a single tweet
and possibly win a pair of Qantas first-class pyjamas and a toiletries kit.
Unfortunately, at the time of the tweet, the airline's entire fleet was grounded due
to union protests. Thousands of passengers were stranded, many of them strug-
gling to get their refunds. The Twitter thread was swarmed by angry travellers
who did not mince their words when expressing their frustration with what was
supposed to be a 'dream experience', but it had become a nightmare. Dissatisfied
employees also joined in the tirade of complaints (Taylor, 2011).

Creative Connections & Commons Inc. (CCCI) is an international language
and translation agency, and CCCI (2020) reported that in 1987, Braniff Airlines
started to widely promote its new leather seats, encouraging travellers to fly with
luxury. Yet in Latin America, it faced translation and localisation mistakes. The
'Fly in Leather' campaign was translated into Spanish as 'Vuela en Cuero'.
Unfortunately, this had different connotations in Spain and Mexico. 'En cueros',
which is pronounced the same as 'en cuero', means 'naked', turning the fancy
tagline into a racy one: 'Fly Naked'. The humourous, unintentional invite became
an embarrassing and costly mistake for Braniff Airlines.

Airport operators are using marketing campaigns through digital channels to
universalise the airport's brand image. In the 21st century, airport and airline
operators combine physical media with interactive media to attract new target customers and satisfy their wants and needs. Some airport operators and governments
make the mistake of not aligning with the values of the city where they are located and
later changing the airport's name and brand image. The image of the airport should
be linked to the city. Airports such as Louisville Muhammad Ali International
(IATA: SDF) in the United States, Hollywood Burbank (IATA: BUR) in the United
States, Liverpool John Lennon (IATA: LPL) in the United Kingdom and Málaga

Costa del Sol (IATA: AGP) in Spain have changed their original names to reflect the link to their respective cities since airports are ambassadors of tourist destinations. Indeed, the change of the airport name from Málaga airport to Málaga Costa del Sol was a reality in 2011 after finishing the third terminal, which was opened on 15 March 2010. This change was done for regional tourist interests and to disseminate and promote the Málaga Costa del Sol airport brand in the international tourism market (Florido-Benítez, 2022b, 2022c). 'Costa del Sol' reflects briefly (at the airport name) what visitors will experiment with in the city. Therefore, 'Costa del Sol' becomes a brand image for the airport and city in June 2011. These tourism promotion and communication strategies promote the positioning of the airport brand worldwide.

Halpern and Graham (2022) affirm that airports are increasingly viewed as commercial entities and spheres of influence for commercial activity. There is a high relationship between satisfaction levels and airport image (Ryu & Park, 2019). McCarran International Airport (IATA: LAS) in the United States is localised near the centre of Las Vegas, and this has an active role in creating visitors' impressions of the city of Las Vegas (Nghiem-Phu & Suter, 2018). Airport operators have placed greater emphasis on airport marketing and branding (Florido-Benítez, 2022d). Wattanacharoensil et al. (2021) demonstrated the positive relationships among sense of place, airport image and destination image. Air travellers mentally compare airport performance with the destination image and thus provide consistent promotional messages that will enhance satisfaction levels in airports and destinations.

Airports and airlines provide accessibility, connectivity and frequencies of flights at tourist destinations and tourist attractions like theme parks, museums, national parks, historical monuments and prestigious hotels and buildings, with the aim of facilitating the movement of tourist flows worldwide. Nevertheless, airports' international–national passenger arrivals are susceptible to exogenous and endogenous factors like economic conditions, flight services, fluctuations and shocks. Interoperability among DMOs, airports, airlines and stakeholders is crucial to addressing and preventing times of crisis and planning contingency plans in a situation of uncertainty as to the actual scope of business activities.

In 2017, the Rijksmuseum in Amsterdam, Amsterdam's DMO and the Amsterdam airport Schiphol designed a promotion campaign where passengers picked up luggage at Schiphol airport, and they saw 10 paintings from the Rijksmuseum's collection that were on display at a special baggage carousel bearing reproductions of some of its most famous masterpieces (see Link: https://www.museumnext.com/article/rijksmuseum-covers-schiphol-airport-luggage-belt-dutch-works-art/). Moreover, Rijksmuseum and Schiphol airport implanted a small museum exhibit of the original classic paintings in the Schiphol terminal, in the area behind the passport control, at the Holland boulevard. Tourists prefer tourist attractions close to hotels for their comfort and the trip's time optimisation. These joint strategy alliances increase the number of tourists in the cities and visitors at museums, particularly in this period of pandemic crisis. Readers can see YouTube's joint promotion campaigns at this link (https://youtu.be/oqRz1zcL-XEw). In 2020, most Dutch citizens stopped travelling in and out of the country, and their trips dropped by 55%. Moreover, 20% of people expect to fly less in the future after the coronavirus (de Haas et al., 2020). It can be expected that the demand for travel will reduce, and that people will travel less by public transport (De Vos, 2020). With marketing promotion and communication techniques, the sales volume objectives of the museum products can be achieved, the awareness of the museum image can be improved and the museum attendance can be increased (Florido-Benítez, 2023a).

More effort should be placed into promoting and developing new tourism products through physical and digital marketing strategies like advertising and providing information that includes positive messages associated with international tourists (Lai et al., 2022). Large capitals and the monumentalisation relationship and marketing promotion strategies reinforce one another, with both benefiting from the other's capacity to communicate the city's brand identity. Sutcliffe (1979) suggests that the monumentalisation of large capitals was employed for geopolitical and tourism purposes. These were especially designed to impress most tourists who visit these large metropolitan cities. On 4 May 2022, Emirates Airlines showed its new customised Airbus-380 livery dedicated to Dubai's newest architectural icon and centre for pioneering concepts and ideas, the Museum of the Future in Dubai. The first aircraft of the Emirates A380 (A6-EVK) is sporting this exciting new livery (Emirates Airlines, 2022). Dubai's DMO is promoting Dubai's Museum of the Future through digital channels as the most beautiful building on earth, and this has become one of Dubai's most uniquely designed structures.

Abdullah et al. (2020) revealed that trip purpose, mode choice, distance travelled and frequency of trips for primary travel were significantly different before and during the pandemic. People still perceive infection risk in means of transport (especially in aeroplanes), and they become more selective when choosing a travel mode during the pandemic crisis. Most trips were made for shopping during the pandemic around the world (Abdullah et al., 2020; Florido-Benítez, 2021a). Factors like interior design, ambience, diversity of products and services and staff's friendliness are analysed by passengers in airport retail stores (Han et al., 2021). As stated by the DMO's Tourism Ireland (2022), three factors are necessary to address tourism recovery:

(1) Consumer motivation to travel: identify when consumers will be ready to consider holidaying again and which markets offer us the best short-term prospects.
(2) Restoration of access: accessibility, connectivity and increase of air frequencies through airlines.
(3) Retaining tourism and aviation industries as strong, internationally appealing industries: empower the relationship between tourism and aviation sectors because they will need to invest in new business models to stimulate and attract tourists to destinations

To support these three factors, DMO's tourism in Ireland established a three-phase plan: restart, rebuild and redesign (3R) tourism and aviation sectors to recover tourism demand through joint promotion and communication campaigns. These are the three scenarios for promoting tourism, travel and leisure activities from overseas to the island of Ireland:

(1) Restart tourism in Ireland with a new consumer campaign called 'The Green Button'.
(2) Rebuild tourism demand supported by the government, airlines and airports for viable inbound initiatives to the island of Ireland.
(3) Redesign tourism and aviation industries and activate trade sales through digital channels.

In this chapter, we are showing a wide variety of sophisticated joint promotion and communication campaigns that cover all marketing mediums to reach the established objectives by airport and airline operators, DMOs and stakeholders. For instance, when the United States' government announced the reopening of borders with the United Kingdom due to the COVID-19 pandemic, British Airways, through its agency Ogilvy, London and New York cities launched a joint promotion campaign named 'NEW YORK. WE'RE BACK', with the aim of restarting the flow of tourists with this airline and the city of New York. Sometimes, DMOs influence certain airlines to cover a specific flight route with the aim of connecting two or three tourist destinations and empowering the growth of these destinations. In the context of marketing, interoperability between DMOs and destination managers is advised to develop a co-branding strategy that is more comprehensive and benefits both airlines and destinations (Al Saed et al., 2020; Pike et al., 2021).

On 4 May 2022, Alaska Airlines joined forces with Disneyland Resort and DMO's Los Angeles to unveil a new Star Wars-themed aircraft. The plane, painted space black with the iconic Millennium Falcon emblazoned on the tail chased by TIE fighters, celebrates Star Wars: Galaxy's Edge, the newest land of adventure inside Disneyland Park in Los Angeles, US. This customised aircraft operates the air route from Seattle-Tacoma International Airport (IATA: SEA) to John Wayne airport (IATA: SNA) in Orange County. Readers can see YouTube's customised aircraft at this link (https://youtu.be/92CxXIyh6FI). This is a real illustration of how joint marketing campaigns may be an opportunity to attract tourists and convince them to visit tourist attractions in cities and tourist destinations. Strategies and marketing tools in tourism are constantly changing. We insist once again that 'everybody plays, and everybody wins', and we think that joint marketing strategies and campaigns are very important to redress the situation of the aviation and tourism industries at tourist destinations in these times of economic and pandemic crisis, Brexit and Russia–Ukraine war.

A report of the impacts on the European aviation industry and economies of the European Union caused by the shutdown of air traffic due to the COVID-19 pandemic by the IATA (2020a) indicated that airlines in Europe lost $21.5 billion in 2020. Spain and the United Kingdom were the worst affected by the pandemic crisis. In the case of Spain, the tourism sector is of major economic importance, as it generates more than 2.6 million jobs, comprising 12.8% of the country's total employment, and contributes 12.3% to its GDP (INE, 2020). Spain was the second destination in international tourist arrivals in 2019. In 2020, this country showed one of the largest decreases, with a 98% drop in international tourist arrivals. In addition, Great Britain decreased by 59% in international tourist arrivals (Moreno-Luna et al., 2021). These shocking statistics have sparked a heated debate among governments, airport operators, airlines, DMOs and stakeholders worldwide, and all of them must work together to build an environment conducive to tourism and aviation activities. At this juncture, we believe all efforts should be pooled to make our common goals a reality and find a practical solution acceptable to all, with the aim of making a successful exit from the economic and pandemic crisis and shaping the next sustainable, efficient, decarbonisation and environmentally friendly business models.

Table 3 lists the latest economic impact figures for selected European states (IATA, 2020a). These data underscore the importance of relations established between airports and airlines and countries, which helps to provide a clear global vision as important as connectivity, accessibility and economic impact in cities. Improving these data should be a priority for all governments, airport operators and airlines in the coming years. Readers need to interpret the data displayed in

Table 3. Impact of COVID-19 on European Aviation in 2020.

Country	Passenger Impact	Impact Origin-Destination Passengers (Million)	Impact Airline Revenues ($Billion)	Impact Employment Total	Impact Gross Value Added ($Billion)
Austria	−61%	−17.5	−2.8	−55,300	−4.8
Belgium	−63%	−19.3	−2.7	−68,900	−6.5
Czechia	−65%	−11.3	−1.4	−36,000	−1.3
Finland	−63%	−10	−1.5	−42,000	−3.7
France	−65%	−94.6	−16.7	−46,6100	−41.5
Germany	−65%	−117.6	−20.2	−550,800	−38.7
Greece	−61%	−30.7	−4.4	−273,700	−11.8
Hungary	−63%	−10.5	−1.3	−45,500	−1.8
Ireland	−65%	−22.7	−2.9	−93,100	−13.4
Israel	−59%	−14	−3.4	−92,600	−8
Italy	−63%	−98.2	−13.4	−369,100	−25.2
Netherlands	−62%	−33.7	−6.2	−183,500	−14.9
Norway	−79%	−27.3	−3.8	−110,300	−12.1

(Continued)

Table 3. *(Continued)*

Country	Passenger Impact	Impact Origin-Destination Passengers (Million)	Impact Airline Revenues ($Billion)	Impact Employment Total	Impact Gross Value Added ($Billion)
Poland	−61%	−24.3	−2.8	−68,600	−2.2
Portugal	−64%	−30.4	−4.2	−200,200	−8.5
Romania	−63%	−13.1	−1.5	−57,900	−1.3
Russia	−62%	−71.9	−9.6	−458,200	−10.5
Spain	−63%	−132.7	−17.9	−1,049,500	−69.1
Sweden	−69%	−23.6	−3.1	−115,800	−11.6
Switzerland	−64%	−31.8	−6	−128,000	−17
Turkey	−59%	−62.5	−7.4	−598,900	−26.5
Ukraine	−59%	−11.5	−1.4	−86,300	−0.8
UK	−65%	−165	−30.6	−780,000	−59.3

Source: Adapted from IATA (2020a).

Note: Please note that the sum of the passenger and revenue impacts in this table are not additive. They include the impacts from all carriers irrespective of airline registration region.

Table 3 and the urgency and serious nature of the situation in economic and social terms. That is why marketing strategies, their tactics and promotion campaigns through digital channels are as important as the effectiveness thereof. Promotion and communication campaigns, social influence and price value have a positive influence on hedonic motivation to go to tourist destinations.

On 19 August 2021, Munich and Düsseldorf airports launched a combined marketing campaign for advertising space, with clients benefiting from packages that ran across both locations. Six packages were available, tailored to different target groups and customer needs. The 'Digital Welcome' package featured two prominent digital advertising spaces that could be seen by most arriving passengers. With the 'Big Departure' package, clients could benefit from passengers' waiting time before the security check. The advertising messages were displayed on five large digital and analogue screens. Both airports focused on economically strong regions with highly mobile target groups with high purchasing power (The Moodie Davitt Report, 2021).

Each year, we all see delays or restrictions on flights by weather or strikes of workers fighting for better working conditions at airports. These circumstances provoke a bad passenger's experience, product and service shortages in airports and airlines and irrecoverable leisure time by passengers. Airport operators and airlines need to manage this situation in the best possible way to reduce passengers' stress and to be efficient and effective when resources are scarce. Elbaz et al. (2022) suggest that to reassure customers that the service failure would not ruin their travel experience, airlines and airports should leverage customer willingness to downgrade. For instance, if an airline realises it does not have enough vegetarian meals, then they need a way of knowing which customers are willing to eat a non-vegetarian meal or opt out of having a meal altogether. As a result, the airline can ensure that the customers who would be most upset at not having the correct meal are served appropriately.

Interoperability between airports or airlines in data and information terms is vital to designing new lines of products and services through marketing strategies. Furthermore, sharing information and data helps airport operators to be able to change faster product and service ranges and brands, which are generally not bought by visitors or passengers in the airport's retail firms. Airports' business portfolio is of utmost importance to the development of tourism in cities and countries. Moreover, shopping is a major reason for people to travel.

Airports are required to be more attractive to airlines and passengers with relevant investments in commercial policies. Airports are no longer just a physical infrastructure where aeroplanes take-off and land. Airports are vital economic generators, providing a gateway to their territories. In a competitive environment, airports require expanding and enhancing their appeal to increase their share of air travel and tourism, including innovation and a strong focus on customers' experiences (ACI, 2017; Florido-Benítez, 2022b). The air connectivity of low-cost and legacy carriers has a high impact on airports and tourist destinations that are managed by DMOs. Nevertheless, Felsenstein and Fleischer (2003) and Beeton (2004) discuss the role of tourism promotion with public assistance in boosting the regional economy. The European Commission encourages marketing agreements corresponding to effective marketing needs for regional development. DMOs cannot be subsidies to airlines to operate in an airport (Florido-Benítez, 2021b). Indeed, the local Association for the Promotion of Touristic and Economic Flows and Ryanair's marketing agreement at Montpellier airport was found illegal under EU State Aid rules (European Commission, 2019).[1]

7.5 Mobile Marketing as a Promotion Tool

One of the most striking features of today's society is the consumption not only of goods and services but of images and information as well, giving rise to an image culture. Most people have a smartphone, and it has become a part of us as if it were another vital organ, a lifeline. If we are not conscious of the opportunities offered by mobile devices or of the fact that interactive media is the future of commercial activities, then we are not only going to lose customers but also sales

---

[1]The European Commission (2019) State Aid Guidance to airports and airlines states that public subsidies may be used by regional airports or regional authorities to attract price-sensitive airlines to an airport under specific conditions. Subsidies are, for example, lower airport charges, discounts to airport charges, success fees or incentive payments to airlines as remuneration for alleged services, especially marketing.

and revenues. The competitiveness and positioning of any tourist destination depend significantly on its airport. Hence, positioning is the perception that real or potential customers have in their minds about a product and how this perception is reflected in their preference for some competitors over others, particularly in a complex business environment and a power struggle between companies through promotion and communication campaigns on mobile devices.

An image is recognised by its graphic design and the visible elements surrounding it, which are developed by companies through various codes such as logotypes, corporate colours, architecture, visual applications and uniforms, among other things, and then projected onto various outlets with a communicative intent (Florido-Benítez, 2016c). In this same vein, Conde et al. (2010) affirm that a tourist destination's positioning is measured according to the image a tourist holds of it. The aviation industry constitutes a challenge for airport operators and marketers due to the high dynamics of the provision of information. Companies in the aviation sector use mainly mobile marketing. Airlines and airports strive to communicate more and more effectively with passengers (Szymczak, 2018).

Airports and companies that coexist in their microenvironment are being transformed into e-commerce driven companies that are willing to use mobile devices as their new direct sales channel or commercial information adders to favour and improve the sale of products to users. Florido-Benítez (2016a) indicates that large airports are taking advantage of the consolidation of smartphones to create airport applications' brand and communication strategies. Airport operators manage the airport's brand image according to the nature and role of brand loyalty (see Fig. 37).

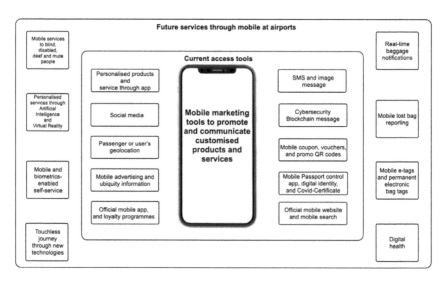

Fig. 37.   Present and Future of Mobile Tools to Promote and Communicate Customised Products and Services. *Source:* Compiled by the author.

An airport's brand image is a competitive advantage when it has a good reputation worldwide. In fact, Lee and Park (2016) found that social media, transparency and social responsibility had a significant influence on airport business performance and its brand image. For instance, in 2016, a research project was conducted by the International University of Bad Honnef, Florido-Benítez and Düsseldorf airport (IATA: DUS), with the aim of improving the app of this airport in terms of communication, management, screen interface and loyalty programme. Nowadays, the Düsseldorf airport app has become an indispensable tool for passengers, and this airport was awarded as the second-best regional airport in Europe and fifth-best regional airport in the world in 2021 by Skytrax.

Airports and airlines use mainly smartphones as support for conducting promotion and communication campaigns. Mobile marketing is characterised by customisation of products and services, and companies have the chance to monitor and measure users' reactions and conduct satisfaction surveys more quickly during the customer's purchasing process. Obviously, airport operators must provide free Wi-Fi high-speed internet (5G) access as an amenity for travellers. These indicators are very important to create and stimulate continuous interactions between airport operators and passengers. The airport's app is the most suitable channel for receiving information at airports since passengers could access real-time information and manage themselves more effectively (Chingchuang et al., 2020).

Mobile marketing is uniquely suited to help potential customers find you or learn about your products precisely when they need them, especially in promotion and communication campaigns. Connecting with mobile customers helps businesses keep them informed and updated about various issues such as launching new products or services, special offers, sales periods, special promotions and gaining more credibility in comparison with their competitors (see Amirkhanpour et al., 2014; Florido-Benítez, 2016a; Krum, 2010; Pantano & Priporas, 2016). Every airport has its own characteristics, niche market and limitations. Indeed, it would not be advisable to implement an airport's app if there are no commercial activities within the terminal. Airports manage the promotion and communication of products and services through the airport's apps because airports' apps are used as sale channels and universalise the airport's brand image. It is quite conceivable that commercialisation via smartphone is integrated into airports. Consequently, airlines and airports will be able to offer special promotions on smartphones.

The Moodie Davitt Report (2020) reported that Los Angeles World Airports (LAWA), Unibail-Rodamco-Westfield Airports (URW Airports) and airport e-commerce platform Grab partnered to launch a new service called 'LAX Order Now', allowing guests to order food and drink from restaurants across the airport terminals using 'touchless service'. Customers can access all the information and services they need through their smartphones. LAX Order Now does not require downloading a mobile app. Airport guests can use their camera app to scan one of many QR codes located throughout the airport or visit https://www.lax-shopdine.com/retailer-category/dine/ directly from their smartphone to search and browse menus from any participating restaurant. This new service offered by Los Angeles airport provides multiple forms of payment including credit and debit cards, Apple Pay and Google Pay. Guests will pick up their orders from a designated pick-up area with seals on all packaging. LAX Order Now provides order updates and alerts to users when their order is ready for pick up at one of the designated pick-up locations, which are clearly signed.

Moreover, the mushrooming of airports' apps worldwide with different brands, services and prices has caused competition to increase in the aviation sector. The airport's promotion and communication campaign is influenced by the management of the brand image as part of the airport's strategic policy implementation, since this is seen as a vital role in the airport's business successes because it generates an effect on the passengers' purchasing behaviours towards products and services offered by the airport and firms that coexist in their microenvironment.

Nevertheless, not everything is an advantage; people cannot be downloading all airport applications around the world when they are travelling to another airport, city or country, which would be crazy, right? We recommend airport operators, European Union and the rest of government organisations worldwide develop a unique website and app platform where the most important airports are included, so airports can provide all necessary information (e.g. safety and hygiene rules, products and services, the airport's map terminal, etc.) and respond to demand by passengers. A unique airport platform facilitates a joint pro-gramming, the exchange of updated information, the development of safety, hygiene and quality standards for on airport activities, as well as providing better access and efficiency of information to users through this global airport platform. This business interoperability would strengthen the international airport networks around the world. Complexity and sometimes a lack of transparency and infor-mation in relationships between airport operators and government organisations can easily create further confusion and a lack of mutual understanding to improve the airport system and the lives of citizens.

Many researchers and experts in digital marketing still question whether mobile marketing will be the perfect marketing tool to carry out sales, promote, communicate and stage the products and services of firms soon. But the reality is that most companies and organisations are already developing new promotion and communication methods to boost sales through AI, VR and hologram tools. The future of mobile marketing will always be conditioned by the ubiquity of information and data existing at the moment that customers require it. The future is in our 'mobile-hands'.

7.6 Encourage Promotion and Communication Campaigns at Air Cargo Industry

Where many studies and organisations see darkness at this moment of pandemic and economic crisis, this book shows how these times of difficulty and uncertainty bring new challenges and opportunities to the aviation and e-commerce sectors. Airports encourage the establishment of companies in the city, and they play an important role in the air cargo, logistics and e-commerce development of firms worldwide. The necessity to serve firms with truly global supply chain requirements and distributive infrastructure has helped stimulate the formation of alliances within the global air cargo industry. 'Like airline passenger services, air cargo carriers have started to cooperate through common product and service options, sales, and compatible information systems and to develop global networks' (Baxter & Srisaeng, 2018; Morrell & Klein, 2018). But the point is that the air cargo industry faces many problems that require some innovative solutions (e.g. improved fuel efficiency, zero emissions and reduced costs), if it is to survive and thrive in the new decarbonisation era, with the aim of emerging from this unprecedented crisis more resiliently.

As we have seen before, the air cargo sector is withstanding the pandemic and economic crisis better than commercial airlines. The air cargo industry plays a role of paramount importance in the global economy, especially when time and safety are crucial factors. Air cargo is employed for the mid to long-distance transportation of urgent goods. Its selling position is speed and reliability. In fact, just 1% of global trade moves by air, but that 1% represents 35% of global trade by value (IATA, 2020b). As an example, transport of high-value, perishable or emergency-related products is generally carried out via air because it is the only mode that guarantees shipping times consistent with the user's requirements and needs. Air cargo transport can be carried out in two ways: first, in the belly space of passenger aircraft, and second, using dedicated full freighter aircraft. The first option offers more flexibility in terms of frequencies and destinations but a limited cargo capacity per aircraft (Bombelli, 2020).

The air cargo market is served by three types of providers: all-cargo airlines, combination carriers and integrators. With e-commerce on the rise and the pandemic approaching 5 years, the integrators profit from this development and the increasing demand for high-quality fast transport services. In addition, they have been instrumental in supporting the health sector and countries around the world, shipping millions of doses of the COVID-19 vaccine worldwide. Every day, 6,849 lives are saved, thanks to supply chain solutions that bring vaccines to their destination to time to be effective (Aircargo News, 2019). Air cargo is critical in flying these temperature-sensitive pharmaceuticals in the best conditions, using cutting-edge technologies and procedures; Europe's air cargo carriers have proven essential in the global fight against the COVID-19 pandemic, transporting over 107,000 tonnes of personal protective equipment (PPE) in 2020, the equivalent of 1,000 fully loaded Boeing 777 freighters. This includes more than 5 billion protective masks and other protective equipment, as well as COVID-19 tests and medical supplies (Airline for Europe, 2021).

Air cargo activity is a great opportunity to diversify airport business models as well as an alternative to reduce the high dependency that airports have on passengers. Some airports, like Memphis International Airport (IATA: MEM) in the United States and East Midlands airport (IATA: EMA) in the United Kingdom have focused on freight activities, and they are taking a great advantage thanks to the e-commerce sector boom and the pandemic crisis. Florido-Benítez (2022c) analysed the air cargo at UK and Spanish airports, and he found that the United Kingdom's East Midlands airport increased the number of cargo aircraft movements by 10% in 2020. This airport has been a strategic point to keep supply chains moving during the coronavirus pandemic. The United Kingdom's East Midlands airport experienced the smallest drop in flight numbers compared with other European airports (Harry, 2020).

Regarding global integrators' market, it consists of moving B2B packages through connecting major metropolitan areas as quickly as possible. The three main operators are FedEx, UPS and DHL, and they compete globally in the air cargo sector. Nevertheless, due to the boom of retail e-commerce, major operators such as Amazon, Shein, Zara, Zalando, Alibaba and eBay, among many other firms, rely heavily on express delivery services, and this has provoked the reshaping of the parcel express industry. The pandemic period highlighted not only the importance of e-commerce but also the increasing demand for cargo transport. This has made airports and airlines across the globe develop new investment and marketing strategies to increase the existing cargo terminals and processing capacities for the transported goods.

Malighetti et al. (2019) indicate that this shift has moved airports and integrators towards a more B2C-centred business model, whose deliveries exhibit quite a different profile from typical B2B models. These are the main reasons why air cargo operators are buying new cargo aircraft models, with more payload capacity and improvements in fuel efficiency, emissions and operating costs. In 2022, Boeing launched the 777-8 Freighter to serve the growing demand for cargo while also enhancing its environmental performance. Qatar Airways, one of the world's largest cargo carriers, ordered up to 50 777-8 Freighters, expanding its commitment to the Boeing 777X family. The 777-8 Freighter will be the world's largest (Boeing, 2022). Governments must play an important role in making the region more attractive by intensifying efforts to increase the air cargo activities by developing new airport capacities on capitals' airports and by supporting airlines in expanding their air cargo activities (Zaharia et al., 2022).

Notwithstanding, each airport faces different challenges due to the heterogeneity of the cargo business, such as international or national cargo, new business models and airports focused on e-commerce and warehouse logistics. The best example is Amazon Air, which is a cargo airline operating exclusively to transport Amazon packages, Cincinnati Northern Kentucky International (IATA: CVG) and Lehigh Valley International (IATA: ABE) airports are the main airport hubs as operational bases in the United States for Amazon Air. Although Amazon Air operates out of more than 40 airports across the United States and operates almost 100 flights per day, in 2017, it changed its name from Amazon Prime Air to Amazon Air to differentiate themselves from their autonomous drone delivery service.

Airports and cargo airlines, or among their own cargo airlines, also agree on business strategies. In 2021, CVG airport was equipped with specialised facilities for package sorting and transhipping to distant cities to allow the airport to become Amazon Air's superhub. The new facilities are dramatically changing Amazon Air's geographic profile. Indeed, the development of the CVG airport was facilitated by an agreement with the DHL company, allowing for the cross-utilisation of facilities. This apparently allows Amazon to use DHL facilities primarily during the day when they are generally underutilised. Through vertical integration, Amazon uses logistical facilities to control distribution flows and channels, allowing it to control how parcels are routed within its distribution, including final deliveries to the consumer (Rodrigue, 2020). Bombelli et al. (2020) suggest that in the air cargo business, the airport catchment area is much larger than for passengers because it relies on road feeder services for the ground leg that are not present in passenger networks.

All the vicissitudes of the air cargo sector have been shown to readers; it is also important to stage and understand marketing strategies (individually or together) through promotion and communication campaigns. In 2022, FedEx Express, a subsidiary of FedEx Corporation, was the main partner of EuroGames 2022. This inclusive sporting event welcomed some 2,000 athletes from July 27 to July 30 in Nijmegen, the Netherlands. This event celebrates diversity and inclusion through a series of sporting activities where everyone can participate (FedEx, 2022). This promotion campaign was published in digital newspapers, social media and on FedEx's official website. Sports sponsorship and event marketing are two of the tools and companies' business strategies for making more money during the event. Firms and marketers understand the importance of social media as a powerful promotion and communication tool and use it as a digital marketing channel to communicate with their customers.

Trustworthy relationships are instrumental in managing sport sponsors; Morgan et al. (2020) affirm that this is because the brand image and strategic compatibility are valued by the sponsor. In terms of relational effectiveness, a clear and compatible strategy, the development of positive inter-organisational culture and interpersonal relationships and economic stability are key to successful and effective promotion and communication management. The relationship between sports sponsorship and the marketing of companies' products and services is very strong. The commercialisation of sports has increased the promotion and sponsorship of sports events. The involvement of businesses in sponsorship programmes results in increased brand awareness and a strengthened brand image (Florido-Benítez, 2023b; Nuseir, 2020). Sporting events, arts festivals, charities or movies are a key influence on generating desired consumer responses to sponsorships (Florido-Benítez, 2022b).

In 2021, DHL launched an international brand campaign to celebrate the release of the new James Bond film 'No Time to Die'. The message the DHL company wishes to convey through this association is that, just like Bond, when it comes to logistics, DHL is the provider of choice you can rely on even if the mission is unusual or complex (DHL, 2021). This promotion campaign was published on social media, TV, digital newspapers, social media and DHL's official website. Readers can see the promotion campaign of 007 *No Time to Die* – DHL official logistics partner, in this link (https://youtu.be/Xks9IjNuLaY). A year earlier, as a part of its plan to strengthen domestic transport operations in Brazil, DHL Supply Chain, the global leader in contract logistics, opened its air cargo hub at Guarulhos International Airport, in São Paulo city. As a dedicated cargo terminal, this DHL's airport hub consolidates, palletises and prepares cargo for domestic air transportation dispatched from São Paulo, providing more agility, safety and efficiency to that kind of operation in the region. The DHL company is the only logistics operator with such a work configuration in Brazil (DHL, 2020).

The third example is United Parcel Service, also known as UPS, an internationally acclaimed company that has set up several marketing activities to promote its brand visibility in the consumer market. Advertisement campaigns are displayed with the help of newspapers, television, billboards and magazines for brand recall. Depending on the size of the order placed, UPS offers subscriptions and bulk discount schemes to its clients. Its delivery vans are a means of promoting brand awareness among its customers, as they are able to reach far and wide places. UPS realises the importance of social media platforms and hence offers service-related information via its website. Advertising campaigns are also shown on its official website to increase brand awareness. The company encourages its employees to offer voluntary services as part of community activities. The UPS company targets business-to-business markets extensively, and the brand enjoys high recognition among consumers in the United States. Also, UPS had a presence among consumer markets through its sponsorship of National Association for Stock Car Auto Racing (NASCAR) and its sponsorship of the Olympics in 1996 (Roy, 2010). UPS has made several sponsorship deals. It is the official logistics partner of several athletic programmes at the university and college levels, and since 2013, it has also become the official logistic and shipping sponsor of Scuderia Ferrari. Besides, this company is the official express carrier and sponsor of the golf tournament The Open Championship (Marketing91, 2019).

In 2022, UPS introduced a new daily flight connection for air cargo from Billund airport (IATA: BLL) in Denmark to Cologne airport (IATA: CGN) in Germany. Businesses in the Jutland region exporting packages to Europe and the rest of the world will benefit from later pick-up times. The new flight path allows Danish businesses, especially small and medium-sized enterprises, to have greater flexibility. The opening of this new air route provides opportunities for all firms in Denmark to expand into global markets faster, thanks to the connectivity, accessibility and air frequency offered by UPS and these two airports. This new air route is helping to develop the European air network to meet the growing e-commerce demand for the region (Aircargo News, 2022).

Air cargo carriers' advertising is placed in digital newspapers, billboards, TV and radio marketing campaigns. These firms use their official websites to promote their products, services and promotional activities. Offers and incentives are posted on their official website and apps. UPS, FedEx and DHL companies also use other social media portals like Facebook, Twitter, Instagram, TikTok and YouTube to remain in direct contact with their customers. Moreover, platforms like LinkedIn help mangers' human resources find, manage and contact the ideal candidates for their teams. This platform aims to save firms' time in finding the right person and engage the world's most qualified talent pool for company recruitment purposes; thus, promotional marketing promotes internal marketing.

Despite the growing interest in promotion and communication campaigns from researchers, marketers and the tourism and aviation sectors, there is still a need for an updated, accessible and in-depth textbook that introduces the principles and practice of airport marketing strategies through digital channels to stage the reality of aviation marketing in the 21st century. A living example of this is the Dallas-Fort Worth International Airport (IATA: DFW), which is managed by the Dallas Airport Board operator. This operator affirms that social media, like traditional media, must be responsive on a 24/7 basis, particularly in times of crisis, because the communication between customers and the DFW airport's staff must be a 2-way communication, communication is dialogue, not monologue. Corporate communications maintain consistency of messaging on social media, aligned with the overall DFW airport's messaging. Social media communication staff responds rapidly to engagement opportunities on social media and coordinates with other airport departments to ensure accuracy and timely response. DFW airport's major social channels are Facebook and Twitter; these two platforms increased exponentially in followers' terms from 2012 to 2015 (see Fig. 38). Users appreciated the clear and updated information about the airport's services and products, and their comments were positively valued, especially in comparison to other US airports (Dallas-Fort Worth International Airport, 2015).

Social media communication staff manage the information and communication of DFW airport's digital media depending on platform audience, marketing and promotion strategies and key performance indicators (KPIs) to measure promotion executions and their possible changes in case of possible mistakes to improve the quality of information provided to customers and promotion and communication campaigns. Sometimes, the management of information and communication on Facebook is different than on Twitter platforms due to the

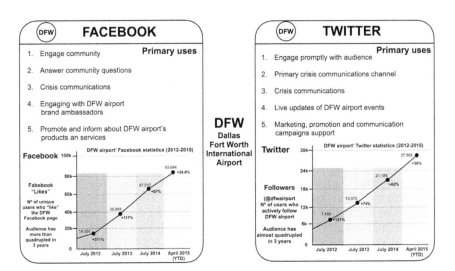

Fig. 38.   Dallas Airport's Management and Use of Facebook vs Twitter Platforms. *Source:* Adapted from Dallas-Fort Worth International Airport (2015).

audience, number of followers or even the user's activity in time and response terms (see Fig. 38). Every contact is an opportunity to build the reputation and influence of airports and airlines and to build relationships with all airport audiences. Social media offers the opportunity to promote programmes and services within airports, in addition to collaborating with airlines, concessionaires and community partners.

Firms' promotion and communication campaigns and slogans at digital channels provide the characteristics of the products and services marketed, illustrate their advantages against their global competitors and communicate and stage the improvement of their products and services to their clients and potential customers. A viral image is more effective than a million flyers and is much cheaper and more efficient. In 2015, Cargolux Airlines International celebrated 45 years of flying with a 'You name it, we fly it' slogan-logo jet on a new Boeing 747-8R7F LX-VCM. This marketing phrase 'You Name It' had propositional content identified as a request from the company to its customers: just name the items to be transported by aeroplane. It offers freedom to the target customers to ship whatever they want to transport. The second phrase, 'We Fly It' referred to the action of the Cargo Lux company to fulfil the customers' wishes. This slogan is a promise by the Cargolux carrier that it will perform an act after getting the customer's acceptance (Arrosid & Munandar, 2018; Searle & Vanderveken, 1985).

The heterogeneity of the airport cargo business generates different challenges at different airports and cargo carriers. Airport and airline operators need to understand the core characteristics of their own airports and also identify airports that have similar features to theirs in order to enable meaningful benchmarking exercises as well as identify the exposure to external influences in the cargo market relative to other airports. In an airport's marketing plans, a benchmarking tool is vital to compare and monitor the network performance against other airports, and this tool helps to ensure the competitiveness of the airport. Memphis International Airport (IATA: MEM) in Tennessee, US, is a worldwide reference point for cargo, performance and productivity activities. It is no coincidence that MEM airport is FedEx's Superhub, and most air cargo carriers operate at this international cargo airport. In 2016, Mayer (2016) identified that the Hong Kong International Airport (IATA: HKG) and Memphis airports were the busiest cargo airports in the world, although these two airports had a very different cargo profile, different centralities within cargo networks and different types of airlines operating passenger and cargo flights from the airport. Indeed, Airport World (2022) reported that HKG airport achieved just over 5 million metric tonnes of cargo in 2021, up 12.5% since 2020 and up 4.5% since 2019, and MEM airport in second place reached 4.5 million metric tonnes with a −2.9% drop in cargo versus 2020 and up 3.6% since 2019.

For the Memphis Shelby County Airport Authority operator, marketing strategies, promotion communication campaigns and customer relations are very important to Memphis' airport because these marketing tools empower the airport's brand image worldwide in terms of air cargo, quality, performance and productivity.

Table 4. Memphis' Five Marketing Actions From 2022 to 2025.

No	Marketing Actions	Target Period
1	Reinvigorate the marketing campaign to increase public awareness of non-stop destination options at MEM airport	2022
2	Implementing a communications plan to introduce the new modernised B concourse	2022
3	Introduction of a communications plan to introduce the new consolidated de-icing facility	2022
4	Launch of a marketing campaign to increase participation in the Department of Homeland Security's Real ID programme	2023
5	Launch a promotion campaign based on the next phase of modernisation and other projects identified by the Master Plan	2022–2025

Source: Adapted from Memphis International Airport (2022).

In 2022, this operator designed five actions to reach between 2022 and 2025. Ongoing five initiatives include maintaining and continually communicating with a database of key community partners (see Table 4). Community outreach is a critical factor for all employee and passenger communications, as well as customer service. The marketing, communication and customer relations area's responsibilities include media relations, management of the airport's social media channels, web and app content, internal and external newsletters, digital and mobile marketing, branding, customer service and communications with airport tenants, community leaders and the travelling public (Memphis International Airport, 2022).

Memphis airport marketing and communication strategies will help to remain the centre of distribution of air cargo in the United States and pave the international firms' path in a globalised market. A marketing plan may be developed by airport staff, through a partnership with a local university, a DMO or even by a consultant. Each of these options will require resources of time and money from an airport. Answering questions about staffing and budget is a good first step towards a new or updated marketing plan. Airport operators make collaborations with brands like food, accommodations, airlines, etc.; vast research has proven that collaboration always drives brand sales. In fact, the airport operator can produce reports on the airport's market share in his country and whether travellers are using his airport or airline as part of a stopover, to design new promotion campaigns.

7.7 A Brief Overview of Promotion and Communication Campaigns at Free International Trade

For more than 8,000 years, the desire for goods and services from distant countries has driven the evolution of complex international trade networks. These trade routes have left a lasting imprint on cultures and markets across the world, which in many cases can still be seen today. Although the first reasonably systematic body of thought devoted to international trade is called 'mercantilism' and emerged in 17th- and 18th-century Europe. Prior to closing Chapter 7, I would like to remind readers of the fundamental principles of free international trade a doctrine formulated by the economist Adam Smith in the 18th century and empowered by the economist David Ricardo in the early 19th century. These two economists affirm that the exchange of goods and services between market agents is advantageous to society because it makes possible the division of labour and specialisation in production and, therefore, an increase in wealth.

This economic theory remains the touchstone justification for free international trade to this day, though increasing numbers of economists, researchers and academics (e.g. Joseph Stiglitz, Friedrich List, Ha-Joon Chan, and Yuval Harari, among many others) are strictly against this economic model because 'it is regarded as a market promoting ideology that serves the interests of corporate business and capitalist elites at the expense of poor countries and marginalized economic groups throughout the world' (Strange, 2020). Nowadays, personal wealth plays a greater role in developed economies than in emerging economies (Monsen et al., 2012).

The World Trade Organization (WTO) is an intergovernmental organisation that deals with global trade rules. It provides a framework for countries to negotiate trade agreements. It also works to promote free trade by reducing barriers to trade, like tariffs, which are taxes on imports or exports from other countries. The WTO is the world's largest international economic organisation (WTO, 2022). In the same line, as stated by the International Trade Administration (ITA), a free trade agreement is a pact between two or more nations to reduce barriers to imports and exports among them. Under a free trade policy, goods and services can be bought and sold across international borders with little or no government tariffs, quotas, subsidies or prohibitions to inhibit their exchange (ITA, 2022). The concept of free trade is the opposite of trade protectionism or economic isolationism. This hands-off stance is referred to as 'laissez-faire trade' or trade liberalisation. Bhagwati (2007) argues that the most important and persuasive argument in favour of free trade is its promotion of economic growth, labour and productivity.

The aviation and tourism industries are strong driving forces for the achievement of economic and social progress in this free international trade because both industries are closely related to technological, energy, financial, innovation, marketing and environmental sustainability activities. The World Travel & Tourism Council (WTTC) reported that in 2019, the travel and tourism sector contributed 10.3% to global GDP, a share that decreased to 5.3% in 2020 due to ongoing restrictions on mobility. The year 2021 saw the share increase by

6.1%. Promotion of marketing activities contributes to further improving the tourism offer through digital channels. On the other hand, aviation's global stature as an economic engine is evident in the statistics. In 2019, the aviation industry contributed 2.5% to global GDP, a share that decreased by -5.3% in 2020 due to the pandemic crisis (WTTC, 2022). Indeed, in 2021, compared to 2019, there was an overall reduction of 40% in the seats offered by airlines (IATA, 2022b). The implementation of concurrent policy measures geared at fostering air access liberalisation and the promotion of marketing efforts contribute to further enhancing tourism demand (Seetanah et al., 2019).

The reader must be aware of tourism and aviation's transversal importance and its progressive economic growth in the global GDP. Marketing strategies, promotion and communication campaigns are the fastest mainline connections to stimulate consumers' consumption of products and services. Marketing activity and free international trade are linked in today's consumer society to impulsive purchases, and this requires the exchange of goods and services among market agents, companies and consumers. For a company's aims, it is crucial to have a good knowledge of impulsive buyers, especially through neuromarketing science. A study of impulse buying conducted by Wang et al. (2021) revealed that the pandemic increased consumers' impulse buying behaviour, and two key elements were: loss of control and anxiety, which mediated the relationship between the pandemic and impulse buying.

May the reader think for a moment about what happened during the COVID-19 pandemic? Which sectors benefited? How important have marketing campaigns been during and after the pandemic?

Surprisingly, the COVID-19 pandemic improved dynamism and expanded the scope of e-commerce worldwide, but the mitigation measures aimed at slowing the pandemic taken over by governments have directly affected the supply, demand and daily operations of the retail sector in free international trade (OECD, 2020a). Lockdowns and social distancing measures affected retailers with physical stores more than online retailers, and this accelerated the ongoing shift from brick and mortar to online retailing. In France, the market share of e-commerce rapidly increased to almost 10% of total consumer goods sales during the confinement period, compared to less than 6% in 2019. In the United Kingdom, the Office for National Statistics reported that the proportion of retail expenses spent online increased from 19.1% in April 2019 to 30.7% in April 2020, reaching a record high (OECD, 2020b).

Fig. 39 presents the growth in searches for essential and non-essential retail items, defined as the unweighted average of the growth rates of the relevant categories. Essential items include the following categories: consumer electronics, grocery and food retailers and pharmacy. Non-essential items include the following categories: luxury goods, home appliances, home furnishings, luggage and travel accessories, apparel and gifts and special event items. Data show us that internet searches confirm diverging trends for essential and non-essential retail items in most OECD econo-mies, especially in countries such as the United Kingdom, Ireland, Colombia, Chile, the United States, Canada, Italy and Spain. For example, in the United States, while the sales of clothing retailers dropped by 89.3% in April 2020 compared to the

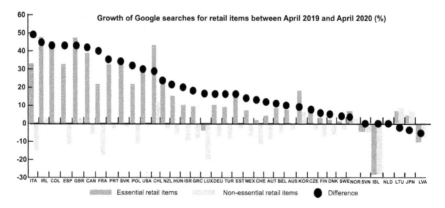

Fig. 39.   Change in Demand for Essential Versus Non-Essential Retail Goods. *Source:* Adapted from OECD (2020b). *Notes:* Google searches are a rough proxy for demand and should be interpreted with great care. In particular, the increase in searches for essential retail items may partly reflect a shift to online shopping for these items, rather than a pure increase in demand. These data have, however, the merit of being available for many countries and allowing comparisons.

previous year, the sales of grocery stores increased by 13.2%. On the other hand, in the EU zone, the sales of non-food products dropped by 23.8% in April 2020 year on year, while the sales of food, beverages and tobacco increased by 1.2% compared to the previous year (OECD, 2020b). Many sectors experienced issues on the supply side as governments curtail the activities of non-essential industries and workers confined to their homes.

Social distancing and lockdown mandates disrupted the buying and shopping habits of consumers along with their consumption patterns (Naeem, 2021). Many companies saw great opportunities during the pandemic, while others were only dedicated to protest. For example, medical, education and health and fitness apps increased downloads and remained 20–35% higher than pre-coronavirus levels. Conversely, apps by companies in the travel, navigation and sports sectors saw the number of downloads dramatically reduced due to the pandemic, especially travel applications, with a drop of 42% in 2019. These sectors are leisure activities, and in periods of crisis, their operations decrease because they are not essential (Florido-Benítez, 2022a; Sensor Tower, 2020). Evidently, education (ZOOM, Microsoft Teams, Google Meet, Skype), technology (Apple, Samsung, Microsoft, Xiaomi, LG), entertainment platforms (Netflix, Disney +, HBO, Amazon Prime, Tencent), grocery and food (Tesco, Amazon, Carrefour, Walmart) and social media (Facebook, Twitter, YouTube, Instagram, TikTok) industries are the most beneficiated in these agitated years of the pandemic, armed conflicts and economic crisis.

Fortunately, in 2022, mobile commerce sales in the United States with smartphones are expected to increase by over 192% compared to 2018, particularly in the tourism and aviation industries. Online travel agencies have developed applications to adapt quickly to the mobile environment as well as to the web (Statista, 2020). Consumers purchase hotel rooms, airline tickets and tourist packages through mobile commerce. In the United Kingdom, 36% of consumers under 34 performed their online holiday booking through mobile phones in 2017 (Statista, 2021). In the paradigm of free international trade, promotion and communication campaigns and marketing strategies designed by companies induce the consumer's impulsive buying. Um et al. (2022) considered four variables affecting consumers' impulsive buying behaviour in tourism mobile commerce (ubiquity, notice of special promotion, convenience and perceived value) as motivating mobile tourism impulse purchase intention. As stated by Islam et al. (2021), perceived arousal through promotion and communication campaigns (digital channels, social media, messages, TV, radio, among many others) had a significant positive relationship with impulsive and obsessive buying. The direct effect of website quality on the urge to buy impulsively reaffirms that an organisation must meet a minimum threshold for website quality. Website quality is a key factor that influences online consumer behaviour and the urge to buy impulsively (Wells et al., 2011). These results show that promotion and communication campaigns through digital channels on/post pandemic have positive and negative effects on companies and consumers.

Nevertheless, like most of my research colleagues, the topic of impulsive buying by consumers unfortunately seems as frivolous and sad as pathological gamblers. Müller et al. (2022) found that with the widespread of e-commerce, many consumers are at risk of developing online compulsive buying–shopping disorder. Pathological gambling affects the gambler's closest family, and financial problems are often encountered. There may be a loss of money to pay for essentials, huge credit card debts and illegal loans, a loss of rent money and eviction. Life in a problem gambler's family is often beset with crises and conflicts, and distress levels are elevated (Custer, 1984). These are also real problems for consumers induced by companies' direct and indirect effects of promotion and communication campaigns. The consumer society model that globalisation has contributed to intensifying appears to be directing the world towards an irrational, absurd and unjust society. I must remind readers that each day, 25,000 people, including more than 10,000 children, die from hunger and related causes (United Nations, 2022).

One noteworthy point is that free international trade brings economic growth, labour and productivity, supported by marketing and promotion activities in the tourism and aviation industries. As a researcher, I am obliged to inform you of the dark side of the business activity of Adam Smith's neoliberal economic model in this book. Not all that glitters is gold. This book also tries to empower and raise awareness among airport and airline operators, DMOs, stakeholders and the rest of the companies to develop responsible promotion and marketing campaigns in their marketing plans because this is an indicator of why companies must be concerned and look after their customers. Hypocrisy and dishonesty can damage a socially responsible campaign and harm your brand's image. We must not forget that airports' profitability depends on their annual passenger throughput, operability, accessibility and connectivity with other airports and destinations.

Indeed, airports with fewer than 1 million passengers per year typically struggle to cover operating costs and often only continue to exist because of government subsidies. In 2014, the European Commission outlined in its 'Guidelines on State Aid to Airports and Airlines' that government subsidies to airports violate European competition law. Therefore, subsidies for regional airports were prohibited. While larger airports had to operate self-sufficiently at once, smaller airports, with less than 3 million passengers per year, were granted a 10-year grace period until 2024 to adapt to the changes. Although very small airports, with passenger volumes below 200,000 per year, are exempt from this directive, the new guidelines are expected to have far-reaching implications. It is estimated that more than 50% of all airports within the EU operate on state aid, and this creates an inefficient market and distorts competition in a democratic system (European Commission, 2014; Florido-Benítez, 2022b; Grimme et al., 2018; Volkhausen, 2022). This would distort competition in the open aviation market, which we are trying to improve within the EU.

The 21st century is known as the Digital Innovation Era, and airports, airlines and all companies want to be well positioned in digital media through promotion and communication campaigns to get the consumer's attention. The evolution of marketing campaigns from ancient Egypt to the present has changed little in terms of trade relationships and actors (B2C and B2B), and the market remains a common space where goods and services are exchanged. The disruptive change came with the staging of products and services through digital channels and the audio's function appearance with more punch and range.

In the era of digital consumption, the tourism and aviation industries sell wonderful dreams, and they use fine words in promotion campaigns. Each TV, YouTube video or image is another little legend about how to consume a certain product or service to make our lives better.

Advertising campaigns on digital channels and social media are exceptional because of the fast reach of a broad target audience, content marketing and inter-activity, all of which are wrapped in a magical, romantic and travelling atmosphere. Romanticism, which promotes variety, fits well with tourist consumerism. This wonderful union, which I call 'Romantourism', has given rise to the infinite 'experience market' on which the modern tourism industry is based. The beginning of the 'Gran Tour' in the 17th century was based on the principles of Romanticism-Tourism-Freedom and only undertaken by the very rich, mainly the sons of the aristocracy, who often travelled abroad under the care of a tutor. The chief destinations were the great cities of the Renaissance (Paris, Turin, Milan, Venice, Florence, Verona, Mantua, Siena and Rome) and the remains of classical civilisations, which usually included the excavations at Herculaneum and Pompeii in Naples.

The tourism industry does not sell airline tickets, visits to the Caminito del Rey in Malaga, Spain (it is a walkway pinned along the steep walls of a narrow gorge), dinners in Michelin star restaurants or hotel rooms; it 'sells experiences.' New York is not a city, nor is Spain a country, both are experiences, the consumption of which is supposed to broaden our horizons, satisfy our needs and human potential and make us happier. Thanks to the democratisation and connectivity of air travel, new technologies, the evolution of airports in large cities and mass marketing campaigns, the use of standardised package products and mass consumption became the so-called phenomenon of mass tourism. Welcome to the world of tourism, its wonderful dreams and experiences and its free international trade.

On the contrary, Turner and Ash (1975) defend that societies have created 'Pleasure Peripheries' to which they can withdraw from the strains of urban living. These are fantasy places that provide a totally artificial life. Most often, they are in areas of extreme poverty, social injustice and primitive culture, but for the tourist, they are exotic and picturesque. Tourism brings with it enormous economic and political problems. The city of Varadero in Cuba is an example of the contradictions that 'capitalist and neoliberal' tourism may generate in a socialist country, where the tourism and urban model are sometimes planned according to capital from international hotel chains (González et al., 2014). According to Wang and Wall (2007) in the island province of Hainan (China), the economic benefits of tourism growth were considered more important than their social consequences, such as the forced displacement of the population of a village.

The pandemic spurred a new wave of marketing creativity as companies were forced to innovate. Since then, what the consumer needs from brands has changed, their behaviour has become more sophisticated, emotional and purpose-driven and it's up to companies to dig deeper to formulate campaigns that will resonate with their targets. In the years to come, large tourism and aviation companies will display new tourism experiences under the umbrella of AI, virtual reality (VR), metaverse, hologram, augmented reality (AR) and nanotechnology tools, which will enable consumers to choose and enjoy their trips at home. The reader can see an example of metaverse tourism in this link (https://youtu.be/U9MsTzMwRpo), Nike Japan's Air Max Day 3D billboard advertising in 2022 (https://youtu.be/N6v7HQiCNiQ) or another brand (https://youtu.be/gZ_8YwxjYS4). The pandemic and war crisis are the beginning but not the end, and both have the potential to affect not only the daily airport's operations but also the extensive array of potential stakeholders like airlines, hotels, rental cars, restaurants, shopping and logistics, among many others, in this globalised and free trade economy.

References

Abdullah, M., Dias, C., Muley, D., & Shahin, M. (2020). Exploring the impacts of COVID-19 on travel behavior and mode preferences. *Transportation Research Interdisciplinary Perspectives*, *8*, 100255.

ACI. (2017). Airport digital transformation. https://aci.aero/Media/98748da4-556a-468d-b6e4-2cb36778bc71/gjg-8A/About&hx0025;20ACI/Priorities/IT&hx0025;20-&hx0025;20New/Documentation/Airport&hx0025;20Digital&hx0025;20Transformation&hx0025;20V1.0.pdf. Accessed on August 12, 2022.

Adler, L. (1966). Symbiotic marketing. *Harvard Business Review*, *44*, 59–71.

Aircargo News. (2019). Poster campaign for consumers: How air cargo delivers the goods. https://www.aircargonews.net/business/supply-chains/poster-campaign-for-consumers-how-air-cargo-delivers-the-goods/. Accessed on August 14, 2022.

Aircargo News. (2022). UPS adds Billund freighter flight. https://www.aircargonews.net/airlines/freighter-operator/ups-adds-billund-freighter-flight/. Accessed on August 13, 2022.

Airline for Europe. (2021). Europe's air cargo carriers pivotal in COVID-19 fight. https://a4e.eu/publications/europes-air-cargo-carriers-pivotal-in-covid-19-fight/. Accessed on August 8, 2022.

Airport World. (2022). Cargo volumes in Hong Kong exceed five million tones in 2021. https://airport-world.com/cargo-volumes-in-hong-kong-exceed-five-million-tonnes-in-2021/. Accessed on August 9, 2022.

Al Saed, B., Upadhya, A., & Saleh, M. H. (2020). Role of airline promotion activities in destination branding: Case of Dubai vis-à-vis Emirates airline. *European Research on Management and Business Economics, 26*(3), 121–126.

Amirkhanpour, M., Vrontis, D., & Thrassou, A. (2014). Mobile marketing: A contemporary strategic perspective. *International Journal of Technology Marketing, 9*(3), 252–269.

Arrosid, I., & Munandar, A. (2018). Illocutionary acts in online airline advertising slogans. *Lexicon, 5*(1), 46–54.

Baxter, G., & Srisaeng, P. (2018). Cooperating to compete in the global air cargo industry: The case of the DHL express and Lufthansa cargo A.G. joint venture airline 'AeroLogic'. *Infrastructure, 3*(1), 7.

Beeton, S. (2004). Rural tourism in Australia has the gaze altered? Tracking rural images through film and tourism promotion. *International Journal of Tourism Research, 6*(3), 125–135.

Bhagwati, J. (2007). *In defense of globalization.* Oxford University Press.

Boeing. (2022). Boeing launches 777-8 freighter to serve growing demand for cargo, enhanced environmental performance. https://boeing.mediaroom.com/2022-01-31-Boeing-Launches-777-8-Freighter-to-Serve-Growing-Demand-for-Cargo,-Enhanced-Environmental-Performance. Accessed on August 9, 2022.

Bombelli, A. (2020). Integrators' global networks: A topology analysis with insights into the effect of the COVID-19 pandemic. *Journal of Transport Geography, 87*, 102815.

Bombelli, A., Santos, B. F., & Tavasszy, L. (2020). Analysis of the air cargo transport network using a complex network theory perspective. *Transportation Research Part E: Logistics and Transportation Review, 138*, 101959.

Buhalis, D., & O'Connor, P. (2005). Information communication technology revolutionizing tourism. *Tourism Recreation Research, 30*(3), 7–16.

Camilleri, M. A. (2018). The promotion of responsible tourism management through digital media. *Tourism Planning & Development, 15*(6), 653–671.

CAPA. (2015). *Airport advertising – An overlooked revenue opportunity. CAPA's guide to the state of the art.* https://centreforaviation.com/analysis/reports/air-%20port-advertising–an-overlooked-revenue-opportuni-%20ty-capas-guide-to-the-state-of-the-art-220188. Accessed on July 24, 2022.

CCCI. (2020). Big brand's international marketing and localization mistakes. https://ccci.am/big-brands-international-marketing-and-localization-mistakes/. Accessed on July 29, 2022.

Chen, Y.-C., Huang, H.-H., Chiu, S.-M., & Lee, C. (2021). Joint promotion partner recommendation systems using data from location-based social networks. *ISPRS International Journal of Geo-Information, 10*(2), 57.

Chingchuang, C., Ono, K., Watanabe, M., & Paskevicius, A. (2020). The study of information system and its suitability for each media channel at airports in Thailand. *Journal of the Science of Design*, *4*(1), 59–66.

Conde, E. M., Ramirez, R., & Fernández, A. (2010). Evaluation of the tourist positioning of a destination, manzanillo case, Mexico. *TURyDES*, *3*(8), 1–29.

Custer, R. L. (1984). Profile of the pathological gambler. *The Journal of Clinical Psychiatry*, *45*(12), 35–38.

Dallas-Fort Worth International Airport. (2015). *Social media strategy executive overview.* https://silo.tips/download/dfw-international-airport-social-media-strategy-executive-overview. Accessed on August 10, 2022.

Darmawan, A., Wong, H., & Thorstenson, A. (2018). Integration of promotion and production decisions in sales and operations planning. *International Journal of Production Research*, *56*(12), 4186–4206.

de Haas, M., Faber, R., & Hamersma, M. (2020). How COVID-19 and the Dutch 'intelligent lockdown' change activities, work and travel behaviour: Evidence from longitudinal data in the Netherlands. *Transportation Research Interdisciplinary Perspectives*, *6*, 100150.

De Vos, J. (2020). The effect of COVID-19 and subsequent social distancing on travel behavior. *Transportation Research Interdisciplinary Perspectives*, *5*, 100121.

DHL. (2020). DHL supply chain expands its operations in the air cargo transportation with an exclusive hub in the main airport in Brazil. https://www.dhl.com/br-en/home/press/press-archive/2020/dhl-supply-chain-expands-its-operations-in-the-air-cargo-transportation-with-an-exclusive-hub-in-the-main-airport-in-brazil.html. Accessed on August 14, 2022.

DHL. (2021). DHL launch international brand campaign to celebrate the release of the new James Bond film 'No time to die'. https://www.dhl.com/global-en/home/press/press-archive/2021/dhl-launch-international-brand-campaign-to-celebrate-the-release-of-the-new-james-bond-film-no-time-to-die.html. Accessed on August 22, 2022.

DMO's Tourism Ireland. (2022). *Tourism Ireland's submission to the joint committee on media, tourism, arts, culture, sport and the Gaeltacht.* https://niopa.qub.ac.uk/bitstream/NIOPA/13326/1/SUBMISSION-TO-JOINT-COMMITTEE-ON-MEDIA%2C-TOURISM%2C-ARTS%2C-CULTURE%2C-SPORT-AND-THE-GAELTACHT%2C-APRIL-2021_2.pdf. Accessed on July 31, 2022.

Duarte, P. A. D. O., & Silva, S. C. E. (2018). The role of consumer-cause identification and attitude in the intention to purchase cause-related products. *International Marketing Review*, *37*(4), 603–620.

Dublin Airport. (2019). Dublin airport wins social media award. https://www.dublinairport.com/latest-news/2019/05/31/dublin-airport-wins-social-media-award. Accessed on July 31, 2022.

El Kssaimi, F.-Z., & Develi, E. L. (2022). 'Neuro-marketing' perspective on consumer behaviour. *Journal of Industrial Policy and Technology Management*, *5*(1), 57–73.

Elbaz, A. M., Soliman, M., Al-Alawi, A., Al-Romeedy, B. S., & Mekawy, M. (2022). Customer responses to airline companies' service failure and recovery strategies: The moderating role of service failure habit. *Tourism Review*, *78*(1), 1–17.

Emirates Airlines. (2022). Emirates takes Dubai's vision of tomorrow to the skies, launching museum of the future custom A380 livery. https://www.emirates.com/

media-centre/emirates-takes-dubais-vision-of-tomorrow-to-the-skies-launching-museum-of-the-future-custom-a380-livery/. Accessed on August 2, 2022.

European Commission. (2014). Guidelines on state aid to airports and airlines. *Official Journal of the European.* https://eur-lex.europa.eu/legal-content/EN/TXT/?uri=CELEX%3A52014XC0404%2801%29. Accessed on August 15, 2022.

European Commission. (2019). State air: France to recover $8.5 millions of illegal aid to Ryanair at Montpellier airport. https://ec.europa.eu/commission/presscorner/detail/en/IP_19_4991. Accessed on August 13, 2022.

FedEx. (2022). FedEx express main partner of EuroGames 2022. https://newsroom.fedex.com/newsroom/europe-english/fedex-express-main-partner-of-eurogames-2022. Accessed on August 14, 2022.

Felsenstein, D., & Fleischer, A. (2003). Local festivals and tourism promotion: The role of public assistance and visitor expenditure. *Journal of Travel Research, 41*(4), 385–392.

Fisher, C. E., Chin, M.-D. L., & Klitzman, R. (2010). Defining neuromarketing: Practices and professional challenges. *Harvard Review of Psychiatry, 18*(4), 230–237.

Florido-Benítez, L. (2016a). La implementación del mobile marketing. In *Como herramienta multidisciplinar en el sector turístico y aeroportuario.* Editorial Académica Española.

Florido-Benítez, L. (2016b). The influence of demographic and situational characteristics in satisfaction and decision of tourism activities via mobile marketing. *Cuadernos de Turismo, 38,* 143–165.

Florido-Benítez, L. (2016c). Mobile apps: Improve airports' brand image and differentiate among competitors. *ARA Journal of Tourism Research, 6*(1), 39–53.

Florido-Benítez, L. (2020). Seville airport: A success of good relationship management and interoperability in the improvement of air connectivity. *Revista de Turismo Estudos e Prácticas, 5*(2), 1–30.

Florido-Benítez, L. (2021a). The effects of COVID-19 on Andalusian tourism and aviation sector. *Tourism Review, 76*(4), 829–857.

Florido-Benítez, L. (2021b). The supremacy of airports generates a high dependence on the tourist destination Spain. *Revista de Turismo Estudos & Prácticas, 10*(2), 1–31.

Florido-Benítez, L. (2022a). International mobile marketing: A satisfactory concept for companies and users in times of pandemic. *Benchmarking: An International Journal, 29*(6), 1826–1856.

Florido-Benítez, L. (2022b). The impact of tourism promotion in tourist destinations: A bibliometric study. *International Journal of Tourism Cities, 8*(4), 844–882.

Florido-Benítez, L. (2022c). The safety-hygiene air corridor between UK and Spain will coexist with COVID-19. *Logistics, 6*(52), 1–22.

Florido-Benítez, L. (2022d). The world airport awards as a quality distinctive and marketing tool for airports. *Journal of Airline Operations and Aviation Management, 1*(2), 54–81.

Florido-Benítez, L. (2023a). The location of airport an added value to improve the number of visitors at US museums. *Case of Studies on Transport Policy, 11,* 100961.

Florido-Benítez, L. (2023b). The role of the top 50 US cargo airports and 25 air cargo airlines in the logistics of E-commerce companies. *Logistics, 7*(1), 8.

Florido-Benítez, L. (2023c). Bridges: A tourist attraction and iconic element at urban cities' tourism promotion websites. *International Journal of Tourism Cities, 9*(3), 771–787.

Florido-Benítez, L., & del Alcázar, B. (2020). Airports as ambassadors of the marketing strategies of Spanish tourist destination. *Gran Tour, 21,* 47–78.

González, J. M., Salinas, E., Navarro, E., Artigues, A. A., Remond, R., Yrigoy, I., Echarri, M., & Arias, Y. (2014). The city of Varadero (Cuba) and the urban construction of a tourist enclave. *Urban Affairs Review, 50*(2), 206–243.

Gould, K. T. (2019). Meeting today's challenges in travel retail with digital commerce marketplaces. *Journal of Airport Management, 13*(3), 245–253.

Grimme, W., Maertens, S., & Schröpfer, A. (2018). Options for traffic growth at smaller European airports under the European commission's guidelines on state aid. *Transportation Research Procedia, 35,* 130–139.

Gu, H. (2019). Airport revenue diversification. *Journal of Management Science & Engineering Research, 2*(1), 25–28.

Habel, J., Alavi, S., & Linsenmayer, K. (2021). From personal to online selling: How relational selling shapes salespeople's promotion of e-commerce channels. *Journal of Business Research, 132,* 373–382.

Halpern, N., & Graham, A. (2022). *Airport marketing* (2nd ed.). Routledge.

Halpern, N., Mwesiumo, D., Suau-Sanchez, P., Budd, T., & Bråthen, S. (2021). Ready for digital transformation? The effect of organisational readiness, innovation, airport size and ownership on digital change at airports. *Journal of Air Transportation, 90,* 101949.

Han, H., Quan, W., Gil-Cordero, E., Cabrera-Sánchez, J.-P., & Yu, J. (2021). Performance of retail stores at airports and their role in boosting traveler satisfaction and willingness to repurchase. *Sustainability, 13*(2), 590.

Harari, Y. N. (2016). *Homo Deus. A brief history of tomorrow.* Harvill Secker.

Harry, R. (2020). East Midlands airport experiences cargo growth amid Covid-19 outbreak. 2020. *Aircargo News,* 1. https://www.aircargonews.net/cargo-airport/east-midlands-airport-experiences-cargo-growth-amid-covid-19-outbreak/. Accessed on August 7, 2022.

IATA. (2020a). *Impact of COVID on European aviation (August 2020).* https://www.iata.org/contentassets/c0b84098b8d845d2a01f78f637521dbe/impact-covid-european-aviation-august-2020.pdf. Accessed on March 16, 2024.

IATA. (2020b). *The value of air cargo. Air cargo makes it happen.* https://www.iata.org/contentassets/4d3961c878894c8a8725278607d8ad52/air-cargo-brochure.pdf. Accessed on August 6, 2022.

IATA. (2022a). *Global outlook for air transport. Times of turbulence.* https://www.iata.org/en/iata-repository/publications/economic-reports/airline-industry-economic-performance—june-2022—report/. Accessed on July 23, 2022.

IATA. (2022b). *Economic performance of the airline industry.* https://www.iata.org/en/iata-repository/publications/economic-reports/airline-industry-economic-performance-june-2020-report/. Accessed on August 15, 2022.

INE. (2020). Contabilidad regional de España. Resultados por Comunidades y Ciudades Autónomas. https://www.ine.es/dyngs/INEbase/es/operacion.htm?c=Estadistica_C&cid=1254736167628&menu=resultados&idp=1254735576581#!tabs-1254736158133. Accessed on August 15, 2022.

Insider Intelligence. (2021). *Worldwide digital ad spending 2021 report.* https://www. insiderintelligence.com/content/worldwide-digital-ad-spending-2021. Accessed on July 24, 2022.

Islam, T., Pitafi, A. H., Arya, V., Wang, Y., Akhtar, N., Mubarik, S., & Xiaobei, L. (2021). Panic buying in the COVID-19 pandemic: A multi-country examination. *Journal of Retailing and Consumer Services, 59*, 102357.

ITA. (2022). Free trade agreement overview. https://www.trade.gov/free-trade-agreement-overview. Accessed on August 7, 2022.

Krum, C. (2010). *Mobile marketing: Finding your customers no matter where they are.* Pearson Education Inc.

Lai, M. T. H., Yeung, E., & Leung, R. (2022). Understanding tourists' policing attitudes and travel intentions towards a destination during an ongoing social movement. *Journal of Hospitality and Tourism Insights, 6*(29), 874–891.

Lawrence, J. M., Crecelius, A. T., Scheer, L. K., & Patil, A. (2019). Multichannel strategies for managing the profitability of business-to-business customers. *Journal of Marketing Research, 56*(3), 479–497.

Lawrence, J. M., Scheer, L. K., Crecelius, A. T., & Lam, S. K. (2021). Salesperson dual agency in price negotiations. *Journal of Marketing, 85*(2), 89–109.

Lee, N., Chamberlain, L., & Brandes, L. (2018). Welcome to the jungle! The neuromarketing literature through the eyes of a newcomer. *European Journal of Marketing, 52*(1/2), 4–38.

Lee, Y.-K., & Park, J.-W. (2016). Impact of a sustainable brand on improving business performance of airport enterprises: The case of Incheon international airport. *Journal of Air Transport Management, 53*, 46–53.

Lim, W. M. (2018). Demystifying neuromarketing. *Journal of Business Research, 91*, 205–220.

Lindstrom, M. (2010). *Buy ology: Truth and lies about why we buy* (1st ed.). Crown Business.

Los Angeles International Airport. (2022). LAX guides, tips, art & amenities. https:// www.flylax.com/lax-guides-tips-and-amenities. Accessed on July 28, 2022.

Luisetto, M., Almukhtar, N., Ghulam, R.-M., Rafa, A. Y., Khan, F. A., Hamid, G. A., Cabianca, L., & Ahmadabadi, B. N. (2018). Endogenous archeological sciences: Anatomy, physiology, neuroscience, biochemistry, immunology, pharmacology, oncology, genetics as instrument for a new field of investigation? Modern global aspects for a new discipline. *Open Access Journal Addiction and Pschology, 1*(3), 1–18.

Makridakis, S. (2017). The forthcoming Artificial Intelligence (AI) revolution: Its impact on society and firms. *Futures, 90*, 46–60.

Malighetti, P., Martini, G., Redondi, R., & Scotti, D. (2019). Air transport networks of global integrators in the more liberalized Asian air cargo industry. *Transport Policy, 80*, 12–23.

Marketing91. (2019). Marketing mix of UPS united parcel service. https://www. marketing91.com/marketing-mix-of-ups/. Accessed on July 30, 2022.

Masa'deh, R., AL-Haddad, S., Al Abed, D., Khalil, H., AlMomani, L., & Khirfan, T. (2021). The impact of social media activities on brand equity. *Information, 12*(11), 477.

Mashrur, F. R., Rahman, K. M., Miya, M. T. I., Vaidyanathan, R., Anwar, S. F., Sarker, F., & Mamun, K. A. (2022). An intelligent neuromarketing system for predicting consumers' future choice from electroencephalography signals. *Physiology & Behavior, 253*, 113847.

Mayer, R. (2016). Airport classification based on cargo characteristics. *Journal of Transport Geography*, *54*, 53–65.

Memphis International Airport. (2022). Strategic overview 2022–2025. https:// flymemphis.com/strategic-overview/. Accessed on August 23, 2022.

Monsen, E., Mahagaonkar, P., & Dienes, C. (2012). Entrepreneurship in India: The question of occupational transition. *Small Business Economics*, *39*, 359–382.

Moreno-Luna, L., Robina-Ramírez, R., Sánchez, M. S.-O., & Castro-Serrano, J. (2021). Tourism and sustainability in times of COVID-19: The case of Spain. *International Journal of Environmental Research and Public Health*, *18*(4), 1859.

Morgan, A., Taylor, T., & Adair, D. (2020). Sport event sponsorship management from the sponsee's perspective. *Sport Management Review*, *23*(5), 838–851.

Morrell, P. S., & Klein, T. (2018). *Moving boxes by air: The economics of international air cargo*. Routledge.

Müller, A., Joshi, M., & Tobias, A. T. (2022). Excessive shopping on the internet: Recent trends in compulsive buying-shopping disorder. *Current Opinion in Behavioral Sciences*, *44*, 101116.

Naeem, M. (2021). Understanding the customer psychology of impulse buying during COVID-19 pandemic: Implications for retailers. *International Journal of Retail & Distribution Management*, *49*(3), 377–393.

Nghiem-Phu, B., & Suter, J. R. (2018). Airport image: An exploratory study of McCarran international airport. *Journal of Air Transport Management*, *67*, 72–84.

Nuseir, M. T. (2020). The effects of sponsorship on the promotion of sports events. *International Journal of Business Innovation and Research*, *22*(2), 191–207.

Obembe, D., Kolade, O., Obembe, F., Owoseni, A., & Mafimisebi, O. (2021). Covid-19 and the tourism industry: An early stage sentiment analysis of the impact of social media and stakeholder communication. *International Journal of Information Management Data Insights*, *1*(2), 100040.

OECD. (2020a). Average daily time spent using internet, mobile internet and social media, 2019. In *OECD digital economy outlook 2020*. OECD Publishing. https:// www.oecd-ilibrary.org/science-and-technology/average-daily-time-spent-using-internet-mobile-internet-and-social-media-2019_9596e864-en. Accessed on August 2, 2022.

OECD. (2020b). *COVID-19 and the retail sector: Impact and policy response*. https:// www.oecd.org/coronavirus/policy-responses/covid-19-and-the-retail-sector-impact-and-policy-responses-371d7599/. Accessed on August 12, 2022.

Orzan, G., Zara, I.-A., & Purcarea, V.-L. (2012). Neuromarketing techniques in pharmaceutical drugs advertising: A discussion and agenda for future research. *Journal of Medicine and Life*, *5*(4), 428–432.

Pantano, E., & Priporas, C.-V. (2016). The effect of mobile retailing on consumers' purchasing experiences: A dynamic perspective. *Computers in Human Behavior*, *61*, 548–555.

Pike, S., Pontes, N., & Kotsi, F. (2021). Stopover destination attractiveness: A quasi experimental approach. *Journal of Destination Marketing & Management*, *19*, 100514.

Plassmann, H., Venkatraman, V., Huettel, S., & Yoon, C. (2015). Consumer neuroscience: Applications, challenges, and possible solutions. *Journal of Marketing Research*, *52*(4), 427–435.

Pratt, S., McCabe, S., Cortes-Jimenez, I., & Blake, A. (2010). Measuring the effectiveness of destination marketing campaigns: Comparative analysis of conversion studies. *Journal of Travel Research, 49*(2), 179–190.

Renvoise, P., & Morin, C. (2005). *Neuromarketing: Le nerf de la vente.* De Boeck Supérieur.

Rodrigue, J.-P. (2020). The distribution network of Amazon and the footprint of freight digitalization. *Journal of Transport Geography, 88*, 102825.

Roy, D. P. (2010). The impact of congruence in cause marketing campaigns for service firms. *Journal of Services Marketing, 24*(3), 255–263.

Ruane, L. (2013). Signs of our times: Airport ads are big business. https://eu.usatoday.com/story/money/business/2013/09/22/airport-ads-big-business/2842833/. Accessed on July 26, 2022.

Ryu, Y. K., & Park, J.-W. (2019). Investigating the effect of experience in an airport on pleasure, satisfaction, and airport image: A case study on Incheon international airport. *Sustainability, 11*(17), 4616.

Savin-Baden, M. (2021). What are postdigital humans? In M. Savin-Baden (Ed.), *Postdigital humans. Postdigital science and education.* Springer.

Schuller, D., & Schuller, B. W. (2018). The age of artificial emotional intelligence. *Computer, 51*(9), 38–46.

Searle, J. R., & Vanderveken, D. (1985). *Foundation of illocutionary logic.* Cambridge University Press.

Seetanah, B., Sannassee, R. V., Teeroovengadum, V., & Nunkoo, R. (2019). Air access liberalization, marketing promotion and tourism development. *International Journal of Tourism Research, 21*(1), 76–86.

Sensor Tower. (2020). Q2 2020. Store intelligence data digest. https://www.appannie.com/en/apps/ios/top/. Accessed on September 1, 2022.

Shahriar, A., Tasnim, M., Taufique, H., & Carolyn, S. (2021). What omnichannel really means? *Journal of Strategic Marketing, 29*(7), 567–573.

Statista. (2020). *Mobile phone usage for online holiday bookings in the United Kingdom (UK) 2017, by age.* https://www.statista.com/statistics/380969/online-holiday-booking-by-device-and-age-uk/. Accessed on August 21, 2022.

Statista. (2021). *Mobile commerce in the United States – Statistics & facts.* https://www.statista.com/topics/1185/mobile-commerce/#dossierKeyfigures/. Accessed on August 22, 2022.

Straker, K., & Wrigley, C. (2016). Translating emotional insights into digital channel designs: Opportunities to enhance the airport experience. *Journal of Hospitality and Tourism Technology, 7*(2), 135–157.

Straker, K., & Wrigley, C. (2018). Engaging passengers across digital channels: An international study of 100 airports. *Journal of Hospitality and Tourism Management, 34*, 82–92.

Strange, G. (2020). Debating free international trade. *The American Journal of Economics and Sociology, 79*, 25–47.

Styvén, M. E., & Wallström, Å. (2019). Benefits and barriers for the use of digital channels among small tourism companies. *Scandinavian Journal of Hospitality and Tourism, 19*(1), 27–46.

Sutcliffe, A. (1979). Environmental control and planning in European capitals 1850–1914, London, Paris and Berlin. In I. Hammarstrom & T. Hall (Eds.), *Growth and transformation of the modern city* (pp. 71–88). University of Stockholm.

Szymczak, A. (2018). The use of mobile applications by airlines in the process of marketing communication. *Marketing of Scientific and Research Organizations, 29*(3), 133–153.

Taylor, R. (2011). Epic fail for Qantas Twitter competition. https://www.reuters.com/article/us-qantas-idUSTRE7AL0HB20111122. Accessed on July 29, 2022.

The Moodie Davitt Report. (2020). *'LAX order now': Los Angeles airport expands mobile ordering, payment and collection.* https://www.moodiedavittreport.com/lax-order-now-los-angeles-airport-expands-mobile-ordering-payment-and-collection/. Accessed on August 5, 2022.

The Moodie Davitt Report. (2021). *Munich and Düsseldorf airports launch joint advertising initiative.* https://www.moodiedavittreport.com/munich-and-dusseldorf-airports-launch-joint-advertising-initiative/#:~:text=GERMANY.,runs%20initially%20to%20year%20end. Accessed on August 4, 2022.

Torres, E. N., Wei, W., Hua, N., & Cheb, P.-J. (2019). Customer emotions minute by minute: How guests experience different emotions within the same service environment. *International Journal of Hospitality Management, 77*, 128–138.

Triantafillidou, A., & Yannas, P. (2020). Social media crisis communication in racially charged crises: Exploring the effects of social media and image restoration strategies. *Computers in Human Behavior, 106*, 106269.

Turner, L., & Ash, J. (1975). *The golden hordes: International tourism and the pleasure periphery.* Editorial Constable.

Ulman, Y. I., Cakar, T., & Yildiz, G. (2015). Ethical issues in neuromarketing: 'I consume, therefore I am!'. *Science and Engineering Ethics, 21*(5), 1271–1284.

Um, T., Chung, N., & Stienmetz, J. (2022). Factors affecting consumers' impulsive buying behavior in tourism mobile commerce using SEM and fsQCA. *Journal of Vacation Marketing, 29*(2), 256–274.

United Nations. (2022). Losing 25,000 to hunger every day. https://www.un.org/en/chronicle/article/losing-25000-hunger-every-day. Accessed on August 4, 2022.

Varadarajan, R., & Rajaratnam, D. (1986). Symbiotic marketing revisited. *Journal of Marketing, 50*(1), 7–17.

Volkhausen, N. (2022). Regional airports and economic growth: Evidence from the single European aviation market. *Regional Economic Development Research, 3*(2), 117–143.

Wang, S., Liu, Y., Du, Y., & Wang, X. (2021). Effect of the COVID-19 pandemic on consumer's impulsive buying: The moderating tole of moderate thinking. *International Journal of Environmental Research and Public Health, 18*(21), 11116.

Wang, Y., & Wall, G. (2007). Administrative arrangements and displacement compensation in. Top-down tourism planning. A case from Hainan Province, (China). *Tourism Management, 28*(1), 70–82.

Wattanacharoensil, W., Fakfare, P., & Graham, A. (2021). Airportscape and its effect on airport sense of place and destination image perception. *Tourism Review, 77*(2), 549–569.

Wei, W., Zheng, Y., Zhang, L., & Line, N. (2022). Leveraging customer to customer interactions to create immersive and memorable theme park experiences. *Journal of Hospitality and Tourism Insights, 5*(3), 647–662.

Wells, J. D., Parboteeah, V., & Valacich, J. S. (2011). Online impulse buying: Understanding the interplay between consumer impulsiveness and website quality. *Journal of the Association for Information Systems, 12*(1), 3.

WTO. (2022). Principle of the trading system. https://www.wto.org/english/thewto_e/whatis_e/tif_e/fact2_e.htm. Accessed on August 4, 2022.

WTTC. (2022). *Economic impact reports*. https://wttc.org/Research/Economic-Impact. Accessed on August 14, 2022.

Yan, K., Hua, G., Cheng, T. C. E., Wang, S., & Dong, J.-X. (2022). Joint promotion of cross-market retailers: Models and analysis. *International Journal of Production Research, 60*(11), 3397–3418.

Yu, H., & Chen, D. (2019). New optimal control decisions for channel system with lagged effect: Dynamic advertising and pricing cases. *IEEE Access, 7*, 75350–75359.

Yu, H., Chen, D., & Huang, C. (2018). A study of dynamic joint promotion strategies in the distribution channel. *Systems Science & Control Engineering, 6*(1), 409–420.

Zaharia, S. E., Pietreanu, C. V., & Flăminzeanu, M. C. (2022). Air cargo transport development in central and eastern Europe and Baltic countries. In *2022 IEEE 6th International Conference on Logistics Operations Management (GOL)*, Strasbourg, France (pp. 1–10).

Chapter 8

Airport and Aviation International Awards as a Promotion Marketing Tool

Abstract

The airport's international recognition and attractive potential by awards' private and public organisations or governments have awakened a great level of interest from airport and airline operators, researchers and academics in the aviation industry. Some of the most important prestigious aviation and tourism accolades worldwide, like the World Airport Awards (Skytrax), Airports Council International (ACI) World's annual Airports Service Quality 'ASQ Awards' (Airport Council International) and the World Travel Awards (World Travel & Tourism Council), recognise and reward the excellence of services and products provided by airports and airlines. Consequently, the winning airports have global recognition depending on the award's category and empower the airport's brand image against its main competitors. These awards have become true marketing windows, where all airports want to win to promote their brand image and distinguish the airport's position as a world leader in the aviation industry. This topic and the dissemination of information at the airport's website and other digital channels will be tackled in Chapter 8.

8.1 Brand Image of Airports

Large airports have established their own brand images as a strategy of positioning in the aviation and tourism industries, helping to improve the location of the airport and city and unifying like-minded passengers based on their choice of airport. Airports' brands represent the quality of service, personalised products and services, access to premium passenger lounges and choice of retail stores, among other benefits that each airport may offer. It is essential to create an airport's brand image through the selection of appropriate brand values and their most efficient use for the airport's brand positioning worldwide. But building a high airport's brand image positioning in the aviation and tourism sectors

Airport Marketing Strategies, 155–164

Copyright © 2024 Lázaro Florido-Benítez

Published under exclusive licence by Emerald Publishing Limited

doi:10.1108/978-1-83608-082-420241008

requires more than just linking an airport with a particular name, logo/isotype/imagotype/isologo symbol and creating a promotion campaign. To create a unique and differentiated airport's brand positioning on digital channels, the airport operator needs to develop strategies related to the needs of passengers, highlight the airport's operability, differentiate and stage its airport business portfolio and design a value proposition meaningfully against its major competitors according to the airport's category and target market.

In line with these priorities defined and applied in the airport's positioning, strategies, goals and actions at the marketing plan and digital channels, these actions will encourage passenger willingness to spend more time at select airports that offer these perks as a means of incentives to stay there longer. Kefallonitis and Kalligiannis (2019) found that the more time passengers spend at an airport, the higher the likelihood of: improving emotional affinity with the airport, building a stronger association with the airport's brand and raising revenue from airport services and stores. In this marketing and positioning context, we wondered: Why should airport operators participate in international award competitions?

8.2 The Positioning of the Airport's Brand Image Through Marketing International Award Organisations

The growth of international awards, events and recognitions, as well as other aspects of airports' activities, by private and public organisations and governments, has awakened a great level of interest from airport and airline operators, researchers and academics in the aviation industry. International awards managed by organisations are the best scenario to position and promote the airport's brand image and products and services around the world because airports play an active role in the promotion and delivery of tourism products and services in their host cities. The COVID-19 pandemic is accelerating the change of the rules of the game in air transport and tourism around the world (Florido-Benítez, 2021a, 2021b). A study carried out by Straker and Wrigley (2016) revealed that airports that are using digital channels as a communication tool are higher ranked compared to those that currently do not utilise them to their full extent. For instance, Florido-Benítez (2022a) proposes that these operational strategies are heavily focused on enhancing consumers' travel experiences at airports and airlines. These operational and technological strategies implemented by airports are highly valued by passenger surveys in the Skytrax World Airport Awards; these are the most prestigious qualities in air transport, and they are known as The Olympics of the aviation industry. Skytrax is a consultancy firm based in London, United Kingdom.

The Skytrax World Airport Awards are voted by customers in the largest, annual global airport customer satisfaction survey. The awards are based on 13 million airport survey questionnaires completed by 106 different nationalities of airline customers during the survey period. Skytrax is a specialised advisor in research and quality for the air transport industry. It advises airports and airlines around the world on quality improvements and quality leadership (World Airport Awards, 2021a). The word 'awards' generally refers to the application processes and ceremonial events through which organisations that have implemented a business excellence framework are formally and publicly recognised (Grigg & Mann, 2008).

Air transport faces the challenge of improving the processes of information communication and transmission, customer experiences and relationships based on real-time information exchange (Queiroz et al., 2021). As stated by Graham (2019), competition in the airport industry assumes three different levels: competition among groups of airports, competition among airports and competition inside airports. With increasing competition between airports, perceived quality and consumer satisfaction have become a key focus of management and the most important tools to maintain a competitive advantage (Florido-Benítez, 2020). Awards can advance knowledge about management and organisational learning theory, standardise processes and assist public, private and non-profit sector managers in determining which strategies are best suited for their organisations (Milakovich, 2004).

Globalisation has affected relations between airports and investors. It has become common for airports to design and justify marketing strategies based on the need to appeal to potential external investors, and it has become equally commonplace for foreign investors to condition airports' goals. One of the results of this has been the competition between airports to attract new investors, a competition in which airports compete to best fulfil the needs and requirements of investors and investment projects.

Airport operators must clearly adapt to the new challenges of aviation and tourism activities. In 2021, the Skytrax World Airport Awards were different due to the pandemic, with major airports falling rank and an entirely new award category (i.e. COVID-19 Airport Excellence Awards) dedicated to the incredible efforts made by the aviation industry. Promoting public confidence in aviation safety through scientific propaganda of safety and hygiene knowledge is vital and a strong impetus for economic recovery around the world. In this complex economic situation and its difficulties, confidence is very valuable. Xiaozheng et al. (2020) found that during the pandemic, airports' safety and hygiene communication was by means of advertising and publicity. Aviation safety knowledge and other relevant information can be directly transmitted to consumers through digital channels to communicate the relationship between production and demand and attract consumers' attention and interest (Florido-Benítez, 2022c).

Fig. 40 displays World Airport Awards by category in 2021, and these recognise airport excellence in customer experience worldwide based on the survey's data. For example, Singapore Changi airport (IATA: SIN) has been the best airport in the world for 8 years in a row, from 2013 to 2020 (World Airport Awards, 2021b). This implemented several proactive strategies to enhance airport revenues through commercial activities, using e-commerce channels to reach out to airport customers. Changi airport turns itself into a destination through business partnership collaborations. Projects at the Singapore Changi airport

Best Website and Digital Services	Best Airport Leisure Amenities	Best PMR and Accessible Facilities	Best Improved Airports	World's Best Airports	COVID-19 Airport Excellence	World's Cleanest Airports	Best Regional Airports
Best Airport Security							Best Airport Hotels
Best Transit Airports		Skytrax World Airport Awards by Categories					Best Domestic Airports
Best Baggage Delivery							
Best Airport Immigration	Best Airport Dinning	Best Airport Shopping	Best Airport Staff	Best Low-Cost Terminal	Best Airport Terminals	Best Airports by PAX Numbers	Best Airports by Region

Fig. 40.   Skytrax World Airport Awards by Categories in 2021.
Source: Adapted from the World Airport Awards.

include the HSBC Rain Vortex, the Shiseido Forest Valley, Canopy Park and the Changi Experience Studio (Chutiphongdech & Vongsaroj, 2022).

The Skytrax assessment is very important because this is an independent institution recommended by the global air transportation industry. Previous studies on airport service quality have shown a link between the quality of services and passengers' satisfaction as well as brand image. More recent research on airport service quality has also brought in big data and public reviews such as those from Google Review, Facebook, Twitter, TripAdvisor or Yelp platforms where passengers can leave their comments and/or ratings of their airport experience after the journey to tackle quality services in the air transport and tourism industries (see Fakfare et al., 2021; Lee & Yu, 2018; Martin-Domingo et al., 2019). The feedback from platforms like Skytrax, ACI World's ASQ Awards, World Travel Awards or Google Review can also help balance the results and allow the airport managers to develop more holistic and comprehensive viewpoints for airport quality improvement and for their own future decisions (Bunchongchit & Wattanacharoensil, 2021). Indeed, there is a high correlation between Skytrax' airport ranking and digital channel usage, like the airport's websites and apps (Florido-Benítez, 2022d).

Needless to say, domestic and international awards have become a popular marketing tool to increase the visibility of award organisers. Table 5 presents a list of international awards in the aviation and tourism industries, like the World Airport Awards, the ACI World's ASQ Awards, the World Travel Awards, the Edward Warner Award, the Aviation Industry Awards, and the Travel Retail Awards, among many others. These international awards are based on

Table 5. Recognised Awards in the Aviation and Tourism Industries.

No	Name of Awards	Managed
1	World Airport Awards	Skytrax
2	ACI World's ASQ Awards	Airport Council International
3	World Travel Awards	World Travel and Tourism Council
4	The Edward Warner Award	Inter. Civil Aviation Organization
5	Aviation Industry Awards	Business Rivers
6	The Travel Retail Awards	TR Business
7	ATW Airline Awards	ATW Air Transport World
8	Business Traveller Middle East Awards	Motivate Media Group
9	Travel and Leisure's World's Best Awards	Globehunters
10	Air Transport Awards	Hermes Air Transport Org.
11	Selling Travel Agents Choice Awards	Selling Travel Magazine
12	CAPA's Aviation Awards	CAPA Centre for aviation
13	Air Cargo News Awards	Air Cargo News Magazine
14	DestinAsian Readers' Choice Awards	DestinAsian Media Group
15	Wanderlust Travel Awards	Wanderlust Corporation
16	TTG China Travel Awards	TTG Asia Media Pte. Ltd.

Source: Compiled by the author.

recognising and rewarding the excellence of services and products and changes in the culture and performance provided by airports and airlines. Hartley and Downe (2007) indicate that international awards are used both as recognition for an organisation that has developed total quality management and to spread the quality message through digital channels. Many organisations and countries have their own national award schemes to improve quality systems. The ACI EUROPE Awards (2020) recognise excellence and outstanding achievement across a whole range of activities. They cover five traffic categories of airports, including the new category named 'Over 40 million passengers'. They also include the Eco-Innovation Award, the Accessible Airport Award, the Digital Transformation Award, the HR Excellence Award and the World Business Partners Recognition Award.

Over the past decade, there has been a proliferation of award schemes for public and private service organisations like airports, airlines, tourist destinations and online travel agencies. These awards exclusively recognise the quality, safety, performance and innovation in service delivery and governance in the aviation and tourism sectors. International awards are seen as a means both of celebrating high performance and contributing to the dissemination of good practices, with the aim of improving airports' services. In addition, the airport's brand image is universalised, which means that the airport becomes an ambassador of the city. This is localised through airport branding, which includes architectural, cultural, artistic and gastronomic characteristics. For this reason, benchmarking has become a valuable tool to improve the quality and safety of services offered by airports and airlines because it compares organisational processes and performance outputs with those of other airports or companies.

Domestic and international awards serve as a cost-effective way to disseminate knowledge about best practices for managing personnel, technology and an organisation's operability. This eliminates much of the risk approach to different improvement strategies, and it creates a demonstration effect where champions are identified as leaders of specific processes and disciplines in which they participated or competed (Milakovich, 2004). Providing incentives such as domestic and international awards, charter marks and audit standards to achieve organisational goals encourages airports and airlines to promote their brand images in the aviation and tourism industries.

These awards have become true marketing windows, where all airports want to win to promote their brand images and distinguish the airport's position as a world leader in the aviation industry. Hamad International Airport (IATA: DOH) was named the World's Best Airport by Skytrax for the second year running (2021–2022), and its diffusion by different digital channels such as digital newspapers, TV, radio, social media, tourism and aviation magazines has been overwhelmingly positive from a marketing, positioning and communication point of view. Publicity and advertising activities are an important marketing tool in the tourism and aviation marketing mix because message credibility is critical due to the intangible nature of products and services offered by companies, tourism and aviation sectors promote and sell experiences.

Publicity creates public awareness of an airport, airline, its brand, products and services through digital media coverage and other forms of communication. The free public information provided by digital media has helped to increase positive information about Hamad airport as well as minimise or respond to negative coverage. The main distinction between publicity and advertising is that publicity is a space that is not paid for by a company to promote its products and services, and this does not identify a sponsor. Publicity is media attention for a firm's products and services. It can include traditional news sources, like news shows, digital newspapers, social media, personalised messages, podcasts, blogs, apps and websites. Although publicity is not controllable by firms, it can be influenced in a favourable way, which constitutes the main task of public relations.

Kotler and Keller (2006) affirm that having no control over message content is crucial to companies because publicity might reveal negative information about a company and its products in some instances. Indeed, publicity is more credible due to the fact that communication with consumers via publicity is less common than via advertising, which brings consumers to evaluate information more critically and can lead to more negative cognitions than advertising (Eisend & Küster, 2011; Florido-Benítez, 2022b; Florido-Benítez & del Alcázar, 2020). On the contrary, advertising is a paid communication that identifies the message sponsor. Balasubramanian (1994) revealed that the primary advantage of advertising is the sponsor's control over the content, and its disadvantage is that recipients consider it less objective and more biased than publicity.

Marketing communications through digital channels are the guiding principles companies follow to communicate with their target markets. Airport operators have to be creative in their promotion campaigns and consider how their official websites and social media can be incorporated to better market their products and provide relevant information to their customers and partners. Kar (2014) suggests that the integration of the website with social media platforms presents ample challenges in terms of choosing the best possible way for such integration. Companies' websites and apps can directly engage consumers in the creative process by both producing and distributing information through collaborative writing, content sharing and social networking. In addition, even these websites can enhance the power of viral marketing by increasing the speed at which consumers share experiences and opinions with progressively larger audiences (Thackeray et al., 2008). Many firms have accelerated the development of the international business dimension of their business operations through the stimulus of international marketing activities (Florido-Benítez & Aldeanueva, 2022).

On the contrary, we need strong monitoring, regulation and enforcement efforts that will counter the users and companies' use of fake information through multiple digital means, such as social media, influencers, some digital newspapers, etc. Information quality, updating and accuracy must be guaranteed by each information source. At the end, airports' promotion campaigns are a priority to stimulate passenger demand and foreign investments (Florido-Benítez, 2024).

A major challenge for airport and airline operators is to promote suitable websites and apps for their promotion of marketing campaigns and their prizes awarded by public and private organisations. For example, the promotional benefits depend on which awards they win, particularly on how well publicised they are (Bovaird & Löffler, 2009). From a scientific point of view, the concept of rewards (benefits) from science should not be misinterpreted, as the sole reason for scientists is to obtain social status and financial gains (Florido-Benítez, 2022d; Göktepe-Hulten & Mahagaonkar, 2010). The airport's official website presence allows operators to use all sorts of media–visual, text, sound, video and animation to promote their services, challenges and accomplishments, with the intention of identifying how digital marketing can improve airport performance. The promotion campaign of marketing refers to how marketing communications are used by a company to inform clients and other stakeholders about its commercial activities and its products and services.

In today's media saturated environment, it is important for tourism and aviation operators to understand how publicity and advertising affect each other (Loda et al., 2007). Some domestic and international awards are powerful marketing tools to promote accessibility in the territory, like the Best Airports by Region, the Best PMR and Accessible Facilities or even the Access City Award

2023 competition managed by the European Commission. Airports and airlines that receive domestic and international awards must use benchmarking for self-promotion and to implement newer, more innovative ideas. If effectively implemented, these changes are likely to result in better performance. The distinctive feature of domestic and international awards in the aviation and tourism sectors is that winners have a formal responsibility to disseminate their practices.

Domestic and international wards are viewed as a goal and a badge of external recognition by other organisations, to carry high brand awareness and credibility among both the aviation industry and consumers. Steffan and Denninghaus (2019) suggest that awards are tools to implement inclusion and accessibility in the built environment. All companies value the importance of receiving an independent assessment of the quality of their products and services as a key motivator for participation in competitions. The role that awards play in branding and marketing products and services favours commercial sales through the company's website and apps (Henryks et al., 2016). The exclusivity of the airport's brand is achieved through the quality of products and services offered in the airport's digital and physical environments.

References

ACI EUROPE Awards. (2020). ACI Europe best airport award winners for 2020 announced. https://www.avionews.it/resources/7bb173eb7593bbb22e54dd9fb b6c7621.pdf. Accessed on August 18, 2023.

Balasubramanian, S. K. (1994). Beyond advertising and publicity: Hybrid messages and public policy issues. *Journal of Advertising*, *23*(4), 29–46.

Bovaird, T., & Löffler, E. (2009). More quality through competitive quality awards? An impact assessment framework. *International Review of Administrative Sciences*, *75*(3), 383–401.

Bunchongchit, K., & Wattanacharoensil, W. (2021). Data analytics of Skytrax's airport review and ratings: Views of airport quality by passenger types. *Research in Transportation Business & Management*, *41*, 100688.

Chutiphongdech, T., & Vongsaroj, R. (2022). Critical components of airport business model framework: Evidence from Thailand. *Sustainability*, *14*(14), 8347.

Eisend, M., & Küster, F. (2011). The effectiveness of publicity versus advertising: A meta-analytic investigation of its moderators. *Journal of the Academy of Marketing Science*, *39*, 906–921.

Fakfare, P., Wattanacharoensil, W., & Graham, A. (2021). Exploring multi-quality attributes of airports and the asymmetric effects on air traveller satisfaction: The case of Thai international airports. *Research in Transportation Business & Management*, *41*, 100648.

Florido-Benítez, L. (2020). Seville airport: A success of good relationship management and interoperability in the improvement of air connectivity. *Revista de Turismo Estudos e Práticas*, *5*(2), 1–30.

Florido-Benítez, L. (2021a). The effects of COVID-19 on Andalusian tourism and aviation sector. *Tourism Review*, *76*(4), 829–857.

Florido-Benítez, L. (2021b). The supremacy of airports generates a high dependence on the tourist destination Spain. *Revista de Turismo Estudos & Prácticas, 10*(2), 1–31.

Florido-Benítez, L. (2022a). The impact of tourism promotion in tourist destinations: A bibliometric study. *International Journal of Tourism Cities, 8*(4), 844–882.

Florido-Benítez, L. (2022b). International mobile marketing: A satisfactory concept for companies and users in times of pandemic. *Benchmarking: An International Journal, 29*(6), 1826–1856.

Florido-Benítez, L. (2022c). The safety-hygiene air corridor between UK and Spain will coexist with COVID-19. *Logistics, 6*(52), 1–22.

Florido-Benítez, L. (2022d). The World airport awards as a quality distinctive and marketing tool for airports. *Journal of Airline Operations and Aviation Management, 1*(2), 54–81.

Florido-Benítez, L. (2024). Tourism promotion budgets and tourism demand: The Andalusian case. *Consumer Behaviour in Tourism and Hospitality. 19*(2), 310–322. https://doi.org/10.1108/CBTH-09-2023-0142

Florido-Benítez, L., & Aldeanueva, I. F. (2022). Fusing international business and marketing: A bibliometric study. *Administrative Sciences, 12*(4), 159.

Florido-Benítez, L., & del Alcázar, B. (2020). Airports as ambassadors of the marketing strategies of Spanish tourist destination. *Gran Tour, 21*, 47–78.

Göktepe-Hulten, D., & Mahagaonkar, P. (2010). Inventing and patenting activities of scientists: In the expectation of money or reputation? *The Journal of Technology Transfer, 35*, 401–423.

Graham, A. (2019). Airport management: A perspective article. *Tourism Review, 75*(1), 102–108.

Grigg, N., & Mann, R. (2008). Rewarding excellence: An international study into business excellence award processes. *Quality Management Journal, 15*(3), 26–40.

Henryks, J., Ecker, S., Turner, B., Denness, B., & Zobel-Zubrzycka, H. (2016). Agricultural show awards: A brief exploration of their role marketing food products. *Journal of International Food & Agribusiness Marketing, 28*(4), 315–329.

Hartley, J., & Downe, J. (2007). The shining lights? Public service awards as an approach to service improvement. *Public Administration, 85*, 329–353.

Kar, A. K. (2014). A decision support system for website selection for internet based advertising and promotions. In S. Sengupta, K. Das, & G. Khan (Eds.), *Emerging trends in computing and communication. Lecture notes in electrical engineering* (Vol. 298). Springer.

Kefallonitis, E., & Kalligiannis, K. (2019). The effect of airport branding to air traffic and passenger movement: An overview. In A. Kavoura, E. Kefallonitis, & A. Giovanis (Eds.), *Strategic innovative marketing and tourism. Springer proceedings in business and economics.* Springer.

Kotler, P., & Keller, K. L. (2006). *Marketing management.* Pearson.

Lee, K., & Yu, C. (2018). Assessment of airport service quality: A complementary approach to measure perceived service quality based on Google reviews. *Journal of Air Transport Management, 71*, 28–44.

Loda, M. D., Norman, W., & Backman, K. F. (2007). Advertising and publicity: Suggested new applications for tourism marketers. *Journal of Travel Research, 45*(3), 259–265.

Martin-Domingo, L., Martín, J. C., & Mandsberg, G. (2019). Social media as a resource for sentiment analysis of airport service quality (ASQ). *Journal of Air Transport Management, 78*, 106–115.

Milakovich, M. E. (2004). Rewarding quality and innovation: Awards, charters, and international standards as catalysts for change. In M. A. Wimmer (Ed.), *Knowledge management in electronic government. KMGov 2004. Lecture notes in computer science* (Vol. 3035). Springer.

Queiroz, M. M., Pereira, S. C. F., Telles, R., & Machado, M. C. (2021). Industry 4. 0 and digital supply chain capabilities: A framework for understanding digitalization challenges and opportunities. *Benchmarking: An International Journal, 28*(5), 1761–1782.

Steffan, I. T., & Denninghaus, M. (2019). Awards as tools to implement inclusion and accessibility in the built environment. In S. Bagnara, R. Tartaglia, S. Albolino, T. Alexander, & Y. Fujita (Eds.), *Proceedings of the 20th congress of the international ergonomics association (IEA 2018). IEA 2018. Advances in intelligent systems and computing* (Vol. 824). Springer.

Straker, K., & Wrigley, C. (2016). Translating emotional insights into digital channel designs: Opportunities to enhance the airport experience. *Journal of Hospitality and Tourism Technology, 7*(2), 135–157.

Thackeray, R., Neiger, B. L., Hanson, C. L., & McKenzie, J. F. (2008). Enhancing promotional strategies within social marketing programs: Use of Web 2.0 social media. *Health Promotion Practice, 9*(4), 338–343.

World Airport Awards. (2021b). World Airport Awards. https://www.world airportawards.com/about-us/. Accessed on August 17, 2023.

World Airport Awards. (2021a). World Airport Awards methodology. https://www. worldairportawards.com/awards-methodology/. Accessed on August 11, 2023.

Xiaozheng, L., Mingshi, H., & Fei, W. (2020). Research on the promotion of public confidence in aviation industry by popular science of civil aviation safety. In *2020 IEEE 2nd International Conference on Civil Aviation Safety and Information Technology (ICCASIT)*, Weihai, China (pp. 1035–1038).

Chapter 9

The Importance of Cybersecurity for Airports in Marketing Activities

Abstract

This chapter tackles cybersecurity as a sociotechnical phenomenon in airport marketing activities. The cybersecurity issues at organisations marketing campaigns (e.g. phishing attacks, URL poisoning, man-in-the-middle attacks or distributed denial-of-service attacks) through digital channels are increasingly frequent and dangerous to companies and customers because of the digitisation of business (websites and apps) that has become the companies' main showcase. Airport and airline operators need to develop new avenues of prevention and mitigation approaches related to cyberattacks in the marketing area. A greater understanding of cybersecurity processes will enable airport operators and airlines to develop security level prevention and mitigation strategies in order to address the increasing challenges airports and airlines face within promotion and communication campaigns, which were previously implemented in their marketing plans.

9.1 Exploring Cybersecurity Threats in Airport Marketing Activities

Airports are operating daily with their own official websites and apps and also working with other partners' e-commerce websites for transactions like airline official websites, Destination Marketing Organization's (DMO's) websites, online travel agencies, Google Flights, among many others. All of them are constantly under cyberattack by hackers (e.g. whackers, software cracker, hacker, cyberterrorists and cybercriminals), and these cyberattacks are causing damage to both private and public enterprises. Marketing activity is a vital business function that is often underutilised when a firm suffers a data breach. Air transport is highly dependent on tourism activities, and this is the reason why airports and airlines are very important in the tourism promotion of destinations (Florido-Benítez, 2022a, 2022b).

Airport Marketing Strategies, 165–183
Copyright © 2024 Lázaro Florido-Benítez
Published under exclusive licence by Emerald Publishing Limited
doi:10.1108/978-1-83608-082-420241009

Cybersecurity in airport marketing activities through digital channels is the cornerstone of facing security threats, as the primary objective of any form of online marketing business is to connect a company with its target audience via digital channels. In this context, we must not forget that airports are considered as a critical infrastructure protection (ICP), as indicated in the EU Directive 2008/114/EC (Articles 2 and 3) and can be affected by cyberattacks. In 2023, three armed drones were shot down over Erbil airport in northern Iraq, where US forces and other international forces are stationed. Whereas in 2024, three US service members were killed and at least 34 wounded in a drone attack on a small US outpost in Jordan.

Cybersecurity in aviation refers to the protection of interconnected aviation information and communication technology (ICT) systems and critical infrastructures, against malicious damage as a result of unauthorised access (Lekota & Coetzee, 2019). In the same vein, Kagalwalla and Churi (2019) define cybersecurity in aviation as the way of protecting computer systems against attacks in the aviation sector. In this book, we understand cybersecurity as a safety tool to protect airport operational systems (hardware, software, data, IoT and via the internet) and helps to prevent exploitation of any threats and vulnerabilities against cyberattacks and cybercrimes by hackers and organisations. Usually, disruptions in the operation of airports come from physical and cyberattack hazards on installations and their interconnected systems.

Florido-Benítez (2021) revealed that Spanish airports are exposed to a series of threats associated with the massive use of information and communication systems, which support the vast majority of their business processes. Two key factors are influencing airports' security and tourist destinations: the internet of things (IoT) and a deficit of interoperability and regulation when communicating a vulnerability. There are no 100% safe spaces, the risks exist and airport operators must prevent them. We are aware that cyberattacks are escalating and spreading quickly worldwide, but so far, it is not easy to say what the emerging risks are and what their consequences may be.

The International Air Transport Association (IATA) reported that cyberattacks are increasing in the aviation industry, and airport and airline operators must comply with aviation cybersecurity regulations across the world (IATA, 2023). The economic impact of cybercrime on business is predicted to reach $10.5 trillion by 2025 (Willard, 2023). The potential for cyberattacks on the aviation industry is a pressing issue requiring constant attention and proactive measures. Unauthorised access is the most prominent type of cyberattack in the aviation industry to steal intellectual property, intelligence and private information (Ukwandu et al., 2022). The air transport industry faces increased cyberthreats and cyberattacks due to hyperconnectivity and the lack of standardised frameworks and cybersecurity defences (Nobles, 2019). One hour of operations disruption at a large airport at peak time has an estimated cost of $1 million; in fact, the cost of a cyberattack is estimated at around $1 million in an airport (Airbus, 2020). A cyberattack is an illegal action that directly affects airports and airlines' operations, their corporate image, reputation, reliability and passengers' confidence. The global aviation cybersecurity market size reached $4.6 billion in 2023, and it is expected to reach $8 billion by 2032 (IMARC Group, 2024).

One of the most well-known cyberattacks is social engineering, which relies on manipulating authorised users to gain access to systems or to trick people into divulging sensitive information. The characteristics of a social engineering attack involve tricking employees into believing criminals are from a credible source. The most common form of social engineering is phishing. According to an European Network and Information Security Agency (ENISA) report (2020) revealed that the number of potential vulnerabilities in a virtual or physical environment continues to expand as a new phase of digital transformation arises. Fig. 41 presents the top 14 cyberthreats in Europe; these are of a technical nature, with malware standing strong as the number one cyberthreat in the European Union, with an increase in phishing, identity theft, ransomware, monetisation holding its place as cyber criminals' top motivation and the COVID-19 environment fuelling attacks on homes, businesses, governments and critical infrastructure.

The European Aviation Safety Agency (EASA) estimated that an average of 1,000 attacks will occur per month on aviation systems in 2020 (EASA, 2021), thus becoming a real threat to airport safety, security and reputation. Cybersecurity risks will only become more significant until airports develop a holistic approach to tackling them. Airlines continue to be an irresistible target for cybercriminals, this involves by 61% of all detected aviation cyberattacks in 2020 and losing around $1 billion a year from fraudulent websites alone. Add to that data theft, card fraud, air miles fraud, phishing, fake invoices and more, and you have a perfect storm for a part of the industry that continues to reel from the pandemic (EUROCONTROL, 2021).

Cybercrimes are on the rise globally, including damage and destruction of data, stolen money, lost productivity, theft of intellectual property, theft of personal and financial data, embezzlement, fraud and phishing attacks on customers and companies (International Telecommunication Union, 2019). In fact, the techniques employed by cybercriminals have become increasingly sophisticated over the years, with victims finding it more and more difficult to notice any red flags.

The Federal Bureau of Investigation, known as the FBI's Internet Crime Complaint Center (2020), counted 467,361 complaints of suspected internet crime, with reported losses of more than $3.5 billion in 2019. The top three crime types reported by victims in 2019 were phishing, vishing, smishing, pharming, non-payment, non-delivery and extortion. For this reason, researchers, academics, companies and governments need to understand types of hackers and their motivations as they evolve and map the vulnerabilities within aviation infrastructures most commonly subject to persistent attack campaigns, as hackers are more proficient and well financed than earlier (Chng et al., 2022; Florido-Benítez, 2021; IATA, 2021).

The aviation sector includes many industries, ranging from airlines, airports, technology providers and subcontractors, all of which are prime targets for cyberattacks. For an overview of cyberattacks in the aviation industry to understand and assimilate existing threats in this complex area, Table 6 displays a review documented of cyberthreats and attacks in the civil aviation industry from 2001 to 2021 by ENISA (2016a,b) and Ukwandu et al. (2022), and their results showed that of all attacks studied, 71% focused on the theft of login details such

1°	Malware	It refers to malicious software that is designed to disrupt or steal data from a computer, network, or server.
2°	Web-based attacks	Web-based attacks are an attractive method by which threat actors can delude victims using web systems and services as the threat vector.
3°	Phishing	It occurs when a cybercriminal sends you a fraudulent email, text called 'smishing,' or a phone call called 'vishing'. If you reply with sensitive information, such as your password, they can use it to take over your accounts.
4°	Web app attacks	Serious vulnerabilities allow criminals to gain direct and public access to databases in order to churn sensitive data, this is known as a web application attack. Many of these databases contain valuable information (e.g., personal data and financial details), making them a frequent target of attacks.
5°	Spam	It is the organised and unauthorised use of an app to send thousands of messages to its users. These messages are sent by fake or hacked profiles and often include unreal advertisements and links to which real users are asked to click on.
6°	DDoS	It is a type of cyberattack in which cybercriminals aim to crash a computer system or server, making sites and services unavailable to customers. These attacks are commonly used by hacker groups to force websites to go offline.
7°	Identify theft	It is also known as identity fraud, is a crime in which an imposter obtains key pieces of personally identifiable information, such as Social Security or driver's license numbers, to impersonate someone else.
8°	Data breach	A data breach exposes confidential, sensitive, or protected information to an unauthorised person. Anyone can be at risk of a data breach, from individuals to high-level enterprises and governments.
9°	Insider threat	It is the potential for an insider to use their authorised access or understanding of an organisation to harm that organisation. This harm can include malicious, complacent, or unintentional acts that negatively affect the integrity, confidentiality, and availability of the organisation.
10°	Botnets	Botnets are networks of hijacked computer devices used to carry out various scams and cyberattacks. Assembly of a botnet is the infiltration, stage of a multilayer scheme. The bots serve as a tool to automate mass attacks, such as data theft, server crashes, and malware distribution.
11°	Information leakage	It refers to the unintended loss of information by an organisation. This usually occurs as a result of employees passing information to others, and sometimes unwittingly.
12°	Ransomware	It is an extortion software that can lock a company's computer and then demand a ransom for its release.
13°	Cyber espionage	It is a type of cyberattack conducted by a threat actor (or cyberspy) who accesses, steals, or exposes classified data or intellectual property (IP) with malicious intent, in order to gain an economic, political, or competitive advantage in a corporate or government setting.
14°	Crypto jacking	It involves the unauthorised use of people's devices (computers, smartphones, tablets, or even servers) by cybercriminals to mine for cryptocurrency.

Fig. 41.   Top 14 Cyberthreats in Europe. *Source:* Adapted from ENISA (2016a, 2016b).

Table 6. Cyberattacks in Civil Aviation Industry From 1997 to 2021.

Year	Class	Incident Attack	Source	Location	Description
1997	Confidentiality	Cyberattack	OTRN	US	A teenager exploited a vulnerability in a local airport's telecommunications service infrastructure in Wosceter, Massachusetts. This DoS attack exposed a weakness in the system the reliance on an infrastructure's unfailing availability.
2003	Availability	Slammer worm	OTRN	US	One of the Federal Aviation Administration (FAA)'s administrative servers was compromised through a slammer worm attack. Internet services were shut down in some parts of Asia as a result of this attack, and this slowed down connections worldwide.
2006	Confidentiality	Cyberattack	OTRN	Alaska, US	Two separate attacks on the US's FAA internet services that forced it to shut down some of its air traffic control systems.
2008	Confidentiality	Malicious hacking	OTRN	US	Hackers stole the administrative passwords of FAA's interconnected networks when they took control of their system. By gaining access to the domain controller in the Western Pacific region, they were able to access more than 40,000 login credentials used to control part of the FAA's mission-support network.

(Continued)

Table 6. (*Continued*)

Year	Class	Incident Attack	Source	Location	Description
2009	Confidentiality	Malicious hacking	OTRN	US	A malicious hacking attack was conducted on FAA's computer, through which hackers gained access to the personal information of 48,000 current and former FAA employees.
2011	Confidentiality	Hacking and phishing	OTRN	Italy	The website of Catania–Fontanarossa Airport (CTA) in Italy was hacked and shut down for a few hours. A 22-year-old suspect was believed to have illegally accessed and damaged data.
2013	Confidentiality	Hacking and phishing	OTRN	US	More than 75 US airports reported phishing e-mails that attempt to defraud users into revealing financial information.
2013	Confidentiality	Malware	OTRN	Turkey	Shutting down of the passport control system at the departure terminals of Istanbul Ataturk and Sabiha Gokcen airports due to a malware attack, leading to the delay of many flights.
2013	Confidentiality	Hacking and phishing	OTRN	United Arab Emirates	The Dubai International Airport (DXB) had 50 email addresses and associated passwords stolen by a team of hackers from the Portugal Cyber Army and the HighTech Brazil HackTeam.
2014	Integrity	Malicious hacking	OTRN	US	US airport computer and communications systems were among the targets announced by the Tunisian Hackers Team in April 2014.

2014	Integrity	Cyberattack	OTRN	India	The Airports Authority of India's enterprise resource planning system was successfully hacked, resulting in the system becoming inoperative, but more importantly, resulting in the loss of personal data on employees.
2015	Availability	DDoS	OTRN	Poland	A distributed denial-of-service (DDoS) attack by cybercriminals that affected LOT Polish Airlines flight-plan IT Network systems at the Warsaw Chopin airport. The attack rendered LOT's system computers unable to send flight plans to the aircraft, thus grounding at least 10 flights, leaving about 1,400 passengers stranded.
2016	Integrity	Hacking and phishing	OTRN	Vietnam	The defacement of a website belonging to Vietnam airlines and flight information screens at Ho Chi Minh City and the capital, Hanoi, displaying messages supportive of China's maritime claims in the South China Sea by Pro-Beijing hackers.
2016	Availability	Cyberattack	OTRN	Ukraine	A malware attack was detected in a computer on the IT network of Kyiv's main airport, which includes the airport's air traffic control system.
2017	Availability	Human error	OTRN	UK	British flag-carrier computer systems failure caused by disconnection and reconnection of the data-centre power supply by a contracted

(Continued)

Table 6. (*Continued*)

Year	Class	Incident Attack	Source	Location	Description
					engineer. This accident left about 75,000 passengers of British Airways stranded.
2018	Confidentiality	Data breach	OTRN	Hong Kong	Cathay Pacific Airways data breach of about 9.4 million customers' personally identifiable information.
2018	Confidentiality	Data breach	OTRN	UK	British Airways data breach of about 380,000 customers' personal identifiable information.
2018	Confidentiality	Data breach	OTRN	US	Delta Air Lines Inc. and Sears Departmental stores reported a data breach of about 100,000 customers' payment information through a 3rd party.
2018	Availability	Ransomware	OTRN	UK	An attack on electronic flight information screens at Bristol Airport. This resulted in the screen being taken offline and replaced with whiteboard information. There was no known adverse effect from this attack.
2018	Confidentiality	Mobile app data breach	OTRN	Canada	Air Canada reported a mobile app data breach affecting the personal data of 20,000 people.
2018	Confidentiality	Data breach	OTRN	US	A data breach on a NASA server that led to possible compromise of stored personally identifiable information (PII) of employees in 2018.

Year		Type		OTRN	Country	Description
2018	Confidentiality	Ransomware		OTRN	US	Boeing was hit by the WannaCry computer virus, but the attack was reported to have minimal damage to the company's internal systems.
2018	Availability	Cyberattack		OTRN	Sweden	Cyberattack launched by a Russian APT group (APT28) that blocked Sweden's air traffic control capabilities, grounding hundreds of flights over a 5-day period.
2019	Availability	Bot		OTRN	Israel	About 3 million bots attacks were blocked in a day by Ben Gurion Israel's airport authority as they attempted to breach airport systems.
2019	Confidentiality	Cyberincident		OTRN	France	A cyber incident that resulted in unauthorised access to Airbus (Toulouse) 'Commercial Aircraft business' information systems. There was no known impact, according to the report on Airbus' commercial operations.
2019	Confidentiality	Ransomware		OTRN	US	Albany International Airport experienced a ransomware attack on Christmas of 2019. The attackers successfully encrypted the entire database of the airport, forcing the authorities to pay a ransom in exchange for the decryption key from a threat actor.
2019	Confidentiality	Crypto mining malware infection		OTRN	Europe	Cyberbit researchers discovered through their security software, known as EDR, a network infection of more than 50% of the European airport workstations by cryptocurrency mining malware.

(Continued)

Table 6. (*Continued*)

Year	Class	Incident Attack	Source	Location	Description
2019	Confidentiality	Phishing	OTRN	New Zealand	A phishing attack targeted Air New Zealand Airports customer. This attack compromised the personal information of approximately 112,000 customers, with names, details and numbers among the data exposed.
2020	Confidentiality	Ransomware	OTRN	US	A cyber-incident that involved the attacker accessing and stealing company data, which was later leaked online (Denver).
2020	Confidentiality	Ransomware	OTRN	US	Data breach suffered by ST Engineering's aerospace subsidiary in the United States that later led to a ransomware attack by Maze Cyber-criminal.
2021	Integrity	Software error	OTRN	UK	A software error in the IT system could not recognise mass discrepancies between the load sheet and the flight plan, leading to the aircraft having 1,606 kg more take-off mass than required (Birmingham).

Source: Adapted from ENISA (2016b, 2020) and Florido-Benitez (2021).

Note: Online Technical Report and News (OTRN).

as administrative passwords and malicious hacking to gain unauthorised access to the IT infrastructure. Denial-of-service (DoS) attacks, which compromise data availability, ranked second at 25%. Third and last were attacks related to corrupting the integrity of files by 4% of all attacks. Furthermore, in this Table 6, we added other cyberattacks from the Florido-Benítez (2021) study related to cybersecurity risks in Spanish airports.

Airports, airlines and DMOs nowadays utilise promotion and communication campaigns in digital channels, since these are pretty helpful in maintaining and attracting passengers and tourists, as well as providing updated information about their products and services. This digital dynamic interaction of relationship between company and customer, which has become ubiquitous and generalised through companies' websites and apps, customized emails, QR codes or bar codes, is the perfect scenery for cyberattacks on content management systems, and distributing malware, trojan horses, takes over a session between a user and the server. It is called 'session hijacking', password attacks or even ransomware where the victim's system is held hostage until they agree to pay a ransom to the attacker. Most citizens are not conscious of the dangers and risks we face in today's world.

Security threats mostly come from compromised user accounts; even marketers' accounts have higher risks because they are allowed higher permissions and access rights. Cybersecurity breaches adversely affect airport performance by leveraging the vulnerabilities of operational and ICT systems.

Airports and airlines' vulnerabilities are in operational systems, payment methods, business and marketing activities in the airport's terminal, IoT, crews, their authentication, security practices for devices, route planning and integration in the cockpit present areas to address. Cyberattacks are associated with social, political, economic and cultural conflicts. Indeed, it is advisable for airports, airlines and companies to use blockchain technology in digital marketing and marketing management because this tool is very effective in providing solutions to both existing and upcoming challenges and situations in the tourism and aviation sectors. Konyeha (2020) indicates that using email as a as means of digital marketing severely risks being hacked by internet thieves.

Hackers might exploit businesses' email accounts to disseminate spam messages that include viruses, forcing other websites hosted on the same server to be blacklisted as a result.

Blockchain security tools work by assessing risks, analysing a blockchain ecosystem and identifying dangers to data, applications and digital assets. Rabby et al. (2022) revealed that blockchain security tools can influence digital marketing by removing intermediaries and delivering trusted cybersecurity services with a high level of transparency and accountability to increase consumer trust and security. The European Union Agency for Cybersecurity provides eight recommendations for enhancing the security and resilience of airports in Europe, tailored specifically towards decision-makers, airport operators and industry. These recommendations are shown in Fig. 42. Each recommendation has been developed based on the information and analysis presented by public and private organisations related to cybersecurity's certification, rules, information security management and security software activities (ENISA, 2016). Perceived

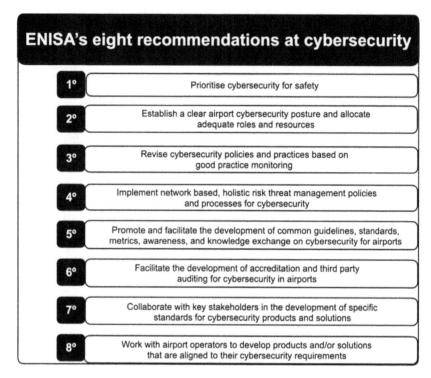

Fig. 42.   ENISA's Eight Recommendations for Airports'
Cybersecurity Activities. *Source:* Adapted from ENISA (2016a, 2016b).

cybersecurity risk harms and plummets firm reputation, and it is indirectly related
to a firm's idiosyncratic risk (Mathur, 2019).

The Société Internationale de Télécommunications Aéronautiques (SITA)
reported that the air transport industry has cybersecurity as a top priority, with
95% of airlines and 96% of airports investing resources in major cybersecurity
programmes or pilots. Most airports worldwide have a cybersecurity Aviation
Security Operations Centre (SOC). It acts like a cyber-control tower with an
integrated combination of processes, people and technology to detect, analyse,
respond to and report on cybersecurity incidents (SITA, 2018). With the
increasing complexity of attacks, it is imperative to safeguard the IoT networks of
smart airports and ensure the reliability of services, as cyberattacks can have
tremendous consequences such as disrupting networks, cancelling travel or
stealing sensitive information (Koroniotis et al., 2020).

An airport that uses cybersecurity's protocols as a safety tool can promote it
on its official website and app as a marketing tool to build consumer trust.
Developing and maintaining good relationships and credibility are critical in
context of the international trade for airports' marketing campaigns. The broad

spectrum and combination of the airport's marketing with cybersecurity activities have induced various advanced perspectives on joint marketing strategies to protect users' personal data and ensure their privacy. This marketing and cybersecurity approach is indispensable to an airport's safety and business activities because the mix of marketing–cybersecurity is the responsibility of the airport operator to guarantee the commercial and operational activities of the airport and the rest of the companies that operate within it.

Konyeha (2020) indicates that security threats mostly come from compromised user accounts; even marketers' accounts have higher risks because they are allowed higher permissions and access rights. Excessive access requests, daily downloads and changes in account information pave the way for access to compromises or threats. Malware attacks can be curtailed using anti-malware measures by encrypting transaction data files and covering up security patches to avoid security breaches. Being able to face cybersecurity issues in a proactive way is a key driver for preserving companies' competitive advantage in terms of economic growth and market position strengthening (Barbier et al., 2016; Corallo et al., 2020). The range of possible motives for cyberattacks presents a challenge for our understanding of hacking, in fact, Holt et al. (2020) note that the consequences of hacks are varied and depend largely on the target and interests of the actor. For instance, a common type of hack involves website defacements, where the attacker replaces the existing content of a website with images and text of their own design, including greetings to peers and taunts to security professionals.

It is worth paying attention to cybersecurity as a safety tool in airport marketing activities because the cybersecurity sector is distinct from all other technological industries, so cybersecurity marketing techniques at airports and airlines must be unique as well. When airport operators are designing marketing strategies in their marketing plans, they should include cybersecurity tools and indicators to measure, prevent, limit or correct vulnerabilities in the operational systems and potential security threats. Naturally, airport operators must monitor everything from promotion campaigns in digital channels to the purchasing cycle of users (see Fig. 43). The airport operator will control and monitor two zones:

(1) Airport operational processes and employees (internal): Operators need to check and update their software every day. A high vulnerability is running unpatched or unsupported software within our operational system, making us more vulnerable to cyberattacks that exploit known vulnerabilities. Moreover, airport operators must supervise the maintenance of databases, protocols of security, the work processes and the environment that employees work in. For example, a simple compromise of a valid email address can serve as a great vector to spread a malicious attachment throughout supply. To protect airport infrastructure, airport cybersecurity teams need real-time intelligence on the latest cyberthreats. In April 2020, unknown persons compromised two San Francisco International Airport websites (IATA: SFO) and injected them with malicious code for stealing user credentials. The attackers' goals were unclear, but airport employees were required to reset their mail and network passwords

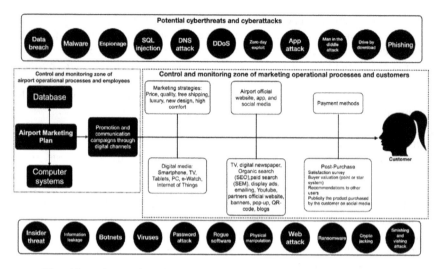

Fig. 43.   Control and Monitoring of Cybersecurity Processes at Promotion Campaigns and the Purchasing Cycle of Users. *Source:* Compiled by the author.

(Kaspersky Daily, 2021). Heathrow Airport was fined £120,000 by the Information Commissioner's Office for the loss of a flash drive containing operating information, including the details of several security service employees (BBC News, 2018). Airports must ensure they are resilient to a range of cyberattacks, from those leading to power supply loss, hardware or software failure and physical damage to attacks that resonate throughout the supply chain. Accordingly, cybersecurity must be treated like physical security and embedded into an airport's infrastructure.

(2) Marketing operational processes and customers (external): Airport operators must tackle vulnerabilities from a proactive point of view, especially in marketing activities, where most companies and users are not conscious of their vulnerabilities or are being attacked by hackers, ransomware or hacktivists. The cybersecurity risk undermines customer relationships. During the period of promotion and communication campaigns through digital channels, airport operators should monitor and assess the security indicators (e.g. KPIs, antivirus software, encryption, network defences) of marketing operational processes and customers, particularly in payment methods, the website and app of the airport, social media, among many others. Implementing mitigation measures, having a plan and building up capacities and contingency measures by airport operators help to better manage the risk of cyberattacks. In March 2022, the website of Bradley International Airport (IATA: BDL) in Connecticut (US) was hit with a cyberattack. The message left by the hackers said: *When the supply of weapons to Ukraine stops, attacks*

on the information structure of your country will instantly stop. America, no one is afraid of you. This type of attack was identified as a distributed DoS. This is when users cannot access information systems, devices and other network resources because of the actions of a malicious cyberthreat actor (Strozewski, 2022).

Airport operators have to develop their own policies to enhance cybersecurity. Securing airports against evolving cyberthreats is a shared responsibility for all aviation stakeholders, including commercial airports, airlines, business associates and regulators (Lykou et al., 2019). For the prevention of malicious attacks, the authorised personnel of the airport must conduct an in-depth analysis of all the security interconnections that were established between different networks (Suciu et al., 2019).

The ability to protect users and operational systems from both external attacks and insider threats is imperative, and this has become a competitive advantage for airports (e.g. Amsterdam Schiphol, Helsinki-Vantaa or Miami International Airport) and airlines (e.g. Qantas, Emirates, Qatar Airways or American Airlines). Indeed, the capacity to protect or defend the use of cyberspace from cyberattacks must be a priority for airport and airline operators. Sometimes, there is no guarantee that hackers will return operators stolen data or information for the payment made, that is, airport and airline operators ought to reflect on the risks of making cyberattack payments. In 2020, half of the US firms that actually paid ransoms were unable to recover all their data, and of the total US companies that suffered a ransomware attack, 68% paid the ransom (HYCU, 2023). These results suggest that paying the ransom also puts airports and airlines at increased risk for a cyberattack in the future and encourages other cybercriminals to repeat the same cyberattack.

Considering the spectrum of the variety of possible attacks, it is necessary to describe a given phenomenon in more detail, a phishing attack. Three and one phishing incidents were perpetrated in airports and airlines, respectively. This type of attack has increased during and after the COVID-19 pandemic, particularly in airports, stealing sensible information and data, money and causing operational disruptions (ElMarady & Rahouma, 2022; Singh & Loura, 2022). The European Air Traffic Management Computer Emergency Response Team (EATM-CERT) agency detected that 15,493 accounts of 30 airlines were offered for sale on the dark web, worth over 400 thousand euros, possibly all of these data were stolen through phishing and data breach attacks (EUROCONTROL, 2023). In 2019, the personal data of over 120,000 customers were compromised following a phishing attack on two members of staff. The attackers used the information gained through phishing to access Air New Zealand's frequent flyer programme, from where they were then able to obtain extensive personal data relating to passengers on the programme (Phillips et al., 2022).

Airports have always been an attractive target for cybercrime. In 2018, a data breach impacted 500,000 customers of British flag carrier British Airways. The data breach involved login details, payment card details and travel booking details being compromised. This data breach went undetected for over 2 months. As credit card details were being entered, these data were being stolen. There was a difficulty in the system because it was not checking a particular area of the network. These payment system attacks create multiple victims who are not part of the airport. The airports are open, and the planes are flying, but there are thousands of people's details flying around the dark web (Mann, 2022). The interaction between a company's informational resources, such as customer perceptions of cybersecurity risk, and its complementary deployment capabilities, such as social media marketing capabilities, is crucial for a firm to address changing market needs (Mathur, 2019). Management plans by DMOs and governments must generate an optimal benefit to improve tourism as well as reduce society's vulnerability in turbulent times (Florido-Benítez, 2022c).

If the tourism sector can boast of anything, it is the speed and integration of digitalisation in the companies that make up this activity, from airports, tour operators to hotels. The ubiquity of information and new technologies have empowered tourists, adapting to the demand of an increasingly informed and demanding consumer, with great capacity for influence and living at the click of a button, has caused that not only has occurred a transformation in the processes or in the products offered, but it demands accessible and satisfactory experiences in the whole process of your trip (Florido-Benítez & Aldeanueva, 2022; Florido-Benítez & Castillero, 2022; Florido-Benítez & Dogra, 2022). Travel and tourism companies must be transparent in how they use consumers' personal information and how they communicate the potential benefits and risks of sharing their data. In this context, airport and airline operators must make it clear that when a cyberattack hits an airport or airline, its negative consequences involve all public and private organisations, as well as customers and tourists (Florido-Benítez, 2024).

Even though the future is uncertain, it is our responsibility to think about the challenges, opportunities, threats and possibilities that exist in the future that can be shaped by tourism and aviation research in an impactful way. The more awareness we have of our marketing and sales processes, the more relevant customers we get. Airports and airlines should have a good messaging service about cybersecurity sales. This plays a big part in building a cybersecurity marketing strategy. Airport operators need to be aware of the importance of having cybersecurity to protect their aeronautical and non-aeronautical activities, and to take into account the consequences, such as the business losses, that might happen to them if they do not practice a proactive culture of cybersecurity.

References

Airbus. (2020). 5 actions to protect your aircraft from cyberattacks. https://aircraft.airbus.com/en/5-actions-to-protect-your-aircraft-from-cyberattacks. Accessed on February 3, 2024.

Barbier, J., Buckalew, L., Loucks, J., Moriarty, R., O'Connell, K., & Rieger, M. (2016). *Cybersecurity as a growth advantage*. https://www.cisco.com/c/dam/assets/offers/pdfs/cybersecurity-growth-advantage.pdf. Accessed on August 23, 2022.

BBC News. (2018). Heathrow fined for USB stick data breach. https://www.bbc.com/news/business-45785227. Accessed on August 28, 2022.

Chng, S., Lu, H. Y., Kumar, A., & Yau, D. (2022). Hacker types, motivations and strategies: A comprehensive framework. *Computer in Human Behavior Reports, 5,* 100167.

Corallo, A., Lazoi, M., & Lezzi, M. (2020). Cybersecurity in the context of industry 4.0: A structured classification of critical assets and business impacts. *Computers in Industry, 114,* 103165.

EASA. (2021). Cybersecurity overview. https://www.easa.europa.eu/domains/cybersecurity/overview. Accessed on September 6, 2022.

ElMarady, A. A., & Rahouma, K. H. (2022). The impact of COVID-19 on the cybersecurity in civil aviation: Review and analysis. In *2022 international telecommunications conference (ITC-Egypt)* (pp. 1–6). IEEE.

ENISA. (2016a). Smart airports: How to protect airport passengers from cyber disruptions. https://www.enisa.europa.eu/news/enisa-news/smart-airports-how-to-protect-airport-passengers-from-cyber-disruptions. Accessed on August 23, 2022.

ENISA. (2016b). Securing smart airports. https://www.enisa.europa.eu/publications/securing-smart-airports. Accessed on August 23, 2022.

ENISA. (2020). ENISA threat landscape 2020: Cyber attacks becoming more sophisticated, targeted, widespread and undetected. https://www.enisa.europa.eu/news/enisa-news/enisa-threat-landscape-2020. Accessed on August 27, 2022.

EUROCONTROL. (2021). EUROCONTROL Think Paper #12 – Aviation under attack from a wave of cybercrime. https://www.eurocontrol.int/publication/eurocontrol-think-paper-12-aviation-under-attack-wave-cybercrime. Accessed on August 21, 2022.

EUROCONTROL. (2023). European air traffic management computer emergency response team. https://www.eurocontrol.int/service/european-air-traffic-management-computer-emergency-response-team. Accessed on January 21, 2024.

FBI's Internet Crime Complaint Center. (2020). FBI releases the internet crime complaint center 2019 internet crime report. https://www.fbi.gov/news/press-releases/press-releases/fbi-releases-the-internet-crime-complaint-center-2019-internet-crime-report. Accessed on August 21, 2022.

Florido-Benítez, L. (2021). Identifying cybersecurity risks in Spanish airports. *Cyber Security, 4*(3), 267–291.

Florido-Benítez, L. (2022a). The impact of tourism promotion in tourist destinations: A bibliometric study. *International Journal of Tourism Cities, 8*(4), 844–882.

Florido-Benítez, L. (2022b). International mobile marketing: A satisfactory concept for companies and users in times of pandemic. *Benchmarking: An International Journal, 29*(6), 1826–1856.

Florido-Benítez, L. (2022c). COVID-19 and BREXIT crisis: British Isles must not kill the goose that lays the golden egg of tourism. *Gran Tour, 6,* 61–100.

Florido-Benítez, L. (2024). The cybersecurity applied by online travel agencies and hotels to protect users' private data in smart cities. *Smart Cities, 7,* 475–495.

Florido-Benítez, L., & Aldeanueva, I. F. (2022). Fusing international business and marketing: A bibliometric study. *Administrative Sciences, 12*(4), 159.

Florido-Benítez, L., & Castillero, L. E. (2022). Analysis of the value chain of Avanza mobility ADO company. *Revista Transporte y Territorio, 26,* 240–275.

Florido-Benítez, L., & Dogra, J. (2022). Study of relationship between Spanish airport and destination marketing: Insights for destination management organizations. *Revista Turismo & Desenvolvimento, 39*, 177–200.

Holt, T. J., Leukfeldt, R., & van de Weijer, S. (2020). An examination of motivation and routine activity theory to account for cyberattacks against Dutch web sites. *Criminal Justice and Behavior, 47*(4), 487–505.

HYCU. (2023). Ransomware attacks – Never pay the ransom (Here's Why). https://www.hycu.com/blog/ransomware-attacks-dont-pay-the-ransom#:~:text=Organizations%20must%20also%20be%20aware,of%20Foreign%20Assets%20Control%27s%20regulations. Accessed on January 22, 2024.

IATA. (2021). Aviation cybersecurity. https://www.iata.org/en/programs/security/cyber-security/#tab-1. Accessed on August 22, 2022.

IATA. (2023). Annual review 2023. https://www.iata.org/contentassets/c81222d96c9a4e0bb4ff6ced0126f0bb/annual-review-2023.pdf. Accessed on January 1, 2024.

IMARC Group. (2024). *Aviation cybersecurity market report by solution type.* https://www.imarcgroup.com/aviation-cyber-security-market. Accessed on February 22, 2024.

International Telecommunication Union. (2019). *Statistics' International Telecommunication Union.* https://www.itu.int/en/ITU-D/Statistics/Pages/stat/default.aspx. Accessed on August 20, 2022.

Kagalwalla, N., & Churi, P. P. (2019). Cybersecurity in aviation: An intrinsic review. In *2019 5th International Conference on Computing, Communication, Control and Automation (ICCUBEA)*, Pune, India (pp. 1–6).

Kaspersky Daily. (2021). Protecting airports from cyberincidents. https://www.kaspersky.com/blog/protecting-airports/42150/. Accessed on August 25, 2022.

Konyeha, S. (2020). Exploring cybersecurity threats in digital marketing. *NIPES Journal of Science and Technology Research, 2*(3), 12–20.

Koroniotis, N., Moustafa, N., Schiliro, F., Gauravaram, P., & Janicke, H. (2020). A holistic review of cybersecurity and reliability perspectives in smart airports. *IEEE Access, 8*, 209802–209834.

Lekota, F., & Coetzee, M. (2019). Cybersecurity incident response for the Sub-Saharan African aviation industry. In *International Conference on Cyber Warfare and Security 2019*, South Africa (pp. 536–545).

Lykou, G., Anagnostopoulou, A., & Gritzalis, D. (2019). Smart airport cybersecurity: Threat mitigation and cyber resilience controls. *Sensors, 19*(1), 19.

Mann, J. (2022). Cybersecurity threats in aviation. https://www.airport-technology.com/analysis/cybersecurity-threats-in-aviation/. Accessed on August 27, 2022.

Mathur, M. (2019). Where is the security blanket? Developing social media marketing capability as a shield from perceived cybersecurity risk. *Journal of Promotion Management, 25*(2), 200–224.

Nobles, C. (2019). Cyberthreats in civil aviation. In *Emergency and disaster management: Concepts, methodologies, tools, and applications* (pp. 119–141). IGI Global.

Phillips, P., Champion, J., & Bettle, P. (2022). Aviation is facing a rising wave of cyber-attacks in the wake of COVID. https://www.shlegal-aviation.com/insight/aviation-facing-rising-wave-cyber-attacks-wake-covid. Accessed on January 23, 2024.

Rabby, F., Chimhundu, R., & Hassan, R. (2022). Blockchain-enabled trust management for digital marketing in the industry 4.0 era. In Y. Maleh, L. Tawalbeh, S. Motahhir, & A. S. Hafid (Eds.), *Advances in blockchain technology for cyber physical systems. Internet of things.* Springer. https://doi.org/10.1007/978-3-030-93646-4_14

Singh, K. D., & Loura, J. (2022). Impact of Covid-19 on operations and cyber-vulnerability of civil aviation. *Amity Journal of Computational Sciences, 5,* 34–39.

SITA. (2018). Air transport cybersecurity insights 2018. https://www.sita.aero/resources/surveys-reports/air-transport-cybersecurity-insights-2018/. Accessed on August 22, 2022.

Strozewski, Z. (2022). U.S. airport hit with cyberattack over Ukraine: 'No one is afraid of you'. https://www.newsweek.com/us-airport-hit-cyberattack-over-ukraine-no-one-afraid-you-1692903. Accessed on August 28, 2022.

Suciu, G., Scheianu, A., Petre, I., Chiva, L., & Bosoc, C. S. (2019). Cybersecurity threats analysis for airports. In A. Rocha, H. Adeli, L. Reis, & S. Costanzo (Eds.), *New knowledge in information systems and technologies. WorldCIST'19 2019. Advances in intelligent systems and computing* (Vol. 931). Springer.

Ukwandu, E., Ben-Farah, M. A., Hindy, H., Bures, M., Atkinson, R., Tachtatzis, C., Andonovic, I., & Bellekens, X. (2022). Cyber-security challenges in aviation industry: A review of current and future trends. *Information, 13*(3), 146.

Willard, L. (2023). Economic impact of cybercrime on business predicted to reach $10.5 trillion by 2025: Cybersecurity ventures. https://www.reinsurancene.ws/economic-impact-of-cybercrime-on-business-predicted-to-reach-10-5-trillion-by-2025-cybersecurity-ventures/#:~:text=The%20economic%20impact%20of%20cybercrime, risk%20appears%20to%20be%20diminishing. Accessed on January 6, 2024.

Printed in the USA
CPSIA information can be obtained
at www.ICGtesting.com
JSHW011759031224
74704JS00004B/114